IT WASN'T
LIKE NOTHING

IT WASN'T LIKE NOTHING

One Marine's Adventure in Vietnam

THOMAS J. HYNES

IT WASN'T LIKE NOTHING
ONE MARINE'S ADVENTURE IN VIETNAM

iUniverse books may be ordered through booksellers or by contacting:

iUniverse
1663 Liberty Drive
Bloomington, IN 47403
www.iuniverse.com
1-800-Authors (1-800-288-4677)

ISBN: 978-1-4917-6579-1 (sc)
ISBN: 978-1-4917-6578-4 (e)

Library of Congress Control Number: 2015905897

Print information available on the last page.

iUniverse rev. date: 04/11/2015

WITH DETERMINATION

With Determination
You fought the war
In that Southeast Asian Nation.
Praise the soldiers who came home
Cherish these who lie alone.
You are not forgotten
The tears that fall at this wall
Flow up to you in your hallowed halls.

By Don Durham

INTRODUCTION

THE WAR IN VIETNAM ENDED on April 30, 1975, when a small contingent of marines was heli-lifted off the roof of the US embassy in Saigon. As the marines flew over the city, they could hear the sounds of the advancing enemy's artillery and see the flash of their exploding shells. Since that time, the war in Vietnam has remained a mystery to the average American. How, they ask, could the most powerful nation in the world be defeated by an ill-equipped third-world army? In an attempt to obtain an answer, they sometimes sought out the veterans of that war and asked, "What was it like in Vietnam?"

Initially, the veteran attempts to tell of his adventures, but after several tries, he finds it is a story that can't be told. The person asking the question simply cannot relate what he is being told to anything he has experienced in the past. The ordeals of the war in Vietnam are indescribable to someone who was not there to share in that experience. After several unsuccessful attempts to describe the war, the veteran learns to respond to the question with a simple "It wasn't like nothing."

Vietnam was not like anything our nation had experienced in the past. It was fought in a forsaken place, over unforgiving terrain, in stifling heat, and in a country whose culture was totally alien to us. But this alone did not distinguish the Vietnam War; Americans have fought under similar conditions in the past. The difference was the enemy, an enemy who refused to face us on our terms, who were masters at guerrilla warfare, and who were willing to make sacrifices beyond our comprehension. The nature of the enemy, combined with the hostile conditions, led to the ultimate defeat of the South Vietnamese forces.

The Vietnam veteran who finds himself unable to tell of his adventures in Vietnam stores them in a secret place within himself. He is accused of not wanting to talk about them, when in reality he can't. This book is an attempt to describe one person's experiences in Vietnam. Whether the author is any more successful in relating these events than the average veteran is up for debate.

The setting of this book is Hill 63 and the Que Son Valley, approximately forty miles south of the large military base at the city of Da Nang. The story takes place in the summer and fall of 1967 and centers on the activities of Second Platoon, Lima Company, Third Battalion, Fifth Marine Regiment, First Marine Division.

Many books have been written about the war in Vietnam, ranging from the description of the political climate in Southeast Asia as it affected the war to the tales of the individual infantryman and the happenings within his squad. All of these stories are important to give us a clear picture of what really happened in Vietnam. The war in Vietnam was about strategies and politics as well as about young men who died in the arms of their comrades. I would hope this book adds a little to our knowledge of America's ill-fated encroachment into the politics of Southeast Asia.

It is important that the reader of works on Vietnam understands the obvious: each story is related through the eyes of the author. The perspective of one writer may be substantially different from that of another. The generals and colonels saw a different war than the privates and corporals saw. The generals worried about moving divisions and regiments while the private's concern may be moving his buddy and himself fifteen feet to the shelter of a trench line. The colonel and his subordinates were interested in enemy body count while the corporal's goal was keeping his fire team alive for one more day.

The stories of the individual infantryman may also vary as a result of their geographical location. The war fought in the rice paddies of the Mekong Delta differed from the war fought at the DMZ. Because of the various viewpoints, we can only get a true picture of Vietnam by reading a wide range of books on the subject.

This book is written from the perspective of a Marine Corps second lieutenant fresh out of OCS and who is undertaking his first command. I was in Vietnam for one reason—I was subject to the draft, and I chose to join the Marine Corps rather than do my time as an enlisted man in the army. I had no intentions of making the Marine Corps my career; once my time was up, I would eagerly return to the civilian ranks. My goal was to survive the war, not win the war. I was more concerned about keeping my troops and myself alive than I was about enemy body count. I was a part of the Marine Corps in the sense that I was fighting a war for them in the rice paddies of Vietnam. I was not a member of the cadre of officers who chose to make the Marine Corps their career.

The war in Vietnam was fought by millions of Americans like me who had no intention of remaining in the military. We referred to the career marines as "lifers," and in many cases, it was not a term of endearment. There were some lifers who fought valiantly and heroically beside us in the rice paddies and jungles of Vietnam. There were many others who were able to avoid the nastiness of the war through their knowledge of the system and their ability to obtain the rear-area assignments. The fact of the matter is—the brunt of the conflict in Vietnam was borne by citizen soldiers who were temporarily in the military, not by the warrior class who had chosen the military as their careers.

The officers who were in the military only because of the draft were the bastard children of the Marine Corps. Since we were officers, we were separate and apart from the enlisted men. On the other hand, we were looked down upon by the career officers who considered us inferior, knowing we would not be around for long under any circumstances. In most cases, we were assigned the unpleasant task of fighting the war; we were in the rice paddies and the jungles while the jobs in the rear were reserved for the lifers. In addition, we were expendable. There was no reason to risk the life of someone who had dedicated himself to the Marine Corps when you could send out a ninety-day wonder whose days were numbered. Most of the staff officers made it through Vietnam. Many of the temporary officers did not. The statistics bear this out: almost 70 percent of the Marine Corps officers killed in Vietnam were either first or second lieutenants.

Those of us fresh out of OCS were able to identify with the enlisted marines who, like us, were in Vietnam because of the threat of the draft. We were in a war not of our making, directed by a cadre of officers who were there to further their careers at our expense. Those of us in the rice paddies had little to gain and everything to lose in this war. The best we could hope for was to return home in one piece. We fought and died so the military could convince the politicians the war was winnable and should be continued for one more day, week, month, or year.

It did not take us long to figure out there was something seriously wrong with our war. We were supposedly fighting on behalf of the people of South Vietnam, but there was no evidence these people cared about who won or lost the war. The peasants in the rice paddies and villages were only concerned about survival; the South Vietnamese soldiers, in most cases, were unwilling to fight and were unconcerned about the plight of the peasants; the South Vietnamese politicians were only interested in lining their pockets with the bounty of the war.

The enlisted marine, barely out of high school, was thrown into this disaster of a war to save a country that was beyond hope. It is little wonder things turned out the way they did. Despite all this, these marines and their counterparts in the army did a superlative job in fighting their highly motivated foe. The acts of valor and the sacrifices made by the grunts of Vietnam were comparable to the deeds of brave Americans who have fought for their country since the Revolutionary War. We were not there for God, country, or Mom's apple pie, but once we got there, we fought bravely for a cause we did not understand.

This book is about the men of Second Platoon and my adventures in leading that platoon. I chose to begin the book with my experiences in OCS and later in the Basic School to give the reader a flavor of the training I received prior to my tour of duty in Vietnam. All marines were well trained before going to Vietnam. Their identities as civilians were taken from them, and they were transformed into marines. Regardless of the shortcomings of the war in Vietnam, they were marines, prepared to sacrifice and die for their country and corps. They may have been civilians at heart, but for a short period of time in the mid- to late sixties, they were marines, and I would put them up against any who have served past or since. This is their story.

1

HEADING FOR VIETNAM

IN THE SPRING OF 1966, I was preparing to graduate from Georgetown Law School and hopefully to get on with the rest of my life. I would return to my hometown of Farmington, New Mexico, and take up the practice of law. A letter from my draft board dramatically changed my plans. I was ordered to report to Fort Polk, Louisiana, for induction into the military service. Uncle Sam was kind enough to give me a choice: I had fifteen days to enlist in one of the branches of the military service; if not, I had better have my ass down to Fort Polk on the assigned day.

My first decision was whether or not I wanted to spend the next two years as an enlisted man in the armed forces or, in the alternative, to become an officer. I quickly chose the latter. My second decision was which branch of the armed forces I wanted to join. Unfortunately, I had watched too many John Wayne movies as a youth, and this choice was easy. I would become a United States Marine.

Actually, I had made this decision three years earlier as an undergraduate at the University of Notre Dame. At that time, I had not made up my mind to go to law school and was faced with the inevitability of the draft. I chose to join the Marine Corps and was admitted to the Officer Candidate School (OCS), which was to begin in the fall of 1963. I had raised my hand and taken the official oath to become a marine. After I decided to attend law school, I returned to the recruiter and told him I had not really meant it when I swore to be a good marine. Surprisingly, they let me out of my obligation, and I went on to Georgetown Law School. I now wondered if the Marine Corps would take me back.

The Marine Corps recruiting office was less than three blocks from the law school. When I entered the recruiting office, I was met by a squared-away young marine sergeant who greeted me as if I were a long-lost friend. When I explained my predicament, he showed even more interest, and within minutes, I was taking tests and filling out forms. After the tests were complete, he explained that he had to get my college transcripts. If everything worked out, I would only have to pass a physical to be accepted into OCS. He told me to check back in a couple of days.

Three days later, I went back to the recruiting office where I was given the news that everything was in order and I should report for my physical. I was directed to the naval yard in Washington, DC, where the examination would be performed. I envisioned being tested by a battery of doctors to ensure I was sufficiently fit to undergo the rigors of Marine Corps training. A rather bored navy doctor took my pulse and blood pressure. He asked me how I felt. I assured him I felt fine, and he declared me fit for duty.

I returned to the recruiting office and later that day was sworn in. I was a marine, if in name only. After being sworn in, I was handed papers that told me to report to Quantico, Virginia, on September 12, 1966, to begin OCS. Immediately after handing me the papers, the recruiter lost all interest in my well-being. I was no longer a prospective recruit; I was now signed, sealed, and delivered to the United States Marine Corps.

I graduated from Georgetown in early June and had the rest of the summer off to prepare myself for OCS. I had heard stories about the physical demands of the program and was determined to get myself in good physical shape before reporting to Quantico. I started a regimen of physical conditioning that lasted less than two weeks. I then said screw it; there was no reason to waste the summer on anything more strenuous than lifting an eleven-ounce beer can. Although I had never been much of an athlete, I was able to win the middleweight boxing championship at the University of Notre Dame. I concluded the Marine Corps could spend its time getting me in shape. Besides, September 12 was a long way off.

September 12, 1966, was an unforgettable day, my first day at OCS. We were introduced to our drill instructor, Gunnery Sergeant Fry, who took an immediate dislike to us. He told us we were a terrible imposition upon him and his Marine Corps. He obviously could not understand how we were chosen to be officer candidates. In his eyes, we were the biggest bunch of screwups he had ever encountered.

After our graduation ceremonies from OCS, we were given two weeks' leave and told to report to the Basic School, where we would be turned into Marine Corps officers. I used the two weeks to accomplish one of the most important things in my life. I married the love of my life, Martha Molina, whom I had been dating for the last two years.

The Basic School, also located at Quantico, was a five-month program designed to get us ready for our future assignments in the Marine Corps. It stressed leadership training as well as the basic skills of being infantry platoon commanders. In addition, it exposed us to the various military occupational specialties (MOS) within the Marine Corps so we could select one at the proper time. The Basic School placed a substantial emphasis on infantry tactics. No matter what MOS an officer chose after Basic School, he would be well versed in the fundamentals of small-unit combat.

Simply graduating from OCS was not a guarantee that someday we would be good leaders. Leadership qualities are something you are born with, but they must be honed and developed through proper training. A major-league baseball player must have natural athletic ability to make it to the big leagues. He must also have the training and coaching to develop his natural talents. Without both, he would never make it as a professional baseball player. The same holds true for combat leaders. An individual may have the natural ability to be a leader of men, but without the proper training, he may never make it in a combat situation. There was no guarantee that those of us who had just completed OCS had the innate ability to be great leaders. We had been exposed to a substantial amount of stress and learned how to handle it. We were potential leaders, and the Marine Corps would attempt to develop that potential during the next several months.

The Marine Corps' primary focus was on the combat infantryman. They truly believed the saying "The deadliest weapon ever created by mankind is the marine and his rifle." As a result, the majority of our training focused on small-unit infantry tactics. We learned to lead grunts into battle. Those of us who grew up watching John Wayne movies might think this would be a relatively easy task—all you needed was a hard-bitten sergeant who yelled, "Charge!" and the individual marines did the rest. In actuality, the task of being a platoon commander was more complex. It is true the effectiveness of the individual marine is the cornerstone of the Marine Corps' success, but the platoon commander and the company commander also play a key role in this success. Those of us fresh out of OCS were about to learn exactly how complex a role this really was.

The fact the Marine Corps was embroiled in a conflict in Southeast Asia had a definite effect on our training at the Basic School. While the Marine Corps stressed basic infantry tactics used to fight a conventional war, they could not ignore the fact they had two Marine Corps divisions committed to the war in Vietnam. As a practical matter, the majority of the graduates of the Basic School would ultimately wind up in Southeast Asia. Many times, the tactics used to fight a conventional war were of little value in combating the guerilla war waged by the Vietcong. While we were still schooled in conventional tactics, there was a strong emphasis placed on waging war against the Vietcong (VC) and North Vietnamese Army (NVA).

After a two-week vacation, I had to report for a flight that left at 0400 hours from Travis Air Force Base, which was just outside of

San Francisco. I caught a midnight flight out of Albuquerque, New Mexico, that would get me into San Francisco a little after 0200, California time. This would give me two hours to get to Travis to check in for my flight to Vietnam. I finally arrived at Travis at 0300 hours, and when I went to the desk to report in, I was told the flight was delayed and to stand by. After a couple of hours, we were informed the flight was canceled and rescheduled for the following day. The next morning, we left on our flight to Okinawa, where we would be prepared for our tour of duty in Vietnam. After three days of processing, it was time to board the jet to Da Nang.

We were on a civilian jet that touched down in Da Nang after a two-hour flight from Okinawa. As we exited the plane, I was struck by both the heat and the smell of Vietnam. Regardless of what you have been told about the beauty of Southeast Asia, the fact of the matter is that it smells like an open sewer and feels like the inside of an oven. It was now time to face reality. We were sent off to a tent area next to the runway to spend the night. The tent we were assigned contained several folding cots without any bedding or pillows. Just outside the tent was a sandbagged bunker for the obvious purpose of giving us shelter in case of an enemy attack.

The most unsettling thing about our new quarters was the fighter jets taking off every few minutes less than two hundred meters from our tent. The noise was deafening, and it felt like you were being blown out of your cot every time one of the jets took off or landed. Obviously, we didn't get much sleep that night.

After several days of preparing us for battle, I was assigned to Lima Company, Third Battalion, Fifth Marines. They were located at Hill 63 some twenty miles south of Da Nang. We were transported there by helicopter, and I proceeded to Battalion headquarters. I was informed that Lima Company was located at the top of Hill 63, and I proceeded to find my way up the hill. I was fortunate to run in to a couple of marines from Lima Company.

I introduced myself and explained I had just been assigned to Lima Company. The other marine said, "Welcome to Lima Company,

Lieutenant. We'll get you up to the CP in no time. I'm Tex, and this is Booger Red. We're Captain K.'s runners."

I asked Tex who Captain K. was, and he answered, "He's the Lima Company commander. His real name is Captain Kolakowski, but everyone calls him Captain K. He's a cool dude, not like most of the lifers around here. He cuts us as much slack as he can, and he looks out for us. You're lucky to be assigned to Lima Company."

I asked, "What's it like around here? Everybody tells me we're in the middle of VC country."

Booger Red replied, "You've got that right, sir. There ain't no friendlies around here. Every one of them motherfuckers out there would just as soon kill you as look at you. 'Course, we've seen worse, but this is pretty bad."

Tex joined in. "It's worse at Que Son. They've got NVA up there. All we got is VC, but that's bad enough. We've been in a firefight every day since we took this hill two weeks ago."

We stopped to catch our breath. Booger Red volunteered, "Our perimeter starts about fifty meters up the trail. I don't like walking around here in the dark. Never know when someone will shoot your ass thinking you're a VC. We'll call out pretty soon and let them know we're coming in."

I asked, "Do you have a password?"

Tex laughed and said, "Shit no, Lieutenant. That's stateside bullshit. Out here, we just tell 'em we're coming in, and they take our word for it."

We proceeded up the hill, and sure enough, Tex called out, and someone answered, telling us to come on ahead. We passed a foxhole where four marines were lying around smoking cigarettes and shooting the shit. They exchanged pleasantries with Tex and Booger Red, and we proceeded on to an area on top of the hill, which Tex identified as the Lima Company's CP. He took me over to a group of marines and introduced me to Captain Kolakowski.

"Captain, this is a new lieutenant who's just been assigned to Lima Company."

I snapped to attention, saluted the captain, and said, "Lieutenant Hynes reporting for duty, sir."

Instead of returning my salute, the captain stuck out his hand and said, "Hi. I'm Henry Kolakowski. Welcome to Lima Company. You can call me Captain K. Everybody else does."

I shook his hand, and he introduced me around. I didn't catch everybody's name, but I shook hands with everyone as I was introduced. Captain K. said, "You got here at the right time. We just got a beer ration. Somebody get Lieutenant Hynes a beer."

I was handed a warm beer, and we all sat down under a shelter made out of ponchos propped up with pieces of bamboo. Since I was the new kid on the block, I thought it would be best to keep my mouth shut and just listen to what everyone had to say. Captain K. explained that while in the field, we didn't salute superior officers. In addition, we didn't wear our rank insignia, since it made too tempting a target for the VC. As the conversation wore on, I removed my second-lieutenant bars as discreetly as possible.

After a couple of beers, I started to relax and joined in the conversations. The group I was drinking with consisted of the company headquarters group. There was Captain K. plus Tex and Booger Red. In addition, there was Charlie Brown, Captain K.'s radioman, and Sergeant Phillips, the company supply sergeant. The most colorful individual of the lot was First Sergeant Louis Schwartz, who monopolized the conversation and had an opinion on just about everything. Since I was new to the company, Sergeant Schwartz gave me his life history. He had joined the Marine Corps in 1943 and landed on several of the beachheads in the Pacific theater during World War II. He had also served in Korea, where he was a corporal but on occasion held the position of platoon commander because everyone senior to him had been killed or wounded. It was difficult to separate fact from fiction in Sergeant Schwartz's stories, but they were entertaining, and it was easy to accept everything he said as true. We drank several beers, and as the evening wore on, Sergeant Schwartz's stories became grander and longer. As the stories ended, I found what looked like a comfortable place on the ground and turned in for the night. I was brimming with confidence and ready to begin my career as an infantry platoon commander, but I think the beer and Sergeant Schwartz's stories were doing the thinking for me.

I suddenly awoke in the middle of the night, and Lima Company's CP was under attack by NVA sappers. We were about to be overrun, and I grabbed my rifle and headed for a pile of rocks that I had noticed when I went to take a piss the evening before. As I dived for the protection of the rocks, I heard a voice say, "What's wrong, Lieutenant?"

It was Booger Red, who was manning the company radio. I realized I had been dreaming, and I lay there totally embarrassed with my mind racing, trying to come up with a logical explanation for my actions. Determining there was no reasonable accounting for my bizarre behavior, I admitted to Booger Red that I had been dreaming and returned to the spot on the ground where I had been sleeping. I went back to sleep, hoping that Booger Red wouldn't tell the entire company what an idiot the new lieutenant was.

The next morning, I awoke with half a hangover and sought out Booger Red to attempt to explain what happened the night before. He just laughed and said, "Forget it, Lieutenant. It happens all the time. At least you weren't screaming at the top of your lungs like some of us."

This eased my mind somewhat, and I set about finding some breakfast. The only thing available was C rations. Although we had eaten C rations back at Quantico, I was not a connoisseur of the mainstay of the infantry platoon. I chose a meal of beans and weenies and attempted to warm them up over a heat tab by setting the can of beans on a flat rock. Booger Red observed my feeble attempts and offered me an improvised stove made out of a discarded C ration can.

After breakfast, I approached Captain K. about getting assigned a platoon. He started the conversation with "Lieutenant, we have a problem. I already have three platoon commanders, and I don't have a place to put you except as weapons platoon commander."

This was fine with me. A platoon was a platoon as far as I was concerned. Captain K. then explained there wasn't a weapons platoon. A weapons platoon normally consisted of six machine gun crews, three 3.5-inch rocket launcher teams, and a sixty-millimeter mortar crew. The machine guns and rocket launchers had been assigned to the rifle platoons. The only thing left was the four-man mortar crew. I was going to be the platoon commander of a phantom platoon. After realizing the significance of my assignment, I was as relieved as I was disappointed. Since I was the commander of a nonexistent platoon, I couldn't screw things up too badly. On the other hand, I felt rather foolish and useless not having a real command. I decided to put the best face on the situation and vowed to be the best weapons platoon commander in all of Vietnam. I probably didn't have much competition in this regard.

After getting over my initial shock, I sought out Sergeant Schwartz to see if I could find what was left of my command, the sixty-millimeter mortar crew. Sergeant Schwartz took me over to a pit that had been dug in a flat area next to the company CP. In the middle of the pit was the mortar surrounded by various mortar rounds. No one was manning the mortar, and I began to wonder if maybe there was a phantom mortar crew, as well. Sergeant Schwartz called to Tex and told him to find the mortar crew and have them report to the mortar site immediately. Shortly, four marines came hustling over to our location. Sergeant Schwartz introduced me to Corporal Ted Hall, who was the leader of the mortar crew, and informed him I was the new weapons platoon commander. Corporal Hall had a quizzical look on his face but took things in stride and said nothing. I could just imagine what was going through his mind. After the introductions, Sergeant Schwartz left us alone so I could begin my career as weapons platoon commander.

Corporal Hall introduced me to the remainder of my command. Lance Corporal Fields was the assistant mortarman while PFC North and Private Hanson were the ammo humpers. After shaking hands all around, I was at a loss as to what to do next. I wanted to inspect the mortar, but I didn't have the slightest idea of what to look for or how it worked. I hoped the men did not realize how ignorant I was about my new job. On the other hand, I was pretty sure they would eventually figure it out on their own. I finally decided honesty was the best policy and admitted my ignorance.

I said, "Guys, I didn't expect to be assigned to the weapons platoon, and I don't know the first thing about this mortar."

The mortar crew's eyes lit up, and they started falling all over themselves showing me how things worked. After several explanations, I had a basic understanding of the mortar, but I would leave the actual operation to the crew. I asked if they needed anything, and they jokingly said that a week of R&R would be in order. I assured them this was beyond my powers.

With nothing better to do, I took a tour of Lima Company's portion of the perimeter set up around Hill 63. Because the hill had just been secured, there were no defensive fortifications built to protect us. There were foxholes strung out along the perimeter about fifty meters apart. Each foxhole was occupied by a four-man fire team. The area closest to the company CP was manned by Second Platoon, which I learned was led by Lieutenant Norman. As I passed through their area, Lieutenant Norman barely acknowledged my presence. Obviously the leader of a nonexistent platoon was not someone you wasted your time talking to. The next platoon in line was First Platoon. As I walked through their lines, I was greeted by a young lieutenant who introduced himself as Chuck Werner. He enthusiastically shook my hand and welcomed me to Lima Company. He also went out of his way to introduce me to his platoon sergeant and three squad leaders. He walked me through his defensive positions, showing me the various fighting holes and explaining why they had been placed where they were. When we completed the tour, he said, "Glad to have you aboard. If you need anything, all you have to do is ask."

As I left First Platoon's area, I felt a little better about my situation. Even if I didn't have a command, Lieutenant Werner made me feel welcome and acted as if I belonged to the company. The same thing was repeated at Third Platoon. The platoon commander was Rich Muler, and he greeted me as warmly as Chuck Werner had. He showed me around and introduced me to various members of his platoon. He also offered to help me in any way he could and invited me back anytime. After meeting the two platoon commanders, I felt much better and concluded I wasn't a total outcast within the company. I returned to the company CP and ran into Sergeant Schwartz. I asked him, "Is there any chance I could go out on a patrol in the near future?"

He responded, "No problem. I'll set something up for you tomorrow morning if that's not too late."

I thanked Sergeant Schwartz and went to sleep eagerly anticipating the next day's activities.

The next morning, I found Sergeant Niel at Second Platoon. He greeted me and introduced me to the members of the patrol. We would take ten men and go out about a klick to the west of the perimeter. Sergeant Niel showed me where we would be patrolling, and I marked the patrol route on my map using a grease pencil on clear plastic that covered the map. This method was taught to us in Basic School. By enclosing the map in a clear plastic envelope and using a grease pencil, you could wipe off the pencil markings after the patrol and continually reuse the map. If you marked directly on the map, the map would soon become useless, marked up with previous patrol routes.

As we exited the perimeter, I was filled with anticipation and some misgivings about my first patrol in the 'Nam. Sergeant Niel appeared very professional in the running of the patrol. He briefed the men prior to the patrol and then assigned one man to walk point. In addition, he assigned each man a position in the patrol. Men were placed on the flanks to provide security on both sides of the patrol. As we exited the perimeter, each man locked and loaded his M16 and appeared to know exactly what was expected of him. The men maintained intervals and walked slowly through the bush, looking in all directions with their rifles at the ready. This being my first patrol, I anticipated an enemy ambush and visually searched out potential sites from which the enemy could launch an attack. After a couple of hours of patrolling, we had taken a circuitous route and were back at the Lima Company perimeter. I was relieved to be back inside the perimeter and thanked Sergeant Niel for the opportunity to accompany him on the patrol. I would later realize the patrol was nothing more than a walk in the park, designed solely for my benefit. We did not go out far enough to engage the VC, and the members of the patrol were simply escorting a boot second lieutenant on his first patrol. At the time, it seemed genuine.

Getting settled in

2

GETTING MY FEET WET

LIEUTENANT MULER REQUESTED PERMISSION TO take out a platoon-size patrol to the village of Tam Li, which was about two klicks northeast of the perimeter. He explained Tam Li covered an entire grid square, which was one thousand meters by one thousand meters. He had not been in that area before and wanted to thoroughly search the village. He stated he suspected the village was a haven for the VC and anticipated enemy contact. Captain K. gave him permission to take out the entire platoon. Captain K. did not ask for a report on the mortar section, and the meeting broke up just as the sun was going down.

After the meeting, Lieutenant Muler approached and asked if I would like to join Third Platoon the next day.

"Sure," I replied, "but I need to check with Captain Kolakowski first."

"If you decide to go with us, you might as well spend the night at our CP," Rich replied as he walked off toward Third Platoon.

I found Captain K. and asked him if it would be okay to join the Third Platoon on their patrol to check out Tam Li. He had no objection, so I grabbed my M16, helmet, and cartridge belt and headed for Third Platoon. When I arrived, Lieutenant Muler was briefing his squad leaders for the next day's mission. As I joined the group, my presence was acknowledged. Rich informed the group they should be ready to go at least one hour before first light. He wanted to arrive at the village as soon as it was light enough to see. He told them we would leave the perimeter and travel to Tam Li in column formation. First Squad would be in the lead, followed by Third Squad, with Second Squad bringing up the rear. He then said, "I'll be between First and Third Squad. When we arrive at Tam Li, I want the First and Third Squad on line as we sweep through the village." Rich asked if there were any questions. When no one replied, he told the squad leaders to make sure their men got some sleep, because it would be a long day. As the squad leaders were leaving, Rich remarked, "By the way, Lieutenant Hynes will be joining us tomorrow. He will travel with Second Squad."

I assumed Rich put me in the safest place in the platoon where I couldn't get in too much trouble. I slept rather fitfully that night, knowing this would be the first real action I would see.

We awoke at 0400 to prepare for the patrol. I cooked a meal of C rations and checked my gear one last time while Third Platoon was forming up. I located Sergeant Coll, Second Squad's leader, and he told me to stay with him during the patrol.

As we left the perimeter, Lieutenant Muler came over and said, "When the shooting starts, get your head down and keep it down." He obviously didn't want a wet-behind-the-ears Second Lieutenant running around playing John Wayne. I wished he had said *if* the shooting started rather than *when*.

We left the perimeter in single file, keeping about eight to ten paces apart. Column formation—or single file, as we would say in civilian life—is not the best way to move a platoon. If you are ambushed at the front of the platoon, there is no way to get substantial firepower on your attackers. Unfortunately, it is the only practical way to move at night. If we tried to travel in a tactical formation, people would be too spread out, and the platoon would become separated.

As we proceeded toward Tam Li, I was surprised at how quiet the platoon was. There were about fifty marines extended over four hundred meters, and I never heard a sound except for the man ahead of me or behind when he brushed against something. We were taking our time and traveled for about forty-five minutes when the platoon came to a halt. Word filtered back that we would remain in position until it was light enough to see. The men around me found a comfortable place to lie down. I copied them, although inside I was much more excited than they appeared to be. Finally, the eastern sky lit up, and the column moved ahead.

As we reached a clearing, I could see the marines ahead of me spreading out. The first two squads got on line, each of them in a wedge formation, one fire team up and two back. Second Squad also got in a wedge formation behind the first two squads. When we started moving, a Vietnamese jumped up to the right of the formation and took off running. Half of the platoon opened up on him. They must have fired five hundred rounds before he fell. I couldn't believe he ran as far as he did before he was hit. Several men ran over to him, but they returned without any weapons.

I asked Sergeant Coll, "How did the platoon know he was a VC before they opened fire?"

"It doesn't matter," he replied. "He never should have run. If they run, they're VC."

Some type of bell began ringing in the village. As a result of the gunfire, the entire population of Tam Li knew of our presence. So much for leaving before first light. After the delay, we started moving through Tam Li.

Tam Li was not as I expected. On the map, it looked like a huge village, but in reality, the hooches were spread out in small groups. Between the clusters of hooches, there were small rice paddies, gardens, and clumps of bamboo. As we swept through the area, we followed the main trail that bisected the village. The front two squads were spread out on each side of the trail, and Second Squad, which brought up the rear, straddled the trail. We traveled about two hundred meters into the village when we started taking fire from the right front. Sergeant Coll yelled for me to get down. His words were wasted, as I was already hugging the ground. These would be the first rounds ever fired in my direction in anger.

The right side of the platoon immediately returned fire. It was hard to determine which rounds were out going and which rounds were incoming. Despite Lieutenant Muler's instructions to the contrary, I crawled forward to his position. He was on the radio while examining his map. He was describing the situation to company headquarters and began calling in an artillery fire mission. His half of the conversation went as follows:

"Connive Lima Six, this is Lima Three, over. Six, we're in heavy contact, and I need a fire mission. Our location is coordinates BT630510, target at BT631510. Azimuth 910. Give me one round of HE in adjustment. I can and will adjust."

Shortly, we could hear a 105 howitzer round whistling in. It struck about one hundred yards left of the location from which we were taking fire. Lieutenant Muler adjusted the fire. "Move right one hundred yards and give me a battery one in effect."

Almost immediately, six rounds came barreling in, right on target. Lieutenant Muler responded, "Repeat with a battery six. Fire for effect."

The artillery responded with thirty-six rounds, which erupted on top of the VC. This silenced the enemy fire, and I assumed we would sweep the area where the artillery rounds landed. Instead, we came under fire from the left front. The left side of the platoon returned fire, and we again started receiving fire from the right front.

Lieutenant Muler obviously did not like the situation and radioed his squad leaders to get ready to move out. By this time, we were getting sniper fire from our rear. Lieutenant Muler gave instructions to his squad leaders to retreat out of the village as soon as the next artillery rounds start landing. He then requested another battery six on the previous target. When the rounds started landing, the platoon began maneuvering back along the trail where we entered Tam Li. Part of the platoon would maneuver while the remainder laid down covering fire. When we arrived at the edge of the village, we set up a perimeter.

Lieutenant Muler adjusted the artillery to where we had received the incoming fire from the platoon's left side and requested another battery six on that area. The enemy fire ceased, and Lieutenant Muler checked with his squad leaders to see if there were any casualties. When he satisfied himself that everyone was in one piece, he radioed back to the company CP to see if we could get a Blackcoat.

Blackcoat was the call sign of an aerial observer (AO). The observer flew in a single-engine plane similar to a Piper Cub. The plane carried two men, the pilot and the AO. The AO could call in artillery or bring in air strikes. In addition, the plane could fire rockets for marking targets for air strikes.

We were informed there were no Blackcoats available. He was also told to hold our position and await further orders. A half hour later, we were ordered back to Hill 63. We maneuvered away from the village for about two hundred yards when Lieutenant Muler concluded we were out of danger. The platoon formed into a column, and we proceeded back to the company perimeter.

On the way back, I had a chance to talk to Lieutenant Muler. He explained he did not like the situation in Tam Li. He was especially concerned when we started taking sniper fire from the rear. The last thing he wanted was to be surrounded by a superior force and cut off from the rest of the company. He assured me we would be back under better circumstances, and things would be different.

We humped back to the company perimeter and reported to Captain K. By this time, it was 1600 hours. I was surprised by the hour and would have guessed we had been at it for little more than a couple of hours. In fact, twelve hours had passed since we awoke and started our mission. Lieutenant Muler briefed Captain K. on what happened at Tam Li. Captain K. agreed that Lieutenant Muler did the smart thing in getting out of there when he did. Lieutenant Muler wanted to return to Tam Li the next day, and Captain K. checked with battalion to see if he could line up a Blackcoat. He received a negative response but was told one would be available the following day. It was decided Third Platoon would return to Tam Li in two days.

I then requested one of the dumbest things that had ever been suggested in Vietnam. "How about taking the sixty-millimeter mortar crew with them?" I asked.

Captain K. didn't bat an eye. He must have known how badly I wanted to be part of the company. He replied, "I think that is an excellent idea."

Lieutenant Muler did not protest but, like Captain K., must have known what a stupid idea this was. His only reply was "Bring your mortar crew over tomorrow night, because we will be leaving before first light."

I was so excited it was all I could do to keep from running over to the mortar crew to tell them the good news. When I found Corporal Hall, I informed him we would be joining Third Platoon on their mission to Tam Li. The mortar crew gave each other "the lieutenant has lost his fucking mind look," but they said nothing. After being assured by Corporal Hall that the mortar was as clean as they could get it and that all members of the crew were present and accounted for, I left them for the night to make plans for the return to Tam Li.

That night, I had a lot to think about. I first reviewed the actions of the day. I was impressed with the way Lieutenant Muler was able to handle the situation. He was calm and collected when the firefight started. In a short period of time, he figured out the enemies' coordinates, shot an azimuth to the target, and got on the radio to call in the artillery fire mission. I wondered if I would ever be as efficient.

I also wondered about the importance of having a Blackcoat with us on our next mission. I would later learn the Blackcoat increased a platoon's or company's effectiveness manyfold. The AO in the Blackcoat could observe the action from above rather than from ground level. This gave him a much better view of the battlefield and allowed him to locate the ground positions on his map. The AO knew the exact coordinates of the marines on the ground and the exact coordinates of the target. The marine on the ground could never be absolutely certain of his location and many times had to guess at the location of the enemy. Also, as a result of having an aerial view, the Blackcoat could adjust the artillery far more efficiently than the marines on the ground.

The biggest dimension the Blackcoat added was air support. The PRC 25 radio, which was standard issue to all rifle companies, could not communicate with the fixed-wing aircraft that dropped the bombs. Although there was one radio issued to each battalion that could communicate with fixed-wing aircraft, it was far too heavy to carry in the field. Without a Blackcoat, the infantry companies and platoons had no close air support. With a Blackcoat, they could rain down death and destruction from the skies. A Blackcoat could not only talk to the fixed-wing aircraft, he could mark targets with his rockets to let them know exactly where to drop their bombs. All the infantry had to do was let a Blackcoat know where the target was, and he would do the rest. Without a Blackcoat, the rifle platoon's only advantage over the VC was its ability to call in artillery. Sometimes artillery was not available, and other times it was difficult to adjust because of the terrain. With Blackcoat, we had artillery that could be adjusted with pinpoint accuracy plus close air support, which could drop napalm as well as various bombs. When we returned to Tam Li with a Blackcoat, the VC had better be ready for a long day.

It should have been immediately obvious that taking the mortar section to Tam Li was a mistake. The mortar and baseplate weighed in excess of fifty pounds. One man had to carry the baseplate, which weighed a good twenty-five pounds, while a second man carried the mortar tube, which weighed about twenty pounds. A third carried the bipod, which weighed another ten pounds. The fourth man carried the radio. This equipment was carried in addition to the gear that the normal rifleman carried. In short, the mortar section was loaded down with all they could carry. The one thing that was left out of the equation was the ammunition for the mortar. A six-millimeter mortar round weighs about seven pounds. I wanted to take thirty rounds with us. This was over two hundred pounds of ammunition that needed to be humped by someone. I went to Third Platoon's CP and found Rich Muler, and I told him of my predicament. It would have been easy for him to explain the futility of trying to take the mortar section with us to Tam Li. Instead, he said, "Bring the ammunition over to the platoon, and I will get each one of my men to carry a mortar round."

Looking back, I realized how patient Lieutenant Muler and Captain K. were with an eager young second lieutenant who wanted to be part of the action. With the availability of the Blackcoat, we had unlimited fire support. The sixty-millimeter mortar was an archaic weapon that was of little use in Vietnam. It was at best a defensive weapon, and trying to hump it in the heat of Vietnam was foolish. I would live and learn.

I spent most of the morning getting the mortar section ready for Tam Li. That afternoon, my relations with Lieutenant Norman of Second Platoon took a turn for the worse. After delivering the mortar rounds to Third Platoon, I returned to the company CP. I ran into Captain K., and he expressed his concern about the company perimeter in the area of Second Platoon. "Why don't you go over and take a look at it and get back to me?" he requested.

I went to Second Platoon's CP to talk to Lieutenant Norman about the problem. He wasn't there, so I walked over to Second Platoon's portion of the perimeter to take a look. The concerns of Captain K. became immediately obvious. Lieutenant Norman had his defensive positions configured in such a manner that there were blind spots between fighting positions. In addition, there were places where you could not see from one fighting position to the next. It was obvious major adjustments had to be made. I reported back to Captain K. and related my observations, and he agreed with me. He then instructed me to go back to the Second Platoon and get the problem corrected. I told him I didn't know where Lieutenant Norman was. He replied, "Don't worry about that. Just find the Second Platoon sergeant and tell him what needs to be done."

I returned to Second Platoon's CP and learned that Lieutenant Norman still had not returned. The platoon sergeant for Second Platoon, Staff Sergeant Niel, who took me on my first patrol, was just walking up as I arrived. I explained to him that Captain K. wanted some adjustments to the perimeter. He and I walked to the perimeter and discussed the situation. We decided to move four of the fighting positions, which tightened up the perimeter and should solve the problems. We found the squad leaders of Second Platoon and explained what needed to be done while walking the perimeter with them. The troops were also present, and it was obvious that they were not happy about the situation. Substantial work had been done on the existing foxholes, and now they had to pick up and start over. They knew better than to express their displeasure in my presence, but I was sure there would be a lot of bitching when I left. I returned to the company CP and gave little further thought to the matter.

An hour later, Lieutenant Norman came storming up to the CP and sought me out. He confronted me and demanded to know exactly what I thought I was doing changing his perimeter.

I replied, "Captain K. told me to get things straightened out. If you have a problem, you should take it up with him. In the meantime, get the fuck out of my face." *This new LT is an Ass hole!*

This was not the reply Lieutenant Norman expected, and he stomped off toward Captain K.'s tent. I stayed around to see what would develop. Lieutenant Norman was in Captain K.'s tent for several minutes when he came walking out red faced and obviously angry. He walked past me, staring straight ahead without saying a word.

I should have left things alone but couldn't resist going to the Second Platoon's CP to rub a little salt in Lieutenant Norman's wounds. I found Sergeant Niel sitting next to Norman and told him, "I'm just checking on the progress Second Platoon is making on the changes in the perimeter."

Sergeant Niel and I walked over to the perimeter. When we got out of earshot of Lieutenant Norman, Sergeant Niel chuckled and said, "Boy, you really pissed off the lieutenant."

It was apparent he didn't like Norman any more than I. Sergeant Niel went on to say, "I told the lieutenant that the perimeter was fucked up, but he wouldn't listen. Now he's pissed off at me as well as you." I assured Sergeant Niel that everything would blow over, and I returned to the company CP.

It was time to gather up the mortar section and head for Third Platoon's CP to get settled in for the night. Shortly after we arrived,

Lieutenant Muler began to brief his squad leaders. The procedure would be the same as before. We would proceed to Tam Li before first light in column formation. When we got to Tam Li, we would put First and Second Squad on line and sweep through the village. Rich placed the mortar section with his command group, which would be directly behind First and Second Squad. After he was finished, there were no questions, and the briefing broke up.

I was even more excited about going to Tam Li this time. I was finally commanding troops, albeit only four. I would also have a radio with which I could communicate with the rest of the company. My call sign would be Connive Lima Four. The call sign for Third Battalion was Connive, and the call sign for Lima Company was Connive Lima. The call sign for a commander of a unit was always six. Therefore, the call sign for the Lima company commander was Connive Lima Six. First Platoon was Connive Lima One, Second Platoon was Connive Lima Two, Third Platoon was Connive Lima Three, and Weapons Platoon was Connive Lima Four. Each squad in the platoon was assigned a radio, and its call sign would be the platoon's call sign plus the number of the squad. For example, the call sign of Third Squad in Second Platoon would be Connive Lima Two Three. Likewise, the call sign of First Squad in Third Platoon would be Connive Lima Three One.

In addition, there was a method for determining who you were talking to on the radio. If you called Connive Lima Two, you would get the radio operator for Second Platoon. If you wished to talk directly to the platoon commander, you would ask for "Two actual." This meant you wanted to talk to the platoon commander, rather than the radio operator. The term *actual* meant the specific commander of the unit you were calling. I was now Connive Lima Four Actual.

To fully comprehend the communication system, you also had to understand the term *net*. A net is the radio frequency assigned to a particular unit. No other unit in Vietnam would be assigned the same frequency. When a radio was set on a certain frequency, it could only communicate with other radios on that frequency. For example, when my radio was dialed in to the frequency of the company net, the only people I could communicate with were members of Lima Company. Captain K. carried two radios in his command group. One was dialed in to the company net, and the other was on the battalion net. He could communicate within the company as well as with Battalion. All of the radio operators had the call signs of other units operating in our vicinity as well as their radio frequencies in case they needed to be contacted in an emergency. Most of the time, we stayed on the company net. If we needed to contact the battalion, we would do so through Lima Six.

That night, we went to sleep early and were up at 0400 ready to head for Tam Li. We proceeded toward Tam Li in column formation and stopped outside of the village, waiting for first light. I told Corporal Hall, who was carrying the radio, to monitor the net and let me know when Blackcoat came on station. Shortly, Corporal Hall handed me the radio handset and said Blackcoat just checked in. I heard Lieutenant Muler's voice, "Roger, Blackcoat. We are ready to move out. Why don't you stay about three or four klicks south of us, and I will call you if we make contact. That way, we won't alert Charlie to your presence."

"Lima Three, this is Blackcoat Two. I copy that you want me to stay south of you until you make contact. I have two fixed wings standing by on the ground. I can have them on station in five minutes. I'll be to the south waiting for your request. Over."

With that, we began our advance on Tam Li in tactical formation. When we reached the edge of the village, the damn bell started ringing again. It was a wake-up call for everyone in the village. We advanced along the same trail that we had used previously. When we arrived at the location of the previous firefight, nothing happened. I assumed the VC must have wised up and got the hell out of Dodge. We traveled another two hundred meters when all hell broke loose. We were taking heavy fire from both the right and left front. I grabbed the handset from Corporal Hall as we dived into a small depression. I could hear Lieutenant Muler on the radio. "Blackcoat, we've got heavy contact. We're about five hundred meters into the village along the main trail. When you get in sight, I will pop smoke. Over."

"Roger, Lima Three. I'm on my way."

We continued to take heavy fire. Shortly, I could hear and then see the single-engine Blackcoat flying toward us. As he approached, Lieutenant Muler threw a yellow smoke grenade.

The Blackcoat responded, "I've got your smoke in sight."

"Roger, Blackcoat. This is Lima Three. The yellow smoke is pretty much in the middle of our position. We are taking fire from our twelve o'clock about one hundred meters out."

"Roger, Lima Three. I will have a fire mission on target in a minute."

The forward elements of Third Platoon were returning fire while the rest of the platoon was maneuvering into a defensive position. My mortar section was setting up the mortar behind a small mound of dirt. Corporal Hall took off the radio and left it with me so that he could supervise the operation. A few minutes later, Blackcoat came back on the radio.

"Lima Three, I have a round on the way. Over."

Seconds later, we could hear the round whistling in. Lieutenant Muler was on the radio to the Second Squad leader, "Lima Three Two, did you mark that round?"

"Roger, Lima Three. We need to bring it about fifty meters closer."

"I copy," responded the Blackcoat. Seconds later, the Blackcoat replied, "Round out."

Immediately, a second round came in. The Second Squad leader shouted into the radio, "This is Three Two—right on target!"

Blackcoat responded, "Battery six on the way." Thirty-six artillery rounds pounded the enemy position. Blackcoat then said, "Lima Three, I have fixed wing on station. Tell me when you are ready to move out."

The ground fire had subsided, and Lieutenant Muler was on the radio instructing the squad leaders to get ready to move.

Blackcoat came back up on the net. "Hold everything, Lima Three. I've got beaucoup VC in front of you. It looks like an anthill down there. Hold your position while I bring in the fixed wing."

The Blackcoat was circling above us when he fired a round from his rocket pod. It was a white phosphorus (WP) rocket, and soon a white plume of smoke rose to our front. I was about to observe my first air strike. Within minutes, we observed an F-4 Phantom approaching from east to west. He made a pass without dropping a bomb. We watched him circle around and make another pass. This time, he dropped two five hundred–pound bombs. Almost immediately, he was followed by a second Phantom, which dropped two more five hundred–pound bombs. As soon as the second plane cleared the area, the first jet made another run, dropping additional bombs. The second jet returned and dropped its remaining ordinance. This was followed by each jet making another pass, strafing the area with cannon fire from their wing guns. The members of Third Platoon watched, much like they would a fireworks display on the Fourth of July. Each time the planes made a pass over the target, a cheer would go up from Third Platoon. After the strafing run, the jets had apparently used up their munitions and left.

The Blackcoat then called in another artillery fire mission. As the rounds were coming in, Lieutenant Muler radioed the Blackcoat and told him we were ready to sweep through the area. The Blackcoat responded, "I've more targets down there than you can shake a stick at. I have fixed wing on station and am ready to bring in another air strike. Hold your position until I can run this mission."

This time, the procedure was the same, except that the fixed wing dropped napalm instead of the five hundred–pound bombs. The napalm brought an even bigger cheer from the troops. This procedure continued for a couple of hours, alternating between air strikes and artillery missions.

After the air strikes, Blackcoat brought in two Huey gunships to run strafing missions over the targets. This was my first opportunity to observe the gunships in action. Although they were not as impressive as the fixed wings, they were able to stay on station longer than the Phantoms. They made pass after pass over the target, firing both rockets and from machine guns mounted on their landing skids. In addition, their door gunners were spraying the area with machine-gun fire.

Around noon, the Blackcoat came up on the radio and said he was running low on fuel, and another Blackcoat was coming on station. Sure enough, another Blackcoat appeared, and the two planes circled the area. The first Blackcoat was familiarizing the second Blackcoat with the enemy's location.

All of a sudden, we heard rifle fire from another area in Tam Li. We could see green tracer rounds lifting up toward the Blackcoats. The VC were firing at the observation planes. Lieutenant Muler reported this to the Blackcoats, and they responded. Almost immediately, fixed wings were swooping in for additional bombing runs.

The bombing runs were starting to become routine when the new Blackcoat came on the radio and said, "Lima Three, I have some enemy movement to your left front about one hundred yards out."

I seized the opportunity and got on the radio. "Blackcoat, this is Lima Four, and I have a sixty-mike-mike mortar. If you will adjust, I can put some rounds on them."

I am sure Blackcoat must have thought, *Who the fuck is Lima Four?*

He answered, "Negative on that, Lima Four. I don't want to be the first Blackcoat shot out of the sky by a friendly mortar round."

Lieutenant Muler responded, "Lima Four, let's save your ammo. We might need it later." This was obviously said to allow me to save face.

The bombing went on into the afternoon. Lieutenant Muler was anxious to get on with his mission and sweep through Tam Li. There should be lots of VC casualties as a result of the ordinance pounding the village. The sooner we got in there, the sooner we could assess the damage being done.

Around 1400 hours Captain K. came up on the radio net. He had apparently been monitoring the situation. He informed us he was trying to get clearance to bring the rest of the company out to assist in the sweep of the village. The air strikes kept on coming, and we continued to try to get clearance to move into the village. By 1600 hours, it was apparent we were not going to sweep Tam Li.

Lima Six informed us he had permission to bring the rest of the company to our location, and we were to stand by for further orders.

An hour later, we were told to secure a location and set in for the night. The rest of the company would join us as soon as they could. Rich Muler checked his map and found a rather large clearing to our rear near the edge of Tam Li. He ordered the squad leaders to get ready to move out. As soon as we began maneuvering, we came under heavy fire from three sides. We returned fire and made it to the new location without taking casualties.

When we arrived at the clearing, we set up a perimeter and awaited the rest of the company. When we left Hill 63, we only expected to be gone for the day and did not bring our backpacks or other provisions. Lieutenant Muler contacted Lima Six and told him of our situation. We were informed the rest of the company would carry our gear to us and to expect them in three hours.

We hadn't eaten since we left the perimeter, and we were getting hungry. We scooped out fighting holes as best we could and awaited the arrival of the rest of the company. After setting up our night defensive positions, I had time to reflect on the day's activities.

The first thing that crossed my mind was we had not incurred any casualties during our two excursions into Tam Li. On both occasions, we had engaged in substantial firefights, and no one on our side was killed or wounded. I estimated we received over a thousand rounds of small-arms fire in the two skirmishes. I would later discover that in a firefight with the VC, involving rifle fire alone, there were very few casualties occurring after the first few minutes. Except in the rice paddies, most of the terrain in our TAOR contained a substantial amount of cover. Once a unit was able to maneuver into a defensive position, the chances of getting shot by a rifle round were minimal.

Of course, this works both ways. Just as we were not taking casualties, it is likely we were not inflicting casualties on Charlie with our rifle fire. We did have M79 grenade launchers that fired an exploding round that could kill or wound an enemy soldier if it landed close to him. Other than the M79s, our small arms could do little damage to an entrenched VC.

The artillery and air strikes were a different matter. Once we dropped these weapons on the enemy's position, it was absolutely no contest. I learned that in firefights involving small-arms fire alone, Charlie was a worthy opponent. He could slug it out with the best of the American units, but he was no match for us if we could effectively use our air and artillery. Unfortunately, Charlie had ways of neutralizing our indirect fire support.

At 2100 hours, I checked on the mortar crew. They had the mortar set up and their aiming stakes in place. They also had a large number of mortar rounds, still in their cardboard canisters, piled next to the mortar. Corporal Hall asked me, "Well, Lieutenant, how are you liking the 'Nam?"

With false bravado, I replied, "It suits me just fine."

Corporal Hall replied, "You'd better get used to it. Today was a walk in the park, and you know what they say—payback is a motherfucker."

Getting my feet wet

3

LEARNING THE HARD WAY

OVER THE NEXT SEVERAL MONTHS, I would hear this expression many times. Whether the enemy kicked our asses or we kicked their asses, one of the troops always responded with "Payback is a motherfucker."

I tried to act as nonchalant as possible when I asked the troops, "I guess it gets a lot worse than this?"

They all started laughing. "Lieutenant, this ain't shit," Lance Corporal Fields replied. "Wait until we get back in the Que Son Valley. That's where the NVA hang out. These fuckers we dealt with today weren't nothing but rice farmers. Tomorrow, they'll be plowing their fields."

Corporal Hall chimed in, "You think the NVA would have sprung that ambush like they did today? Fuck no! They would have waited until First Squad had walked through their front lines before they started shooting. When the NVA ambush you, you're fucked before you know it."

Lance Corporal Fields added, "Remember Operation Union? Half of First Platoon was completely cut off after the first ten minutes of fighting. We couldn't get artillery or air for the first day without wiping them out. Yes, sir, Lieutenant—payback is a motherfucker."

I thought these stories were being embellished for my benefit, but I still listened in fascination. I later learned what they said about Operation Union was more than true.

I finally changed the subject and asked the men if they were ready for the night. They assured me they were. They had the mortar set up so the rounds would land approximately fifty meters outside of our perimeter. If we came under attack, all they had to do was point the mortar toward the enemy and start launching rounds. Despite what seemed to be an eventful day, the mortar section appeared to be unconcerned about a night attack by the VC. They were more concerned about getting something to eat.

Corporal Hall asked, "Heard anything from the company, Lieutenant? My stomach thinks my throat's been cut."

I replied I thought the company would be there shortly and went to check with Lieutenant Muler. I found Rich talking to his platoon sergeant, Staff Sergeant Wells. Sergeant Wells was a career marine and the largest individual in the company. They were discussing the day's events. Neither Rich nor Sergeant Wells could recall when they had seen so many air strikes in one day.

"I don't know what their targets were, but there must have been a bunch of them," commented Sergeant Wells.

Rich replied, "It's too bad we couldn't have swept through the village before dark. By the time we get in there tomorrow, they will have hauled off their dead and wounded."

"I wonder why they let us catch them in the open like that," questioned Sergeant Wells. "It's not like Charlie to make that kind of mistake."

"I don't know," replied Rich. "Maybe we just got lucky. I bet they won't be there tomorrow."

I asked Rich if he heard from Captain K. He told me they probably wouldn't arrive before midnight.

I went back to the mortar section and told them, "We might as well get some sleep. We won't be eating for a while."

I assigned a two-hour watch rotation. Someone would be manning the radio all night long. I lay on the ground and immediately fell asleep.

I was awakened by one of the mortar crew and was informed the rest of the company was about to arrive. Shortly, the company's forward elements were entering our position, and Captain K. joined Lieutenant Muler and me in the perimeter. Captain K. decided to widen the perimeter to make room for the other two platoons, and he told me to get it coordinated. After moving Third Platoon to the east side of the perimeter, the other two platoons filled in the gaps, and we had a company-size perimeter set up. Everything was more crowded than normal, but it would do for the night. Sergeant Schwartz coordinated the redistribution of the C rations as well as getting Third Platoon's backpacks and gear to them. When everything was squared away, I returned to the company CP and cooked a meal of C rations. Shortly, the platoon commanders gathered with Captain K. for a company meeting. We would sweep through Tam Li at first light. The village was divided into three sectors, and each was assigned to a platoon. First Platoon would be responsible for the northern sector, Third Platoon the middle sector, and Second Platoon the southern sector.

Captain K. instructed us to take our time as we swept through the village, making sure we thoroughly searched everything. He said, "I don't care if it takes all day; I want to cover every square inch of that place. Let's make sure that we maintain security. I don't want to get caught with our pants down in there."

Captain K. ordered everyone dug in before we turned in for the night. As the meeting adjourned, he told me the mortar section would be attached to the company command post and for me to stay close to him. When everyone left, Captain K. gathered the first sergeant, the gunnery sergeant, and me together and set up a watch rotation. He wanted the four of us to stand a two-hour watch each. During our watch, we were to make a tour of the perimeter. Captain K. further instructed, "If you catch someone sleeping on watch, contact his platoon commander and let him deal with it. I don't want to know about it unless the platoon commander brings it to my attention." With that said, he assigned each of us a watch, and we turned in for the night.

The fact that marines fell asleep during their night watch was a recurring problem in Vietnam. Each command dealt with it differently. It was a court-martial offense to get caught sleeping on watch. Unfortunately, you can only push men so far. If they are humping day and night, it is sometimes impossible to stay awake. As a practical matter, even the best of troops fall asleep on watch.

The problem was usually dealt with at the platoon level. Each platoon commander had a different punishment for the offender, depending on the circumstances and the number of times the offender had been caught sleeping. If it happened too often, he would be turned over to the company commander for formal punishment.

That night, I lucked out and got an early watch. I walked the perimeter without incident, awoke my replacement, and went to sleep. I was awakened by the noises of the company getting ready for the day's activities. It was still dark, and I asked Corporal Hall what time it was.

"It's 0500 hours, Lieutenant, and the company will be moving out pretty soon."

I hurriedly prepared a meal of C rations and wolfed it down.

I found Captain K. talking to the platoon commanders. "Blackcoat should be coming up on the net pretty quick. As soon as he is in position, we will move out."

The platoon commanders left to join their platoons. Captain K. and I shot the breeze until it was time to move out. We speculated about what we would find in the village. He did not think we would meet much resistance but concluded, "You never know."

We heard the Blackcoat approaching before he came up on the radio net. Captain K. gave the word to move out, and the platoons started sweeping through the village. The company CP followed Third Platoon as they swept through the middle sector of Tam Li. After passing through the area of the previous day's firefight, I observed the results of the air strikes. Surprisingly, the bombs didn't do as much damage as I would have expected.

We moved slowly while the troops checked things thoroughly. They began finding things rather quickly.

Lima Two came over the radio. "I've got lots of blood trails over here. Can't find any bodies, though."

The forward elements of Third Platoon were getting excited as they discovered caches of medical supplies—mostly bandages as well as boxes of syringes and other medication with Chinese writing on them. The other platoons called in, reporting they were also finding substantial amounts of medical supplies. Third Platoon discovered a package of black hoods with clear plastic covers over the eye openings. Someone identified them as primitive gas masks used by the VC. We also found bolts of cloth, which were raw material for the making of bandages. Second Platoon found two sewing machines next to a large pile of bandages.

It became apparent Tam Li was a major distributor of medical supplies to the VC. Captain K. instructed the platoons to bring everything to his central location, and the marines started straggling in with armloads of materials. We piled them up, and Captain K. called battalion to report the situation.

"Connive Six, this is Lima Six. We've discovered a large cache of medical supplies and need instructions on what to do with them. Over."

Captain K. was instructed to continue searching the village and to stand by for further instructions. The more we looked, the more we found, including a tunnel complex, which was checked out by some of the smaller members of the company. The pile of medical supplies continued to grow as the day wore on.

Captain K. was contacted by Battalion and told to stand by for a chopper incoming from the south. Almost immediately, we could hear the *whump-whump* of the rotor blades of the helicopter. We popped a smoke grenade in a clearing, and the helicopter landed. Colonel Brady, the battalion commander, stepped off the chopper with Lieutenant Young, the battalion medical officer assigned to our battalion. They examined the medical supplies, in particular the vials of medicine we found. Lieutenant Young was especially interested in a case of ampules, which he determined to be used in case of a nerve gas attack. After assessing the situation, Colonel Brady took the case of ampules with him and instructed us to burn the rest of the supplies. He then boarded his helicopter and left the area.

As instructed, we burned the medical supplies with the help of a five-gallon can of diesel left by Colonel Brady. As a result, we had a sizable bonfire blazing. The temperature at the time was well over one hundred degrees, and the humidity was around 95 percent. The added effect of a roaring fire created a surreal scene in the middle of Tam Li.

It was getting close to 1700 hours, and the company had to find a place to spend the night. Captain K. ordered us to get ready to move out. We had searched the entire village and were now on its eastern edge. Captain K. located a likely area on his map, and the company maneuvered another two hundred meters east and set up a perimeter.

Captain K. asked me to register artillery targets around the perimeter. This consisted of adjusting artillery rounds on four sides of our position. Once they were zeroed in, the locations were recorded by the fire direction center at the artillery battery. If we were to come under attack during the night, we could call in fire missions on these registered targets immediately. We could also adjust rounds off these targets. I was halfway through this task when small-arms fire broke out on the south side of the perimeter.

Since I had the company radio, which was on the battalion net, I ran in the direction of the firing. I might be able to call in a fire mission if we were under attack. When I arrived at Second Platoon's CP, I discovered three of its men were cut off from the rest of the company. Apparently, they had gathered several canteens and were going to fill them at a well that was approximately one hundred meters outside the perimeter. They were on their third trip to the well and were ambushed while filling the canteens. One of Second Platoon's squads maneuvered its way down to the well. They were taking heavy fire as they tried to get to the trapped marines. The squad leader radioed for a medevac helicopter; he had two wounded marines at the well. Since I had the company radio, I told Lieutenant Norman to inform Lima Six I would call in the medevac.

I got on the radio, advised Battalion of the situation, and requested a medevac. I gave them our location and told them as soon as the medevac was in sight, I would guide it to our LZ. Battalion responded the medevac was on its way and would inform us when it got close to our position. I found one of Second Platoon's radiomen and told him to let me know when the medevac came up on his radio.

I heard that the squad from Second Platoon had picked up the wounded marines and was heading back into the perimeter. The exchange of gunfire had ceased, and I could see the squad returning on the run, carrying the two marines. One of the marines had been hit in the leg and appeared to be in pretty good shape. The other marine had been shot in the chest and had a sucking chest wound. Every time he breathed, you could hear the air entering and exiting his chest through the bullet hole. The corpsman had a cellophane-type material that he was taping to the wound to try to seal the bullet holes. The wounded marine kept moaning and asking the corpsman if he was going to die. The corpsman assured him he would be all right and they would have him out of there in no time.

The Second Platoon radioman told me the medevac had come up on the company net and handed me the radio's handset. I began talking to the chopper.

"Medevac, this is Connive Lima Four. What is your location? Over."

"Lima Four, this is Medevac Three One, and I am inbound five miles north of your position. Once you get me in sight, I'll need directions. Are you taking any fire at this time? Over."

I replied, "Negative on the fire. I can hear you but can't see you at this time."

The medevac came back, "Lima Four, it is starting to get dark, and we need to do this as quickly as possible. When you have me in sight, give me your location and pop a smoke. Once I see the smoke, I will confirm its color and come on in."

A minute later, I could see the approaching chopper and called, "Medevac Three, I have you in sight. I'm at your eleven o'clock, and you're about four hundred meters out. We're popping the smoke. Over."

One of the marines threw a green smoke grenade. "Roger, Lima Four. I have green smoke at my eleven o'clock. Confirm the color, and let me know whether you are taking fire. Over."

"Roger on the green smoke, and the LZ is still secure."

One of Second Platoon's men ran to the green smoke to guide the medevac in with hand signals. The helicopter came directly to the smoke and landed right in front of the marine guiding him in. The two wounded marines were immediately loaded into the medevac, and within seconds, it was back in the air. As the medevac turned and headed back to Da Nang, I got back on the radio and thanked them. Their reply was "Just doing our job, Lima Four."

As the medevac was leaving, Captain K. had arrived at our location. He wanted to know what happened. When he found out the two marines had been wounded outside of the perimeter, he was visibly upset. He took Lieutenant Norman off to the side, and they engaged in an animated discussion.

It was unfortunate the marines from Second Platoon were wounded. It put a damper on what was in general a very successful day. He had found and destroyed several tons of medical supplies and other gear that would have been useful to the VC. We also found several blood trails, indicating the enemy had been killed or wounded as a result of the air and artillery strikes. Unfortunately, the wounding of the two marines evened the score. Although I didn't like Lieutenant Norman, I felt Captain K. was a little unfair when he jumped on him about the casualties. The entire company had become complacent as a result of the day's activities. The lesson to be learned was Charlie was always out there waiting for an opportunity to put a hurt on you. Just when you think things are secure, you can be the most surprised.

A few minutes later, I was introduced to one of the real horrors of war. I resumed the registering of the night artillery targets when I arrived at the north side of the perimeter. There were several marines and a few civilians gathered around a figure lying on a bamboo litter. As I approached the marines, I discovered the figure on the stretcher was a badly wounded *mama-san*. She had been carried in by the villagers and was being administered to by one of the company corpsmen. When I looked closer, I discovered she had taken a piece of shrapnel in her abdomen. Her intestines were protruding from the wound, and she appeared to be near death. She had apparently been wounded by the attack of the previous day. I asked the corpsman what we could do for her.

The corpsman responded, "Lieutenant, it is getting too dark to call in a medevac, and besides, she is too far gone to save."

He suggested we give her a triple dose of morphine, which would be lethal. At the very least, it would stop her pain for a little while. He was not asking my permission to do this but rather voicing his conclusion as to what had to be done. He said nothing more and administered the morphine. With that done, he used sign language to instruct the villagers to pick up the stretcher and remove the old lady from our perimeter.

As I watched them leave, I was overcome with grief as to the fate of the old woman. She was truly an innocent victim of this war. I am sure she lived in a village that was sympathetic to the VC. On the other hand, what happened politically in her village was totally beyond her control. The only rationale that could be given was "That's war."

By now, it was approaching 2000 hours, and Captain K. called a company meeting. The platoon commanders and the First Sergeant attended the meeting along with Captain K. Captain K. began the meeting by reminding us we need to be more concerned about security, obviously referring to the situation with Second Platoon. He then informed us we would be sweeping the company TAOR during the next few days.

"We need to familiarize ourselves with the lay of the land as well as let Charlie know we're around. He obviously thinks he owns this area, and we are going to teach him otherwise," Captain K. told us. "Tomorrow, we will begin sweeping the area by heading in an easterly direction. Expect a lot of changes in direction during the day." He added, "I want the company in a wedge formation with First Platoon in front, Third Platoon in the left rear, and Second Platoon in the right rear. Let's make sure to maintain our intervals and take our time."

Captain K. asked if there were any questions. Lieutenant Werner said, "I don't have a question, but why don't we leave behind a squad in the morning to set an ambush? I'm sure Charlie is still watching us and will probably police up our area when we leave."

Captain K. thought this was a good idea and told Lieutenant Norman to leave behind one of his squads in an ambush position. The company would take their time leaving the perimeter and would stop about five hundred meters out and wait for the squad. If nothing happened in an hour, the squad should rejoin the rest of the company.

This is a tactic that has worked in the past for a couple of reasons. The average rifle company is not very careful in keeping its area policed. It will throw away portions of its C rations as well as leave ammunition and other items useful to the VC behind when it vacates an area. Charlie makes it a point to scavenge a perimeter when the marines move out. A company of VC could survive on what a company of marines throw away. Secondly, Charlie will keep a company under pretty close surveillance and follow it everywhere it goes. They would more than likely slip in behind us as soon as we began our sweep.

The next morning, we were up at first light ready to head out. The squad from Second Platoon had hidden itself in a large grove of bamboo some twenty meters off a trail within our perimeter. They had also set out claymore mines along the trail at both ends of the ambush.

Captain K. gave the orders to move out, and the company headed in an easterly direction. We took our time and made frequent stops, leaving the impression that we were vacating the area. We wanted to give the squad lying in ambush enough time to allow Charlie to wander into its area. We had been traveling for about thirty minutes when we heard explosions and bursts of small-arms fire from the location of the ambush sight. It sounded like our plan worked.

I grabbed the radio handset from Corporal Hall in time to hear the Second Platoon squad leader shouting, "Lima Two, we've got three confirmed kills and a probable wounded VC! There were five or six gooks walking into our kill zone when we sprung the ambush. A couple of them got away. Over."

Captain K. was monitoring the net and commanded Lima Two, "Take the rest of the your platoon back to the ambush site to provide security while they check out the kills. We'll wait here for you."

Second Platoon took off for the ambush site on the run and arrived there in a few minutes. Lieutenant Norman confirmed they had three VC on the ground with three weapons and several Chicom grenades. Captain K. informed Lima Two the rest of the company would move north, and they should rendezvous with us in a village about eight hundred meters north of our present location.

The rest of the morning was uneventful. When we joined up with Second Platoon, they proudly displayed the weapons they had captured in the ambush. The weapons had confirmed the prediction of Corporal Hall that we were dealing with local VC rather than NVA. The weapons consisted of an ancient Russian rifle and two M1 carbines. The M1 carbine was the preferred weapon of the Army of the Republic of Vietnam (ARVN). These two were probably captured from the ARVNs. If we were dealing with the NVA, the weapons would have been AK-47s.

The squad from Second Platoon excitedly related the events of the ambush. As predicted, the VC were policing up the area we had vacated. The squad waited as long as possible to spring the ambush in order to get as many VC as possible in the killing zone. When one of them practically walked on top of the squad's position, they were forced to trigger the ambush. Some of the VC were able to retreat back into the tree line. One of the squad members insisted he had wounded one of those VC. We reported it to Battalion as three confirmed kills and one VC wounded. We might as well give ourselves the benefit of the doubt.

The company continued to sweep through the TAOR without incident for the rest of the day. We would travel in one direction for several hundred meters and then make a ninety-degree turn and travel in another direction. We went from village to village, checking each of them out as we went. The reaction of the villagers was one of studied indifference. A company of marines would appear out of nowhere, and the villagers would act as if they hadn't noticed us. They would continue doing what they were doing without glancing in our direction. Our coming to their village must have been the biggest thing to happen in the neighborhood in many years. We were the first American troops ever to patrol this area, yet the villagers acted like we weren't there.

It was obvious the villagers in this area were not committed to our side. We were never welcomed to a village with smiles from the peasants. Kids did not gather around, begging for food or telling us, "Americans number one. VC number ten." It was obvious the villagers did not want us there and wished we would go away. You cannot blame them for this in that our presence meant nothing but trouble. Firefights tended to break out wherever we went. Civilians were killed, and villages were burned. The peasants were caught in the middle of this war. All they wanted was to tend their fields in peace. They couldn't care less if there was a unified Vietnam. It made little difference to them if South Vietnam prevailed or North Vietnam prevailed. Regardless of who ruled their country, they had to get up every morning to cultivate their fields and hopefully grow enough crops to survive another year. They were only one step away from starvation, and the war made it that much harder to survive

Captain K. instructed me to go with First Platoon. Once we got to our blocking position, I would register artillery targets in the area where we anticipated trapping the VC. After everyone was fully briefed, we saddled up and headed out. First Platoon headed due west toward the railroad tracks, except there weren't any tracks. Apparently, the railroad had been abandoned years earlier. The tracks and crossties had been pulled up. The only thing left was the elevated railroad bed. At one time, the railroad ran the length of the country from north to south and parallel to Highway 1.

After reaching the railroad bed, we moved north several hundred meters to our blocking position. The platoon was spread along the railroad right-of-way for four hundred meters, and we set in to wait for the rest of the company to sweep in from the east.

I registered several artillery targets out in front of the platoon and went over to talk to Chuck Werner, the First Platoon commander. I had recently learned he had attended the Naval Academy. He and Rich Muler graduated in the same class and had been good friends while at Annapolis. Both Chuck and Rich had joined the company at the same time in early April.

Our conversation turned to Operation Union. Lieutenant Werner described the action and explained the operation was the first excursion by US troops into the Que Son Valley. The Que Son Valley ran from southwest to northeast and was a major supply route from the Ho Chi Minh Trail to the southern part of I Corps. The Second NVA Division controlled the Que Son Valley and had never been challenged prior to Operations Union I and Union II.

Operation Union II began with Third Battalion, Fifth Marines being airlifted by helicopter into a huge rice paddy in the middle of the valley. The lead elements into the LZ were Lima and Kilo Companies. It was their job to secure a perimeter for the trailing units. The LZ seemed secure when they first landed, and both companies moved toward a tree line to establish a perimeter. They walked into an ambush laid by an NVA regiment. The NVA let the forward elements of both companies pass through their front lines before they sprang the ambush. Once the forward elements passed through their lines, the NVA opened up with everything they had. They pinned the two companies down in the rice paddies and dropped mortar rounds in on top of them. When the battalion commander tried to land in the command chopper, the NVA blew it out of the sky, killing the battalion commander, the S3 officer, the H&S company commander, and the battalion sergeant major. Three of the four highest-ranking officers and the highest-ranking enlisted man in the battalion were killed in the first hour of the battle.

Kilo and Lima Companies were pinned down for the rest of the day in the rice paddy. Anyone sticking his head above a paddy dike had little chance of survival. It was nightfall before the two companies could consolidate their positions and evacuate their dead and wounded.

The marines who lay in the rice paddy ran out of both water and ammo. The most heroic acts were performed by those who volunteered to move to the rear and bring back water and ammunition. On that day, every officer in Lima Company was either killed or wounded, with the exception of Rich Muler. Chuck Werner was shot in the leg and spent several weeks in the hospital before returning to Lima Company. The company commander was killed, and the Second Platoon commander was badly wounded.

Many medals of valor would have been awarded for the acts of bravery on this day but for the fact that most of the Lima Company command had been killed. Before the operation was over, Third Battalion took a considerable number of casualties. After relating the above, Chuck said, "You might wonder why Rich and I are so cautious when we move our platoons. We don't ever want to go through something like that again."

We moved east to the railroad tracks without incident. As we swept north along the railroad bed, we came across one of the damnedest sights I would ever witness in Vietnam. We discovered a structure that at one time had been a building of some substance. Its walls were made of brick and covered with white plaster. It was probably an abandoned French villa once belonging to a plantation owner. There were no roads leading to the villa, and the only way it could be reached was by the railroad tracks. It was now a bombed-out shell of its former self. Since the railroad was long gone, there was no way to access the villa, and it was now totally isolated. We were really out in the boonies, and the closest road was probably ten klicks away.

The strange thing about the building was the graffiti covering the walls. Graffiti was not unusual on abandoned buildings in Vietnam, and they mostly contained written messages in Vietnamese, which we didn't understand and ignored. This building had graffiti written in English! The message read THE US GOVERNMENT HAS MADE USE OF YOUR LIFE TO WAGE AN UNJUST AGGRESSIVE WAR IN SOUTH VIETNAM. This was a real mindblower not because of the message but rather the location. As I stated earlier, we were the first American troops to patrol this area on a regular basis. Why the VC would choose such an isolated location to leave this message was a complete mystery. The fact that we came upon the message was an accident, and the next American troops may not come through this area for another year. It was like placing a billboard in some remote canyon in the Mojave Desert. Needless to say, we were both amused and taken aback by the message. After taking some pictures of the graffiti, we continued with our mission.

After a while, my thoughts returned to the events of the last couple of days. It is virtually impossible to accurately describe what occurs in a firefight with the enemy. The first word that comes to mind is *chaos*. When the shooting starts, confusion reigns supreme. Bullets are flying, men are scrambling, orders are being shouted. It cannot be compared to anything that we are familiar with in civilian life.

In the midst of the chaos and confusion, there is also a sense of order. The individual marine's first instinct is self-preservation. This may consist of falling to the ground or running to the nearest available cover. Once he obtains a protected position, he attempts to return fire on his enemy. His ability to return the enemy fire depends on his location. If he has a clear field of fire, he is free to commence firing. If there are friendly troops between him and the enemy, he has to hold his fire until he has maneuvered himself into a position to return fire without endangering his fellow marines. This is where the fire team leader comes into play. It is his job to move the members of his fire team so that they can safely direct their fire on the enemy.

At the next level, the squad leader communicates with his fire team leaders in order to maneuver the fire teams into positions from which they can effectively bring the maximum amount of fire on the enemy forces. The squad leader has a dual role when the platoon comes under attack. In addition to getting his fire teams in position to return the enemy fire, he must also communicate with the platoon commander. In most cases, the platoon commander is not in a position to determine exactly where the enemy fire is coming from. He is on the radio to the squad leaders, wanting to know what the situation is and in particular the location of the enemy. Once the platoon commander is given the enemy's position, he can begin calling in artillery fire or request air support through Blackcoat.

The emotions experienced by the individual marines involved in a firefight are also difficult to describe. Immediately, your body injects a shot of adrenaline into your blood vessels, which produces a rush of energy as well as a heightened sense of awareness. Your perception of what is going on around you sharpens, and time seems to slow down. Fear raises its ugly head, and you must deal with that fear. You are afraid of dying and fear the unknown. Is there a handful of rice local VC shooting at you, or is it an NVA regiment getting ready to overrun your position? Your loyalty to the platoon forces you to react to the situation. What is worse—to die or be branded a coward by the platoon? Under no circumstances can you be considered a coward, so you do what you have to do. You get up and maneuver toward your enemy. You fire your rifle, throw grenades, communicate on the radio, and carry your share of the load. In the final analysis, you do what you do because you can't let your comrades down. The fear of failure overcomes your fear of death.

I also reflected on what happened at Tam Li. Why were we able to inflict the casualties and capture the supplies like we did? I am convinced the VC screwed up big-time. Our perception of the VC was they were tactically superior, always one step ahead of us in fighting the war. After all, they had been at war for the last twenty-five years—first with the Japanese, then with the French, and now with us. They were incapable of making tactical errors. This was simply not true at Tam Li. We were probably the first American troops to invade their village. In the past, they had skirmishes with the ARVN soldiers but had never dealt with the Americans. It is my opinion they thought they could stand up to us just like they had done with the ARVN. This local group of VC had no idea of the firepower we could unleash on them. How else do you explain them getting caught in the open or their failure to hide the medical supplies that were lying everywhere? They must have thought they were going to kick our asses when we first arrived at Tam Li. My theory is further confirmed by the fact that, during the next several months, we never got into a firefight in Tam Li, despite the fact that we patrolled it on a regular basis. Charlie learned his lesson and didn't make the same mistake twice.

When I returned to the company CP, everyone was in a somber mood. Word had come over the company radio that Second Platoon had taken three casualties, two of them KIAs. The medevac had just picked up the bodies and was taking them to Da Nang. The facts surrounding the incident were still pretty sketchy, but it appeared they were killed by friendly fire. I found First Sergeant Schwartz and asked him what happened. He said, "Lieutenant Norman had taken the platoon out on a patrol on the west side of the TAOR, and something got screwed up. Apparently, an artillery fire mission was called in on the patrol. Right now, Second Platoon is heading back to the perimeter."

Captain K. came to our position and appeared visibly upset and told Sergeant Schwartz to have Lieutenant Norman report to him as soon as he got in. An hour later, Lieutenant Norman came walking up to the CP and went to Captain K.'s tent. As soon as he arrived, I headed over to Second Platoon's CP and sought out Sergeant Niel. I asked him what happened, and he replied, "It's bad business, Lieutenant. Lieutenant Norman called in an artillery strike right on top of us. I don't know what he was thinking."

I responded, "Sometimes the coordinates get mixed up, and the artillery is fired at the wrong location."

"That's not what happened," replied a distraught Sergeant Niel. "Lieutenant Norman intentionally called in the mission on top of us.

He thought we could get out of there in time and we would catch Charlie sneaking in behind us. He didn't give us enough time to clear the area before the artillery came in, and the guys in the rear squad got killed. Everyone in the platoon is pretty upset right now."

It was obvious that I could not console Sergeant Niel, so I returned to the company CP. When I arrived, Lieutenant Norman was still talking to Captain K., along with a captain from the battalion. I realized this was none of my business, so I left to check out the new mess tent down at the battalion CP. The mess tent was starting to serve chow on a regular basis, and I arrived there in time for the evening meal. Sergeant Schwartz and Lieutenant Werner were sitting together, and I joined them. I commented, "This mess tent is going to beat the shit out of the C rations."

Sergeant Schwartz warned me to go easy on the first couple of meals and let my stomach get used to the new food. He said, "When you go from two meals of C rations a day to real food, your stomach has to have time to stretch. Don't overdo it the first couple of days."

I ignored him and wolfed down my first real meal in two weeks. Captain K. entered the mess tent and after getting his food came over and sat down with us. He told us Battalion was going to conduct an investigation of what happened to Second Platoon, and we should try to keep the troops from talking about the incident. He was obviously shook up in that these were the first troops that had been killed since he took over as company commander. He said, "I can't imagine what Norman was thinking of when he called in that fire mission."

The subject was changed, and we finished our meal. Later that night, Sergeant Schwartz's admonishment came true when I started experiencing stomach cramps from eating too much at the mess tent.

Taking casualties is always hard on a company. It is much worse when someone is killed or seriously maimed. When a trooper receives a less serious wound, the corpsman assures everyone the marine will be all right and probably has a ticket home. Everyone feels that it was too bad he got wounded, but at least he's not in the 'Nam anymore, having returned to the land of the flush toilets.

Speaking of toilets, Sergeant Schwartz told me each platoon would be getting a shitter in the next couple of days. The shitter was a device unique to Vietnam. The first time I saw one, I thought it was an old-fashioned outhouse. It is similar in appearance. It has four holes instead of two and is made out of plywood. The big difference between a shitter and an outhouse was that a shitter has fifty-five gallons drums cut in half to catch the excrement instead of a hole dug in the ground. When the drums started filling up, they were pulled out from under the shitter, and their contents were burned by adding diesel fuel and striking a match. You could always tell when the shitters were being burned by the powerful smell overwhelming the area. The smell of burning shitters is one that is indelibly etched in the memory of every Vietnam vet.

Learning the hard way

4

FINALLY, A PLATOON COMMANDER

AFTER GETTING THE MORTAR CREW lined out, I returned to the company CP. When I arrived, I was told by Sergeant Schwartz that Captain K. was looking for me. I found Captain K. in his tent, and he told me to come in. He came right to the point.

"I'm going to relieve Lieutenant Norman of his command, and I want you to take over Second Platoon."

For a moment, I was speechless. I always thought someone would have to rotate out of the company or get wounded before I got a rifle platoon.

After a few moments, Captain K. said, "I want you to keep this to yourself for the next couple of hours. I haven't told Lieutenant Norman yet, and I don't want him to hear it from anyone but me. I have someone out looking for him, and it will take some time for him to gather his gear and say good-bye to the platoon."

I asked Captain K., "What will happen to Lieutenant Norman?"

He replied, "Battalion has told me they will reassign him to another company outside of the battalion. I feel he deserves another chance at commanding a platoon. With the experience he has gained here and a new beginning, he has an opportunity to be a successful platoon commander. I just don't think the troops in Second Platoon have confidence in him after what happened yesterday."

After assuring Captain K. I would keep my mouth shut about the matter, I left his tent. Being relieved of command is the most ignoble thing that can happen to a Marine Corps officer. For a career marine, it is the end of the line. Although I didn't like Lieutenant Norman, I couldn't help but feel sorry for him. Nobody wanted to succeed more than Lieutenant Norman, and no one tried harder than he did. His biggest problem was he didn't have any common sense; the incident involving the location of his men on the company perimeter was a good example. You don't have to be a rocket scientist to figure out that blind spots in a perimeter are not going to work. If the men manning the perimeter are unable to cover the entire area with fire, the enemy can sneak through these blind spots. The same holds true for the calling in artillery on his own men. That he didn't mark the target and wait until his men cleared the area before requesting the fire mission seemed pretty strange.

In any event, I finally had a platoon. In hindsight, the time spent waiting for a platoon was invaluable. I was able to get a feel for how the company operated as well as hands-on experience in calling in artillery and medevacs. More importantly, I had the opportunity to observe Lieutenants Muler and Werner command their platoons. They were both seasoned veterans and, in my opinion, top notch. Usually, a second lieutenant arrives in Vietnam straight out of Basic School and is given a platoon as his first assignment. The practical aspects of running the platoon are learned through on-the-job training. In my case, I learned from the best, and in the short two-week period, I gained a wealth of knowledge that would allow me to take over Second Platoon with confidence rather than trepidation.

Now that I had my platoon, my thoughts turned to what to do next. I would obviously wait until Lieutenant Norman cleared out. He was walking up toward the company CP as I left Captain K.'s tent. I decided to go talk to Sergeant Schwartz. Since Sergeant Schwartz knew everything about what was going on in the company, I started out the conversation with "Have you heard the news?"

Of course, Sergeant Schwartz had heard the news, and he said, "I think this is really a good move. I have been getting complaints from the troops in Second Platoon for the last few weeks. I passed them along to Captain K. The incident with the artillery was the straw that broke the camel's back. If it wasn't that, it would have been something else. You won't have any problems with the troops' loyalty to Lieutenant Norman, and they should welcome you with open arms."

One of the biggest problems an incoming platoon commander faces is the loyalty the troops have to the departing platoon commander. He generally has been with them for several months and has developed strong ties with the platoon. The old commander has taken them through thick and thin, and they have survived some very tough times. Most of the troops owe their lives to his ability to get them out of serious scrapes with the enemy. In addition, the platoon commander has become an experienced veteran of Vietnam. He knows what to do and what not to do. The platoon has total confidence in its leader's ability and will follow him to the end of the earth. They know the lieutenant will always make the right decision no matter what.

The new platoon commander is usually in a no-win situation. He is obviously inexperienced and as a result lacks self-confidence. In addition, he has to do things his way, which is different from the way the departing lieutenant did things. Anytime something goes wrong, the troops immediately conclude this wouldn't have happened if the old lieutenant was still there. The new lieutenant has to work through this knowing it won't be long before the platoon bonds to him and he becomes accepted as the leader of the platoon.

I asked Sergeant Schwartz if he had any advice for me before I went over to Second Platoon. Sergeant Schwartz was never bashful about giving advice. He told me I would have a problem with Sergeant Niel. He said, "Sergeant Niel is a short-timer and deserves to be taken out of the field. He has served the Marine Corps well but is developing an attitude that will eliminate his effectiveness to the platoon. I will talk to Captain K. and see if we can get Sergeant Niel rotated back to Battalion. You have a couple of NCOs in the platoon who are ready to take over as platoon sergeant."

some stability."

I told Sergeant Schwartz I hoped I could provide that stability. He told me, "Lieutenant, you can do the job if you will treat those marines right. Be fair with them, and they will follow you anywhere. They don't ask for much; if you will look out for them, they will take care of you. There isn't a finer bunch of men than these raggedy-ass marines fighting this war. Those sons of bitches in the rear wouldn't make a pimple on the ass of any marine in Second Platoon. Your job is to keep them in one piece and stick up for them no matter what. If you don't look after them, no one else will."

After talking to Sergeant Schwartz, I went to the mortar crew and told them I would be leaving to take over Second Platoon. I don't know whether I saw a look of relief or regret on their faces when I told them the news. I am sure they were happy to be left alone for a while and not constantly harassed by a second lieutenant with nothing better to do. They wished me well, and Corporal Hall joked, "Remember to take the sixty-millimeter mortar out on all your patrols."

I laughed and responded, "You won't have to worry about me making that mistake again."

I left the mortar squad and went to the company CP and gathered my gear and headed for Second Platoon. The first person I met at the Second Platoon CP was Sergeant Niel. He greeted me with a "Welcome aboard, Lieutenant."

I thanked him and asked him if he had a few minutes, and he replied he had all day.

We sat down in the shade of a poncho and discussed Second Platoon. Sergeant Niel agreed with Sergeant Schwartz that the platoon lacked continuity in its command over the last couple of months. He assured me we had three good squad leaders. All three of them were sergeants E5, which meant they were a rank above corporal and a rank below staff sergeant. The First Squad leader, Sergeant Presno, and Second Squad leader, Sergeant Duff, were career marines, while Third Squad leader, Sergeant Green, had only been in the Marine Corps a short time. Sergeant Green had been in Vietnam for over two years, having extended his tour of duty three times. He was by far the most experienced combat marine in the platoon but the youngest of the three squad leaders.

Sergeant Niel also explained the marines in the platoon were pretty solid. Several of them had extended their tours of duty at least once, and some of them were on a second extension. After your initial one-year tour of duty, you could extend for additional tours of six months each. The incentive for extending your tour was thirty days' leave anywhere in the world. Most marines chose to go home for their thirty days' leave rather than some exotic port of call. The marines on their first and second extensions were pretty salty and could be counted on when the going got tough.

Sergeant Niel went on to say there were some discipline problems in the platoon but nothing that couldn't be handled. "These troops will want to please you, and all they ask in return is for you to be fair with them. Life is hard out here, but these men are just as hard. They can take anything Charlie can dish out and give as good as they get. If you will provide the leadership, they'll follow."

I told Sergeant Niel I would like to meet with the squad leaders, and he instructed the platoon radioman, Lance Corporal Moreno, to get them on the radio and have them come to the platoon CP. They arrived shortly and must have heard the news of Lieutenant Norman being replaced, because they didn't act surprised to see me. Sergeant Niel introduced me to the squad leaders, and we sat down and discussed the platoon. I explained there would be no immediate changes and that, for the first couple of days, I would be getting my feet wet. I also explained I initially would be relying heavily on them and for them not to be afraid of making suggestions. I also told them

I expected them to handle discipline matters within their squads and not bring them to me unless they felt it necessary. I assured them they would have my full support in dealing with the marines in their squads, and under no conditions would I undermine their authority. I asked them if they had any questions, and when no one responded, I told them I would like to meet with the platoon at 1800 hours there at the CP. I wanted every member of the platoon present, and we would delay sending out the night ambush until after the meeting. Everyone left, and I sat down to figure out what I was going to say to the platoon.

I called the platoon meeting to give the members an opportunity to meet me and to hopefully set the tone for my leadership. I obviously wanted to instill confidence in my abilities to lead. Words alone would not do this, of course, but it would be a first step toward developing my role as their leader. I also wanted to let the platoon know what I expected of them and what they could expect from me. In addition, I wanted to communicate my priorities as a platoon commander, what I thought was important, and what was not important. At 1800 hours, the platoon started forming at the CP.

I started the meeting by telling the platoon Lieutenant Norman was gone and I was the new platoon commander. I told them they should not expect immediate changes but to be aware of the fact I had a way of doing things and, in the future, things would be done my way. I then attempted to set forth my view of my role as platoon commander. I told them my priorities were not going to be enemy body count but rather the safety of the men within the platoon. If I had anything to do with it, we would never risk the lives of the marines in Second Platoon for the sake of enemy body count. On the other hand, we had a job to do, and it involved substantial risk as a result of which we would take casualties. Casualties were inevitable. It was my job to minimize those casualties.

I went on to explain, in my opinion, casualties were the direct result of carelessness and laziness within the platoon. If we tried to cut corners or slacked off on the basic rules of survival, we would take unnecessary casualties, and such behavior would not be tolerated. I would not accept conduct by any member of the platoon that endangered his life or the lives of the rest of the platoon. I told them I didn't care if every man in the platoon hated my guts if it meant everyone went home in one piece. While we were in a combat situation, I would be on their asses every minute to make sure everything possible was being done to minimize casualties. I felt strongly about this subject and believed the job of getting these marines safely back home fell squarely on my shoulders.

I further explained I believed in the chain of command, and when they received an order from their squad leader or fire team leader, they could assume that command came directly from me. Any insubordination to the squad leaders or fire team leaders would not be tolerated under any circumstances. If they had a problem, they would first take it to their fire team leader. If it could not be resolved at that level, the fire team leader and squad leader would meet with them to try to resolve the problem. If the problem could still not be resolved, they were free to come to me with their fire team leader and squad leader to discuss their problem and hopefully resolve it. What I didn't tell them was that, as a practical matter, I always had to back the squad leaders. I may discuss the matter later on in private with the squad leader, but in front of the trooper, I always had to support the squad leader.

After discussing the importance of discipline in the field, I told them I really didn't give a shit what they did when we were in the rear. As long as they didn't get caught, what they did was none of my business. The only problem was these marines seldom got to the rear areas, so cutting them slack while in Da Nang was not that big of deal. I ended the meeting by telling them I would commit that I would be the very best platoon commander I could possibly be. In return, I expected them to be the best marines they could be. If everyone did their jobs to the best of their ability, hopefully we would minimize casualties and get as many people home in one piece as possible.

The meeting broke up, and I spent the rest of the evening talking to Sergeant Niel. The mission of Second Platoon for the present was to maintain security around the battalion perimeter and construct the defensive positions on the perimeter. Sergeant Niel and I decided it would be best to rotate the squads so that each of them would get its share of the various jobs. In order to maintain security, we ran two squad-size patrols a day in Second Platoon's TAOR as well as a night ambush. Second Platoon's TAOR was in the area northwest of the battalion's perimeter extending from the perimeter to five klicks outside the perimeter. We would usually run one patrol in the morning and one in the afternoon. We tried to leave at different times and take different routes so that we never established a particular pattern; we didn't want Charlie anticipating when and where we would run our patrols. The night ambushes usually consisted of one four-man fire team that was supposed to go out several hundred meters from the perimeter. I always had my doubts about how far out the ambushes really went.

The work of building the perimeter defenses would be shared by all the squads. Since it was too hot during the middle of the day to do hard physical labor, we worked on the defenses in the morning and the evening. The squad who had the afternoon patrol worked on the defensive positions in the morning; the squad who patrolled in the morning worked that evening. The remaining squad sent out the ambush, and those who went on the ambush did not have to work the following day while the members of that squad who didn't go on ambush were expected to work both the morning and afternoon shift. As I previously said, all the squads would be rotated so no one group could complain they were getting stuck doing too much of any one task.

Sergeant Niel and I also talked about strategy that we could use for the patrolling of the TAOR. Sergeant Niel said, "Every time we get near the railroad bed, we get in a firefight. It's mostly hit and run, but Charlie always seems to know when we're coming. He must have a system of picking us up when we leave the perimeter, because no matter which route we take, he is always waiting for us. If we could figure out a way to get in there without Charlie knowing we're coming, I think we could do some good."

I concluded the key to solving the problem was to figure out how Charlie knew when we were coming. He must have some lookouts posted on these hills and a method of signaling our approach. Our first job would be to figure out how he was doing this, and then we could come up with a solution to the problem. In the meantime, we would maintain our present pattern of patrolling.

The platoon command group consisted of six individuals, which included Sergeant Niel and me. The other marines in the group were Lance Corporal Moreno, the platoon radio operator; Doc Blake, the navy corpsman; Private First Class Wynn, my runner; and Corporal Stang, the platoon right guide. The platoon runner and right guide were archaic positions but were needed to operate the command group efficiently. The platoon's radio had to be monitored twenty-four hours a day. If someone from the company CP wanted to contact us, they did so through the radio. In addition, the platoon constantly had patrols and ambushes out in the bush whose only contact with the platoon was through the radio. Therefore, we needed four people to stand radio watch. During the day when we were inside the perimeter, the radioman, the runner, and the right guide would share the duties of monitoring the radio. At night, Doc Blake would also share the duty, and each of them would stand a two-hour watch.

Both Sergeant Niel and I would get up at least once a night to check Second Platoon's lines. It would usually take me about two hours to make my rounds. I discovered walking the perimeter was a great way to get to know your troops. I made it a point to stop and talk to each marine on watch for about ten minutes. Initially, I did this to get to know them. Once I became acquainted with the men, I stopped and shot the shit with them about their families and anything else that would come up. It was a good method of gauging the morale of the men and finding out if anything was bothering them. It also helped pass the time for the marine on watch. Two hours in the middle of the night was a long time with nothing to do but stare at the wire surrounding the perimeter.

As previously mentioned, sleeping on watch was a reoccurring problem. My approach was to make every effort not to catch a marine asleep on watch. I always made it a point to whistle a tune as loud as I could when approaching a sentry. If he was dozing off, this would usually wake him up. If I had a suspicion that he was still asleep, I would throw a rock into the wire, hoping to make enough noise to wake him up. We always had empty C ration cans filled with pebbles strung along the wire so if the wire moved, the pebbles in the can would rattle and alert the sentry that something was amiss. Throwing a rock into the wire normally created enough noise to wake the dozing marine. If I was unsuccessful in rousing him, I would be forced to approach him and catch him in the act of sleeping. A marine caught sleeping on watch would always deny he was asleep once you woke him up. I would normally take his rifle without awakening him and continue the rounds. When I got back to the platoon's CP, I would call the marine's squad leader and order him to fetch the offending marine and report to the platoon CP immediately. When the marine arrived, I would ask him how it was that I had his rifle in my possession. Initially, he would attempt to come up with some rational explanation but eventually would concede he must have been asleep. I would instruct the squad leader he needed to deal with this problem and reminded both of them that if I were a VC, the entire squad would be dead by now. Usually, we did not have many repeat offenders caught sleeping on watch.

The next couple of days were uneventful as far as patrolling the perimeter was concerned. We ran our daily patrols and on most occasions had minor contact with Charlie. The engagement would consist of a brief hit-and-run skirmish in which contact was broken off before we could call in artillery or air. We didn't take any casualties but probably didn't inflict any casualties, either.

The battalion area was progressing by leaps and bounds, and it seemed like every day something new was happening. When Lima

Company first occupied Hill 63, conditions were extremely primitive. We lived out of our backpacks. Captain K. occupied a tent, and the rest of us slept on the ground covered by our ponchos. We ate C rations and had to fetch our drinking water from a local well. We treated the water with heliozoan tablets to rid it of any microbes that might make us sick. Things were dramatically changing.

The Eleventh Marines moved in an artillery battery of 105 howitzers, and a tank platoon now occupied the southern end of the perimeter. A water point was established near the battalion CP, which meant we would now have treated water available to us and would not have to drink water from the wells. All of this meant that certain luxuries started filtering down to us. As predicted by Sergeant Schwartz, a shitter showed up for Second Platoon, along with a tent for the platoon CP. The tent was big enough to sleep a dozen men. Along with the tent came folding cots, which meant we no longer had to sleep on the ground. A road was cut by the engineers along the perimeter, and we could now get vehicles back to our area. Pretty soon a "water buffalo" was delivered full of treated water. A water buffalo was a tank able to hold over a hundred gallons of water that was mounted on a trailer so it could be hauled behind a truck. When the water buffalo was empty, we just contacted Battalion, and it was refilled. In addition, the mess hall was fully operational, and we could get three hot meals a day from the mess tent, albeit we had to walk a quarter of a mile over the top of Hill 63 to get to it.

For the marines of Lima Company, we were now living in the lap of luxury. The company hadn't had it this good in several weeks. We still didn't have the luxuries of the rear, like cold beer, hot showers, and electricity. While a few of us had folding cots, most of the men still slept on the ground. A clean change of clothes was out of the question, and a trip to the PX was unimaginable.

The disparity between the conditions in the rear and those in the field were the biggest gripes of the combat marine. You would think the huge supply system established by Uncle Sam would be designed to get the gear down to the grunt that was fighting the war in the rice paddies and the jungles. Instead, just the opposite was true. The logistics system was like a huge river in which the water was continually drained off as it flowed to the sea. By the time the supplies got to the grunts, every rear echelon group imaginable had siphoned off everything of value. Sometimes I wondered how we ever got anything at all. What finally trickled down to us was what no one in the rear wanted or needed. We always had plenty of ammo and enough C rations. The troops in the rear had no need for ammo and wouldn't stoop to eating C rations.

It is little wonder the grunts referred to those in the rear as REMFs, or rear-echelon motherfuckers. We could go out and kill Charlie; all we could do is complain about the REMFs. The grunts could identify with the enemy in that their living conditions were worse than ours. The REMFs were something that could only be treated with disdain by the grunts. While the jungle fatigues literally rotted off our backs, the REMFs changed daily into a freshly washed and ironed set. A cold drink of water was something we only dreamed of, while the beer coolers ran twenty-four hours a day back in Da Nang.

The only thing the REMFs didn't have was the title of "grunt." They would never belong to the most elite fraternity in the United States Marine Corps. We knew when we got back to the world, the REMFs would strut around as war heroes, telling of their harrowing experiences in the 'Nam. In Vietnam, the line between grunt and REMF was very clear. Approximately 15 percent of the troops fought the war, while the remainder stayed in the rear with the gear. You could tell the difference between the two just by looking at them. The grunt was underweight, raggedy ass in his dress, and had a look as hard as nails. The REMF looked like the marine on the recruiting poster. You could see the REMF on television when you watched the Bob Hope Christmas show from Vietnam. You could also see the grunt on television; he was the one covered with bandages getting his ass loaded on a helicopter.

I also believe there wasn't a marine in Second Platoon who would trade places with a REMF. No matter how much we complained about our living conditions, we had something the REMFs didn't; we had each other. The bond between men in a combat unit cannot be compared to any other type of human relationship. We were drawn together by our hardships. Our relationship was cemented with the blood of our dead and wounded comrades. The worse the conditions got, the closer we became. The majority of the marines in Second Platoon went through a living hell in Operation Union II, and as a result, they were extremely close knit.

I had not been with the platoon long enough to be accepted. I was still being observed and evaluated by the men of Second Platoon. Hopefully, I would measure up.

I soon set my mind to try to figure out the system the VC were using to detect the presence of our daily patrols. I decided I needed to get a firsthand look at the situation. I gathered Lance Corporal Moreno, Private First Class Wynn, and Corporal Stang and told them to be ready to go at 0400 hours the next day. There was a hill about a klick west of the perimeter that offered a pretty good view of the platoon's TAOR. We would move down there before first light and hopefully get set up without being detected by Charlie. We would then have First Squad run its normal patrol and see what happened. I planned to take my field glasses with me to give me a better view of the TAOR.

The next morning, the four of us were leaving the perimeter before first light, sneaking our way down to our planned observation post. We reached the top of the hill well before dawn and concealed ourselves among the rocks. When it finally got light enough to see, I discovered we had an excellent view of the TAOR. Just as it was getting full light, Private First Class Wynn whispered, "We've got movement on our left front."

My first thought was I wished I had brought more men. We hunkered down, and I whispered for everyone to hold their fire until whoever it was got out in front of us. Pretty soon, an old man came walking out in a clearing about one hundred meters to our front. He was about fifty years old and was unarmed, so we let him pass. I assumed he was a farmer going somewhere to tend his fields or maybe to visit his cousins in the next village. Instead, he started climbing the hill we were on and sat down about sixty meters in front of us. He was looking back toward Hill 63, observing the trail we had used to get to our present position.

I began my surveillance of the TAOR through the field glasses and discovered three other individuals sitting on the sides of hills just like the old man below us. They were too far away to determine if they were armed, but they were damn sure in a position to observe any patrols exiting the perimeter at Hill 63. The question of how Charlie knew when the patrols were coming had just been solved. Because of the proximity of the old man, I was barely able to whisper into the radio to tell First Squad to start its patrol. I didn't want to alert the *papa-san* to our presence, because I wanted to see what was going to happen next. I was sure he would have shit in his pants if he knew there were four marines hidden less than one hundred meters above him.

First Squad would exit the perimeter and patrol due north for several hundred meters and then swing to the west and south and eventually pick us up on the way back. The old man sitting below us was not in a position to observe First Squad as it began its patrol, but there was another observer who would be able to see the squad when it was a couple of hundred meters outside of the perimeter. Sure enough, when sufficient time elapsed for First Squad to clear the perimeter, one of the spies on the north side of the perimeter got up and started walking to the west. He had obviously observed the patrol as it was heading north from the perimeter. He walked to the top of another hill and sat down to continue his observation. As the patrol moved north and then west, the individual who first spotted them moved from hilltop to hilltop, keeping the patrol under observation. I could never see the patrol itself, but I knew its predetermined route and could guess they were under constant surveillance from the individual I was watching through the field glasses.

I got on the radio and instructed First Squad to hold its position for a few minutes. I then told Second Squad to saddle up and start patrolling due west from the perimeter toward our position. It took Second Squad about fifteen minutes to get ready. When Second Squad radioed, it was clearing the perimeter. I told First Squad to continue with its patrol. Just as I expected, when Second Squad got in sight of our position, the old man below us got up and casually walked away on the same trail he had approached us earlier in the morning. He walked to a small hilltop north and west of our position and took up another observation post. I instructed Second Squad to patrol on past our position. I didn't want the papa-san to know we were on to his little game. Second Squad continued on its patrol and moved around the base of the hill we were sitting on. The old man couldn't see them until they emerged from the west side of the hill. As soon as he spotted them, he retreated north and west to another hilltop. I instructed Second Squad to hold up, and the four of us on top of the hill were able to join them without being observed by the old man.

It was now clear what the VC were doing. They used the civilians to spot our movements and keep us under constant surveillance. Although I didn't personally observe this, I can only assume that when the patrols got close enough to Charlie's position, their spies would come running in and tell them of our approach somewhat like the Paul Revere of old—only they would be shouting, "The marines are coming! The marines are coming!"

I ordered First Squad to continue its patrol and informed it that Second Squad would continue to patrol from the south. We would converge on the village located on the northwest side of the TAOR from two directions. This was the same village Lieutenant Norman described to Captain K. when the company was sweeping the TAOR. Second Platoon continued to engage the enemy every time we got in its vicinity. As we were approaching the village, First Squad apparently made contact with Charlie, and we could hear the exchange of gunfire. I contacted First Squad, and they informed me they were taking fire from an area just north of the village. I told them we would maneuver up from the south and try to sweep through the enemy position. We moved about one hundred meters when we started taking fire from our left flank. We returned the fire and attempted to continue moving north to engage the enemy in contact with First Squad. While half the squad laid down fire on the enemy position, the remainder would move to the north toward First Squad. After a few minutes, First Squad informed us Charlie had broken contact. We then turned our attention on the VC who were firing at us, but they immediately withdrew. I determined we had taken no casualties and told First Squad to meet us in the village. We joined up with them and returned to Hill 63.

Finally a Platoon Commander

5

BURNING THE VILLAGE

I WENT DIRECTLY TO THE company CP and found Captain K. to tell him of our adventure. I asked if I could take the entire platoon out the next day, because I had a plan to spoil Charlie's little game. He had no problem with this, and I brought up another subject. It was clear to me that the lookouts posted by the VC were retreating back to the village on the northwest side of Second Platoon's TAOR. I expressed my opinion that this village needed to be eliminated and was obviously a haven for the VC. Captain K. suggested we walk over to Battalion headquarters and discuss this with Colonel Brady.

Captain K. and I approached Colonel Brady with my plan. Destroying a village can be a pretty big deal in some areas of Vietnam. Since we knew 90 percent of the villages in our TAOR were controlled by the VC, it made it a little easier to get approval. Colonel Brady had no objection, but he wanted to clear it with Regiment. I suggested he tell them we engaged the enemy every time we got in the vicinity of the village and the VC shooting at us probably lived in the village. Colonel Brady talked to the regimental S2 and got clearance to torch the village if he deemed it necessary. Colonel Brady said, "Go ahead with your plans for tomorrow, and when you get in the village, call in, and we will make our decision then."

When I got back to Second Platoon's CP, I called Sergeant Niel and the three squad leaders together, and we discussed the mission for the following day. First, I wanted to snatch the lookout who sat below us on the hill that morning. Corporal Stang was sitting in on the meeting, and I placed him in charge of this task. I told him to take Lance Corporal Moreno with the platoon's radio and two other men to grab the lookout. I wanted them to set themselves up on the top of the hill just as we did that morning. As soon as the lookout got in position, they were to run down and grab him. I didn't want them to fire their weapons unless absolutely necessary.

"I want that son of a bitch in our hands without Charlie knowing we got him. Once you grab him, let us know, and the rest of the platoon will head out. Your group will bring the lookout back to the battalion CP for interrogation. The rest of us will proceed to the target on the same route Second Squad took this morning. Without their sentry, Charlie won't know we're coming. When we reach the southern edge of the village, we will put the squads on line and sweep through. Hopefully, we'll catch Charlie by surprise. If everything goes right, that village won't be there tomorrow."

I warned the squad leaders not to let the men know we might burn the village. "We don't have final clearance from Battalion, and if the men know burning the village is a possibility, they might start the job too soon. Besides, I don't want to disappoint them if Battalion says no." I closed the meeting by telling the squad leaders to have everyone ready to go by first light.

I was up next morning giving Corporal Stang his last-minute instructions and reminding him of the importance of capturing the VC lookout without firing a shot. Corporal Stang assured me he had it under control, and at 0400 hours, they headed out. At 0430 hours, they radioed in they were in position. By 0530 hours, they had captured the lookout and were holding him on the trail next to the hill. The rest of the platoon headed in their direction. We ran into Corporal Stang about five hundred meters outside the perimeter. I told Corporal Stang to take the prisoner back to Battalion and make sure they knew exactly why we brought him in.

I then gathered the squad leaders to make sure they understood the plan. I wanted to get the platoons on line as quickly as possible when we got to the village. I was sure some of the farmers working their fields would see us as we approached the village, and I didn't want them running back into the village to alert the VC. We moved out along the trail heading west. As soon as we got due south of the village, we turned north and moved as rapidly as possible toward our objective. About two hundred meters south of the village, the squads started fanning out to get on line for the final assault. When we reached the edge of the village, we started taking fire. By this time, the squads were on line, and we opened up on the village. We had finally caught Charlie off guard and were fighting him on our terms.

The VC were fighting a rearguard action trying to get out of the village without getting annihilated. The marines of Second Platoon were cutting them no slack. This was as aggressive as I had seen a marine unit attack since I arrived in country. We finally had the element of surprise on our side, and the men of Second Platoon were taking full advantage of the situation. The fighting was brief but furious. We had swept through the village in a matter of minutes and had three dead and two wounded VC on the ground. When we reached the other side of the village, we set up a defensive position, and I raised Lima Six on the radio. I reported our success and told him we would search the village. I then asked him if he would contact Battalion as to whether or not we could level the place.

While I awaited a response from Battalion, we started a thorough search of the area. A member of Second Squad found evidence the VC had been eating breakfast. The search of the area turned up half a dozen Chicom grenades, a Russian SKS rifle, and two M1 carbines belonging to the VC casualties. As we continued our search, we found a large cache of rice beneath a pile of rice straw. One of the marines from Third Squad really hit the jackpot when he found several rocket-propelled grenade (RPG) rounds hidden under one of the hooches. It was apparent the village was a haven for the VC. I didn't know whether the VC had just taken refuge there or were full-time residents. It really didn't matter, because three of them were dead, and two more were out of action.

Captain K. came back up on the radio and told me we had permission to burn the village. I asked him what he wanted us to do with the wounded VC, and he told me a chopper would be at our location in about an hour to pick them up. I acknowledged his message and called the squad leaders together. I told them the good news about burning the village, and we discussed the best way to go about it. We were concerned about the troops' reaction to the news. Sergeant Green said he had been through this before, and once the troops got started, it was difficult to keep them under control. He continued, "Things can get out of hand in a hurry, and pretty soon, they're out there killing civilians. Right now, they're still pretty worked up over the firefight, and it won't take too much to set them off."

I decided to wait a while before beginning the task of destroying the village. I told the squad leaders to tell their men we would be setting in for a while and they could take a break. I further informed them to maintain as much discipline over their men as possible. I didn't want them to lose control of the situation. I also reminded them everyone would be held accountable for their actions. I finally told them we would start burning the village as soon as the chopper picked up the wounded VC.

As predicted, things got out of hand in a hurry once we started setting fire to the village. Apparently, I wasn't specific enough when I told the troops they could torch the village. They must have thought I meant the entire TAOR. Pretty soon, every hooch within two hundred meters was on fire. The troops obviously had a lot of emotion bottled up inside, and as they say, "Payback is a motherfucker." When it was all said and done, we had burned down every hooch remotely associated with the village.

In the middle of the melee emerged a remarkable sight. Two of my men approached escorting several Buddhist monks. They explained the monks were found in some kind of church that the marines set afire, and the monks refused to leave the building after it started burning. The marines had to drag them out to keep them from burning up. They wanted to know what to do with them, and I replied, "It beats the hell out of me."

The monks solved the problem for us when they sat down in a circle in an apparent protest to our actions. We left them alone and hoped they wouldn't follow us back to the perimeter. After destroying the village, we returned to Hill 63, flushed with victory and full of stories about a most exciting day.

Did the day's action bring us a step closer to victory in Vietnam, or was it a step backward? What happened at the tiny no-named village in the northwest corner of our TAOR was a microcosm of what was going on throughout Vietnam. What was gained by destroying the village? What was lost by destroying the village? The gain was easy: we denied the VC a safe haven. No longer would they be enjoying breakfast in that village while we were out humping in the bush trying to flush them out.

The loss was more complicated and demonstrated the futility of this war. We often hear the war in Vietnam was lost because the American troops did not have a clear-cut objective. I have always disagreed with this theory. Our objective was to establish a South Vietnamese government that could withstand the North Vietnamese, both militarily and politically. In order to accomplish the military goal, we were to provide the ARVN with a respite from the onslaught of the enemy so they could rebuild and retrain. In theory, at least, the South Vietnamese could develop an army that would resist anything the NVA could throw at them, much like what occurred in South Korea. Politically, we were to assist the South Vietnamese government in winning the hearts and minds of the South Vietnamese people. Did that day's action help win the hearts and minds of the peasants in Second Platoon's TAOR?

You obviously don't make friends by burning their houses down. Our random violence toward the people living in the village did little to further the political goals of the United States or the South

Vietnamese government. If we were trying to win the hearts and minds of these peasants, we took a step backward. The war in Vietnam was not lost because we did not have a clear-cut mission but rather because the mission could not be accomplished by the personnel sent to Vietnam.

The marines in Vietnam had a saying that went "Once you get them by the balls, their hearts and minds will follow." To expect the eighteen-year-old marine to act as an ambassador of goodwill toward the people of South Vietnam was just too much to ask. We were there to fight a war, not to win hearts and minds. No matter how much you preached to the troops, the fact was they did not like the people of South Vietnam. The cultural difference between the South Vietnamese and the average combat marine was overwhelming. You could neither get him to identify with the plight of the South Vietnamese peasant nor convince him the war could be won by being nice to the civilians. He was there to fight Charlie, not to help the South Vietnamese people. He could give a shit if they lived or died. When it came to combat, the marines of Lima Company would do anything asked of them. When it came to diplomacy, they were hopelessly lost.

After arriving back at the perimeter, I went to the company CP to show off the munitions captured at the village. When I got to the top of Hill 63, I could still see the smoke rising from the burned village. I found Captain K. and asked him if Second Platoon could take the rest of the day off and forgo the night ambush. He consented, commenting we had done one hell of a job at the village. I then hunted up Sergeant Schwartz to see if he could get Second Platoon a beer ration, explaining we wouldn't be running ambushes that evening. He told me he would see what he could do and would get back to me later. Lima Company normally did not get a beer ration while it was manning the perimeter and running patrols. In Lima Company, beer and the war were kept separate and apart from each other. While fighting the war, you needed to have full possession of your faculties. Hopefully, that night would be an exception.

I returned to Second Platoon's CP, and everyone was in high spirits swapping stories about the day's events. Kicking Charlie's ass always did wonders for a unit's morale and seemed to make everything all right within the platoon. So what if we were halfway around the world from the "real world" and it was 115 degrees Fahrenheit with 95 percent humidity? Death and destruction were our business, and that day, business was good. Tomorrow would take care of itself.

All of a sudden, Sergeant Schwartz showed up driving a mule with several containers on its bed. We walked over to the mule, and a miracle had occurred. Sergeant Schwartz not only had beer, but it was iced down. Don't ask me how he accomplished this, but Second Platoon had died and gone to heaven.

By now, I was starting to get a real sense of the character of the platoon. A marine rifle platoon in Vietnam was made up of approximately fifty men. I use the word *approximately* because the size of a platoon varies depending on the number of men who were fit for duty, on R&R, or on temporary assignment. As I previously discussed, a Marine Corps rifle platoon is made up of three squads. A normal squad has three four-man fire teams, an M79 grenadier, a radio operator, and a squad leader, which totals fourteen men. In Vietnam, the rifle platoons were usually reinforced by the weapons platoon, which added an additional four-man team to each squad within the platoon. Two of the squads had an M60 machine-gun crew consisting of a machine gunner along with an assistant gunner and two ammo humpers. The remaining squad had a 3.5-inch rocket launcher crew consisting of a gunner, an assistant gunner, and two ammo humpers. In theory, a reinforced squad consisted of nineteen men. This was never the case. As a practical matter, most infantry squads consisted of a gun crew, two four-man fire teams, an M79 grenadier, a radioman, and the squad leader, which totaled fifteen men. If you add the navy corpsman, the platoon radioman, the platoon runner, the right guide, the platoon sergeant, and the platoon commander, you arrive at approximately fifty men in a rifle platoon.

One story described how Private Driscol encountered a VC hidden in a spider hole while the platoon was sweeping an area during another operation. A spider hole is a hole dug in the ground with a trapdoor that is camouflaged so it cannot be detected from above. For whatever reason, Driscol spotted the spider hole and noticed movement inside. Driscol immediately threw down his M16, removed his pack and cartridge belt, ripped open the trapdoor, and dove headfirst into the spider hole. It turned out there were two VC in the spider hole instead of one, and he threw both of them out of the hole. He then retrieved their weapons and threw them out of the spider hole, as well.

It is obvious Private Driscol was not one to be trifled with, and everyone treated him with a healthy respect. I cannot say Driscol was the leader of the platoon, because everyone recognized he was at least half a bubble off. He was respected by the members of the platoon for his exploits, but the platoon looked to Sergeant Green as their de facto leader. Although Sergeant Niel outranked Sergeant Green and Sergeants Presno and Duff had more time in grade, Sergeant Green led the platoon. The other three sergeants had one major impediment, which prevented them from being accepted by the platoon as their true leader; all three of them were lifers.

The troops did not identify with those individuals who decided to make the Marine Corps their lives' work. The vast majority of the grunts who fought the war in Vietnam had no intention of staying in the Marine Corps any longer than they had to. The lifer represented the authoritarian side of the Marine Corps, which most of the men in the bush disliked. The average grunt wanted to fight the war, go back to the world, and get the hell out of the military. The discipline and regimentation of the Marine Corps was nothing more than a pain in the ass. Sergeant Green, on the other hand, represented everything the troops admired. He was smart and possessed a vast knowledge of how to keep people alive in the combat situation. He was also cool under fire and had on many occasions demonstrated his bravery. Most of all, he was somewhat of a maverick and was more than willing to bend the rules if it suited the men's needs. It is little wonder the men of Second Platoon accepted Sergeant Green as their leader.

It would be up to me to ally myself with Sergeant Green in order to become an effective platoon commander. If Sergeant Green and I were to butt heads, he could effectively undermine my authority and neutralize my effectiveness as a platoon commander. At the same time, I had to maintain the confidence of Sergeants Niel, Presno, and Duff. They were key members of the platoon. If they thought I was ignoring them in favor of Sergeant Green, they could cause me serious problems. I was walking a tightrope, trying to keep the various factions in proper balance.

Work on the perimeter fortifications was going smoothly, and we were starting to see some positive results. Most of the bunkers were complete, and there were several rows of barbed-wire obstacles strung out in front of our positions. Although we took special pains to try to construct a formidable defensive position, most of our efforts were for naught. It would be a rare situation for the VC to attack an infantry firebase of this size. For one thing, they would be going up against battle-hardened marines whose ability to fight has been tested under fire. The VC had a hard enough time taking us on in the field under conditions most favorable to them. To take us on under our terms would be insane. Secondly, there would be little gained by trying to overrun our base camp. There were no expensive aircraft to destroy and not enough Americans to inflict significant casualties, and the thing was too damn big to defend for any length of time.

Horror stories of American positions being overrun by the VC were constantly being circulated among the troops in Vietnam. In fact, this was a rare occurrence and usually happened to relatively small, isolated units. If a position was overrun, it could always be attributed to some shortcoming within the unit or a blunder by higher command. Sometimes, emplacements were constructed in locations that could not be properly defended, or insufficient troops were assigned to defend the position. Such was the case in the A Shau Valley when a Special Forces camp was overrun and many of the defenders were wiped out. On other occasions, smaller units were overrun because the occupants got sloppy in their defensive tactics. They may not have had sufficient men on watch or those on watch fell asleep, allowing the VC to get inside the wire undetected.

A third situation that allowed the VC to penetrate a fortified position was when you had REMFs defending the perimeter. The VC were not going to mess with a bunch of dug-in grunts. REMFs were another matter. There were occasions when VC sapper units were able to penetrate their wire and wreak havoc inside a perimeter, blowing up aircraft and other valuable equipment. It is frightening to imagine a bunch of REMFs running around with M16s in hand, shooting at everything in sight. The VC were willing to take the risk, because the reward was large and the risk was small. If you could grant the men of Lima Company one wish, it would be that the VC tried to overrun their position on Hill 63. Charlie was not about to grant them that wish.

Second Platoon was continually running patrols in addition to constructing the perimeter. We were still getting daily contact with the VC, but it was of less and less magnitude. It seemed Charlie was accepting the fact we were there to stay and decided to move to an area that was less hazardous to his health. We would still sneak out and find the sentinels posted on the various hilltops, and we harassed them with artillery fire and occasional helicopters, which would fly over and try to catch them by surprise. If we were successful in capturing them, it was hard to make a case they were VC. They could prove they lived in the area, and sitting on a hill was not much of a crime. We sent them back to the rear for interrogation, but I am sure they talked their way out of the situation on most occasions.

As I mentioned earlier, I had my doubts whether the nightly ambushes were going out to their assigned locations. When I would question the troops about this, I either got a blank stare or was told, "Of course we go to the proper position," followed by a laugh. It was the troops' way of telling me they weren't going out to where they were supposed to be. I really couldn't blame them. Many times, the ambush locations assigned to us by Battalion were unrealistic in that they were too far out and far too risky. Battalion may have been willing to risk the lives of the men of Lima Company in order to increase the enemy body count, but the men of Lima Company were not willing to make such foolish mistakes. Besides, why walk out several klicks to stay awake all night when you could sit just outside the wire and get a good night's sleep? When it came to ambushes, the grunts in the field took a much more practical approach than their superiors at Battalion.

I decided to shake things up a little bit and run a platoon-size ambush. I had been to the abandoned railroad right-of-way to the west of Hill 63 on several occasions. I noticed there was a well-worn path traveling down the right-of-way but never observed anyone using the trail. I instructed the patrols to keep an eye on the railroad bed to see if they observed any foot traffic during the day. The patrol leaders reported they had not seen very many people using the trail during daylight hours. Since there was a dusk-to-dawn curfew in Vietnam, the only conclusion that could be reached is that the trail was being used at night by the VC.

The only way to test this theory was to run an ambush along the right-of-way. Since the right-of-way was at least three klicks outside the perimeter, it was too far to send a squad, so I decided to take the entire platoon. I would also be certain the ambush was set up where it was supposed to be. I discussed my plans with Captain K., and he gave his approval. He would move part of First Platoon over to cover our sector of the perimeter while we ran the ambush. After getting Captain K.'s permission, I discussed the ambush with Sergeant Niel and the squad leaders. The initial problem was to get the ambush in place without being discovered. If we left the perimeter while it was still light, we would surely be detected by the locals, and the VC would be alerted to our presence. If we left too late, we could be setting up the ambush while someone was walking down the trail, which would also alert the VC to our presence. We decided to compromise and leave just as the sun was setting. I also decided to have the artillery battery fire several salvos into the hills west of the perimeter as we were leaving to divert the attention of anyone who might be observing the perimeter.

I set up a rendezvous site two hundred meters behind the ambush to give the platoon a place to gather before the ambush and to retreat to if we came under attack. We would leave a fire team to guard the site, and they could also cover our rear in case the VC tried to sneak up behind us. I assigned First Squad the left side of the ambush, Second Squad the middle, and Third Squad on the right. I would be with Second Squad and would trigger the ambush. I had chosen an ambush site that had plenty of cover and was about fifty meters from the railroad bed. We would string out claymore mines in the killing zone in front of the platoon. If we caught the VC in the ambush, they would be instantly cut to shreds by the claymores.

Having gone through the preliminaries with the squad leaders, I explained, "We are going to a lot of trouble to set this thing up. I want the men to be totally silent while we're waiting. I am not going to trigger the ambush until we get several VC in the killing zone. This means I may have to let a couple of stragglers walk past before I let loose. Tell your men to stay put until I set off a claymore. Then they're free to open up on the kill zone."

As evening approached, the platoon was preparing itself for the ambush. Sergeant Niel approached me and asked if I wanted him to go on the ambush with the platoon. I thought this was an odd question and was about to tell him we needed him. I then remembered what Sergeant Schwartz said about Sergeant Niel being a short-timer, and it was obvious from the way Sergeant Niel asked the question that he didn't want to go on the ambush. I replied, "Why don't you stay here and make sure First Platoon gets set in properly on the perimeter?" I thought to myself that I needed to talk to Sergeant Schwartz about Sergeant Niel's status when we got back from the ambush.

Just as the sun was going down, we left the perimeter and headed west. I told the squad leaders we needed to step out and get to the ambush site as quickly as possible. It took us about half an hour to arrive at our rendezvous site, and it was just starting to get dark. I remembered from the night before that there would be a full moon, which should help us get into position and give us a better view of the kill zone. After leaving a fire team to guard the rendezvous area, we moved to the ambush site. Everything went fairly smoothly, and we had the ambush set up in pretty short order. I didn't think our presence had been detected and was sure Charlie wouldn't be expecting us that far from Hill 63. Now it was up to Charlie to do his part and walk into the ambush.

It wasn't long before I heard two individuals walking along the trail in from of us. They weren't making any effort to keep quiet as they were approaching us. They were carrying on a conversation and laughing among themselves. As they approached, they appeared to be two fairly young Vietnamese men. They weren't carrying weapons, and they acted like they were out for an evening stroll. I don't know what they would have done if they had known that a platoon of marines was lying in wait less than fifty yards away. I decided to let them pass and hoped that bigger fish would come along.

Nothing happened for the next couple of hours, and I began to worry that our efforts were not going to be rewarded. All of a sudden, a figure appeared in front of us on the railroad bed moving from south to north. Unlike the two previous individuals, he was carrying a rifle and moved slowly, making little noise. He was obviously paying attention to what was going on around him and kept looking from side to side. I concluded he must be a forward element of a larger unit and decided to let him pass, hoping his buddies weren't far behind. He stopped in the middle of the ambush site, turned around, and started walking back south along the trail. I assumed he was going to give the rest of his unit the all-clear sign and they would be in the kill zone shortly.

The anticipation was indescribable. If we could get a large number of VC in the kill zone, we would rip them to shreds in seconds. The minutes ticked off, and the entire platoon held their collective breaths.

The minutes turned into an hour, and then another hour passed without any sign of the VC. By that time, I could have kicked myself in the ass for not springing the ambush when the lone VC was in the kill zone. In hindsight, a VC in hand would have been worth two in the bush. Just before dawn, we packed it in and headed back to Hill 63. The lone VC must have detected our presence and turned back to warn whoever was following him along the trail. Unfortunately, we would never know for sure.

The next morning, I went to the company CP and found Sergeant Schwartz to discuss the situation regarding Sergeant Niel. It was obvious that it was time to take Sergeant Niel out of the field. He had served his country and the Marine Corps well over the last year, and it would be a real tragedy if he were killed or wounded during these last few weeks. Sergeant Schwartz agreed and told me he would talk to Captain K. about finding a safer place for him in the company headquarters group. I did not want to approach Captain K. directly, because he might think I was displeased with Sergeant Niel's performance, which couldn't have been further from the truth.

The platoon sergeant plays an important role in the operation of the platoon. Various platoon commanders deal differently with their platoon sergeants. Sometimes the platoon commander will give his orders directly to his platoon sergeant who then deals with the squad leaders. The squad leaders report directly to the platoon sergeant, who reports to the platoon commander. I did not like this arrangement for two reasons. First, the members of the platoon can become unclear as to who is really running the platoon. I did not want any member of my platoon to ever have a doubt as to who was in charge. Secondly, since I was ultimately responsible for whatever happened to the platoon, I wanted this responsibility to rest squarely on my shoulders. If something went wrong, it was because I made a mistake and not because the platoon sergeant screwed up. As a result of my approach, I gave my orders directly to the squad leaders, and they always reported directly to me. The platoon sergeant was there to consult with me, and I always valued his counsel, but the ultimate decisions were always mine.

A short time later, Sergeant Schwartz came by Second Platoon's CP and approached me with Sergeant Niel in tow. He told me Battalion had ordered Lima Company to send them a sergeant to be assigned to Battalion headquarters on a temporary basis. Since Sergeant Niel had substantial time in country and was about to rotate back to the States, he thought it would be best to send him up to Battalion. Sergeant Schwartz said, "He wanted to check with me first to make sure I had no objections."

I assured both Sergeant Schwartz and Sergeant Niel we would have a hard time replacing Sergeant Niel, but if Battalion needed someone, they couldn't find a better man. Sergeant Niel seemed relieved by the turn of events, but I could also tell he would miss Second Platoon. He gathered his gear and made the rounds to say good-bye to the men. His departing words to me were, "Make sure you look out for these guys, because if you don't, I'll have to come back here and do the job. If you need anything, you'll know where to find me." I assured him I would do my best to keep the platoon in one piece, and I would be by to see him in next time I went to the battalion CP.

I was now faced with the task of finding a new platoon sergeant. I had to pick from one of the three squad leaders, which would not be an easy choice. As usual, I sought out Sergeant Schwartz for his advice, and as usual, he had an opinion on the subject. His first choice was Sergeant Green of Third Squad. He felt the men looked up to Sergeant Green, who had a wealth of experience as a result of his many tours in Vietnam. I pointed out that Sergeant Green was the junior sergeant of the three squad leaders, and this might cause some problems with the other two. Sergeant Schwartz responded the welfare of the platoon was the most important thing, and if the other two squad leaders didn't like it, that it was just too bad. I decided to take Sergeant Schwartz's advice and go with Sergeant Green. Unfortunately, it was the only bad advice ever given me by Sergeant Schwartz and would cause me problems down the road.

That evening, I announced my decision to the three squad leaders. There wasn't a lot of reaction by any of the three sergeants, and I assumed I had made the right decision. We discussed who would take over Third Squad, and Sergeant Green suggested Corporal Hale. Corporal Hale was the M79 man in Third Squad and the senior corporal in the squad. I agreed with the choice and told Sergeant Green to make the necessary arrangements. Sergeant Green asked when we were going to make the switch, and I told him there was no time like the present. He left to get his gear, and Sergeant Duff, the Second Platoon leader, approached me to question my decision of appointing Sergeant Green as platoon sergeant. He pointed out he was the senior NCO in the platoon, and by right, the position should have been his. I explained the thoughts behind my decision. Sergeant Duff shrugged his shoulders and walked off, obviously disappointed.

The next morning, Captain K. told us he had gotten word from Battalion that we would begin a battalion-size operation the following day. Lima, Kilo, and India Companies would sweep the area east and south of Hill 63 in what was planned as a two-day operation. The three companies would be on line, and we would sweep along the west bank of the Song Ly River in a southerly direction for about seven klicks and then sweep back to Hill 63 on the west side of Highway 1. We would spend the night at the southern end of the sweep. Captain K. further informed us Lima Company would be on the eastern edge of the sweep, and we would have the Song Ly protecting our left flank. Kilo Company would be on our right flank, and India Company would be on the western edge of the sweep. Captain K. told us to make sure we took enough rations to last three days, just in case we ran into the unexpected. Breakfast would be served at 0400 hours, and we would assemble outside of the battalion mess tent at 0500 hours to depart on the operation.

I returned to Second Platoon's CP and told Corporal Stang to find the squad leaders and tell them we would have a meeting within the hour. When all the squad leaders arrived, Sergeant Green and I briefed them on the upcoming operation. I told them to cancel the night ambush and to move up the afternoon patrol so that everyone was inside the perimeter by 1600 hours. I wanted all the troops fully supplied and ready to go by 1800 hours, at which time I would hold an inspection of the platoon. I did not want to be scrambling around in the dark the next morning trying to get everyone ready to go. When I was sure everyone understood what was expected, I dismissed the squad leaders and sat down with Sergeant Green to discuss the operation.

Since I had never been on an operation bigger than the company sweep of the TAOR, I was a little apprehensive. Sergeant Green had been on his share of operations and assured me Second Platoon would be able to handle the situation. Sergeant Green went on to say, "Operations can be a real pain in the ass, and people get killed and wounded. We really lose control of the situation because the idiots in Battalion and Regiment are in charge. We have to do things at their pace and not at ours. In addition, they dictate the route and set up the objectives. What looks good to them on a map may not look so good on the ground. Unfortunately, it's the poor son of a bitch on the ground who pays for their mistakes."

I told him we would take our time and not take any unnecessary risk. He laughed and said, "Lieutenant, when we get out there, they will tell us how fast we go and where we go. They don't give a shit about the risk. All they're concerned about is having things look good on the maps and trying to get some enemy kills. They would march us through the gates of hell if they thought it would increase the body count. Just wait and see."

I challenged Sergeant Green's assertions and said I didn't think the Marine Corps would unnecessarily risk our lives. Sergeant Green became very serious and responded, "Look around you, Lieutenant. How many lifers do you see in the platoon? How many lifers do you see in the company? This war isn't being fought by lifers; it's being fought by civilians like you and me. The Marine Corps knows in a couple of years we ain't going to be around. We're expendable; you don't see them risking the life of a major or colonel or the lives of them fat fuckers back in Da Nang. If we get killed or wounded, it's just too damn bad. They couldn't care less."

I argued we hadn't taken that many casualties since I had joined the company, and hopefully, that would continue.

"Lieutenant, we've had it easy since you've been here," he replied. "Wait until we start running operations. You'll find out what it's really like. We will be humping day and night, and it will be payback time for Charlie. He'll catch us in some God-awful situation and will fuck us over big-time. Remember, payback is a motherfucker, and we haven't been paid back lately."

Sergeant Green then started in on the war by saying, "You know, Lieutenant, if they would just tell us how many gooks we've got to kill to win this war, I wouldn't mind taking the risk, but it don't matter how many of them sons of bitches we kill. There are always more just around the corner. We get men killed and wounded for what? So that some fucking colonel can tell the general what a great job we're doing. We ain't winning this war; we're killing Charlie, and he's killing us. What the fuck does that prove?"

I didn't have a good response to his argument, so I changed the subject by asking him if he had ever been in the area we were going to run the operation. He said, "We came through there when we took over Hill 63. It ain't nothing but rice paddies and dikes. I don't think we will have any major problems."

Sergeant Green left to check on the C rations and ammo for the operation, and I studied my map. Since I had not been in the area of the next day's operation, I felt it was important I familiarize myself with the lay of the land. The operation was to take place along the west bank of the Song Ly River, which ran between Highway 1 and the South China Sea. We would depart from Hill 63 and head due east until we hit the Song Ly. Once we arrived there, we would anchor the left side of our sweep to the riverbank, and the companies would spread out to the west. In theory, we would catch Charlie in the middle of our sweep, and he would have nowhere to go. If he tried to move east, he would have to cross the Song Ly, and we would be able to spot him moving across the river. If he tried to move to the west, he would run into Kilo or India Company.

The maps showed the terrain as mostly rice paddies. There were a substantial number of dikes in the area, and the land was generally flat with a few small hills scattered here and there. We would be passing through several small villages consisting of scattered hooches and one rather large village. If we were going to engage the enemy, it would be more than likely local VC. This type of terrain did not favor the NVA in that there was no place to hide large concentration of troops. From all appearances, it looked like this would be a walk in the park. Lima Company would leave at first light and be the lead company in the march to the west bank of the Song Ly. Once there, the companies would get on line and start sweeping south.

That evening, I conducted an inspection of the platoon. I checked each man's pack to make sure he was carrying enough ammo and food to last him through the operation. The men always wanted to carry as little weight as possible when they went on operations, and sometimes they scrimped on the essentials. I was more concerned about the amount of ammo they were carrying than anything else. The men, having been through this before, seemed to share my concerns, and all of them were well supplied with ammunition. When I was satisfied everything was in order, I instructed them to turn in early and to form up outside the mess tent at 0500 hours.

The next morning, I finished breakfast, and the platoon commanders had one last meeting with Captain K. before we headed out. He told us we would be moving to the Song Ly in wedge formation with First Platoon in the lead, followed by Second Platoon on the right flank and Third Platoon on the left flank. We would march to Highway 1 in column formation and form up there into our tactical formation. He then said, "We need to move as quickly as possible, because Battalion wants us on the bank of the Song Ly by 0600 hours to start sweeping south."

I quickly calculated we would be traveling approximately six klicks in little more than one hour. It would be a long way to go in a short time if we were going to maintain any semblance of tactical integrity. It appeared that Sergeant Green's predictions were coming true sooner than expected.

We began without incident, arriving at Highway 1 a little after 0500 hours. We had less than an hour to cover the remaining 4,500 meters to our initial objective. The problems raised by Sergeant Green were starting to hit home. On a map, 4,500 meters does not look like much. If the terrain is flat and unobstructed, the 4,500 meters could easily be covered in an hour if the company were to move at a brisk pace. Unfortunately, the maps do not show the terrain as it actually lies, and it is impossible to determine what obstacles would hinder the grunts trying to reach the objective. Under ideal circumstances, we would be able to reach the riverbank by 0600 hours, but the circumstances were never ideal.

As we began maneuvering toward our objective, it became apparent we would run into problems. We encountered gullies that were covered with brush and had steep slopes on both sides. The company also slowed down as we tried to find trails through bamboo thickets. In addition, the terrain was dictating our tactical movement. Instead of being spread out in a wedge formation as planned, we started funneling together into a column formation. There were times when Second Platoon was no more than thirty meters from the flank of Third Platoon, and both platoons were almost single file as we worked our way through the obstacles. Under normal conditions, we would have slowed down and gotten the platoons spread out, but we were pressing to get to our first objective.

All of a sudden, a firefight broke out in front of the formation. The fighting appeared to be furious, and we could hear the explosion of grenades and M79 rounds, along with small-arms fire. Second Platoon was too far back to return fire on the enemy positions. I noticed a small hill to our right front and ordered the squad leaders to get the platoon up on top of the hill. It took us approximately five minutes to get in position. Once there, we were able to observe the area where the firefight was taking place. I didn't know the exact location of First Platoon and was afraid to direct fire into their vicinity. I set up the M60 machine guns, and we started pouring fire into an area well in front of what should have been First Platoon's forward positions. I don't know if our machine-gun fire had any effect, but it certainly wouldn't hurt anything.

The firefight stopped as quickly as it started, and I could hear the First Platoon radio operator requesting an emergency medevac. Apparently, they had taken some casualties in the firefight. Since the situation seemed secure, I took my radioman and headed for Captain K.'s position. As we were walking in that direction, my radioman told me they changed the status of the medevac from emergency to routine. I was relieved to hear this and assumed the casualty was not in that bad of shape. When I arrived at Captain K.'s CP, there was a shocked look on the faces of the marines standing there. I looked on the ground and was frozen by the sight of a dead marine lying at the feet of Sergeant Schwartz. I asked who it was, and someone said it was Lieutenant Werner. I felt like I had been hit in the stomach with a sledgehammer. I had come to know Chuck quite well over the last several weeks and was totally stunned by what happened. As I looked around, it was apparent that everyone was visibly upset. Sergeant Schwartz, being the veteran that he was, took control of the situation and was on the radio trying to coordinate the medevac and informing Battalion of what had occurred. I noticed Lieutenant Muler standing by himself, and I walked over to try to console him. I knew of the bonds of friendship between Rich and Chuck, and there wasn't much I could say. I asked Rich how it happened, and he informed me Chuck was shot in the thigh, and apparently, the bullet severed the artery that ran down the leg. He bled to death in a matter of minutes, and there was nothing the corpsman could do to stem the flow of blood. It was obvious Rich was devastated by this loss and was doing everything he could to hold himself together.

I heard the sound of the medevac approaching as Sergeant Schwartz was directing it to our location. I walked over to Lieutenant Werner's body to see what I could do to help. Sergeant Schwartz told me we needed to strip him of his equipment before we put him on the chopper. I went through his pockets and pack and got his maps, compass, and other items that would be useful to us. By this time, the chopper was landing, and three marines rolled Lieutenant Werner's body onto his poncho and loaded him onto the medevac. As the medevac disappeared over the horizon, Captain K. told me, "Put Second Platoon on the lead, and get us to the Song Ly."

I radioed Sergeant Green to have the men saddle up, meet me in front of the company, and start moving toward the riverbank. When I joined up with Sergeant Green, I radioed the squad leaders to sweep through the area where the firefight took place to see what we could find and then head due west toward the river. As we moved through the battle site, we could see where Charlie had been concealed awaiting our approach. There were spent shell casings scattered everywhere and several American-made hand grenades lying on the ground. A closer inspection revealed that the pins of the grenades had been pulled, but the spoons were still held in place by black tape. About a month earlier, Battalion came down with an order directing the spoons of all grenades should be taped to prevent a detonation in the event the pins were to accidentally work loose. Apparently in the excitement, the marines of First Platoon forgot to remove the tape before they threw the grenades, and as a result, they fell harmlessly among the enemy. The taping of the grenades was one more brilliant idea thought up by someone from Regiment who had never been in a firefight in his life. We gathered up the grenades and detonated them by removing the tape and throwing them over an embankment. We then moved out and headed for our objective, the west bank of the Song Ly.

The death of Chuck Werner weighed heavily on my mind as we moved toward the river. We obviously had been moving too quickly in an effort to get to the objective in the time frame set for us by Battalion. Did this contribute to Chuck's death? Would things have been different if we were taking our time and maintaining tactical integrity? How many VC would we have to kill to pay back for the death of Chuck Werner? These questions would never be answered, but it was clear one of America's finest had been lost and would never be replaced. The grief that would be suffered by his family was unimaginable, and he would not soon be forgotten by the men of Lima Company. Despite that, the war continued, and we had to get to the Song Ly as quickly as possible to satisfy the demands of our superiors.

I radioed Captain K. that my forward element had reached the banks of the Song Ly. He ordered the platoons to get on line to begin sweeping south. When everyone was in position, we got word from Battalion to move out, and we started our sweep as planned. The left flank of Second Platoon was protected by the Song Ly River, and our right flank was covered by Third Platoon. We proceeded for several hundred meters when rifle fire broke out to my left front. I proceeded to the area of the firing and discovered three marines from Second Squad standing over the body of a dead Vietnamese. I asked them what happened, and one of them said, "This guy jumped up right in front of us and started running, so I capped his ass."

I had my doubts about that. The Vietnamese was unarmed and looked like any other villager who inhabited the area. I was not in a position to argue the point and was not sure I really cared. The VC who killed Chuck Werner probably had breakfast with this bastard, and wasn't payback supposed to be a motherfucker? I radioed Lima Six we had one confirmed VC killed with no weapons, and we continued moving south.

As we continued our sweep, the terrain became more and more difficult to traverse. What appeared as dikes on the map started to become steeper and higher, and we were crawling up and down some that were several meters high. I couldn't figure out what purpose the dikes served, except maybe to control flooding during the monsoon season. As I was crawling up the side of one of the dikes, I received an excited call over the radio from Sergeant Presno of First Squad.

"Lima Two, we've got a sampan trying to cross the river in front of us. Over."

I told him to fire warning shots in front of the boat and I would be right there. I could hear the M60 machine gun opening up as my radioman and I ran toward the bank of the river. When I arrived at Sergeant Presno's position, I observed a large motorized sampan trying to cross the river to our left front. The warning shots seemed to have little effect as the boat kept chugging along in front of us. I told the machine gunner to take the boat under fire and then told Sergeant Presno to get some LAAWs over there as quickly as possible.

The term *LAAW* is an acronym for Light Antitank Assault Weapon and is nothing more than a rocket-propelled round in a disposable launcher. Each squad carried a couple of LAAWs with them, and they were brought to the riverbank in short order. By the time the LAAWs arrived, the machine-gun team had poured several hundred rounds into the sampan and was running out of ammo. Despite the punishment received from the machine gun and the rounds being fired by the troops from their M16s, the sampan kept making its way toward the far bank of the river. The first LAAW fired at the sampan missed its mark—as did the second; the third round was the charm, as it cut the sampan in half. We couldn't discern any passengers in the sampan, but it was obviously being driven by someone and could have carried several others. We continued to fire our M16s at the sampan until it sank, and we satisfied ourselves that there were no survivors. I radioed an after-action report to Captain K. that we killed six VC in the escaping sampan. That should make the day for some general in Da Nang whose job it was to add up the body count, and who's to say there weren't six VC on the sampan?

As the day wore on, the heat continued to rise, and we moved into an area covered by white sand. The sand was so white it looked like the ground was covered with snow. As the temperatures went over one hundred degrees, it was more and more difficult to maintain the pace expected by Battalion. The sand reflected unbearable heat, and it was apparent that if we didn't do something, we would start suffering heat casualties—a serious problem that can lead to death. An individual can pass out from heat prostration, and if he is not cooled down immediately, it will turn into heat stroke, which can be fatal. I felt we were being pushed by Battalion as a result of their frustration in not making contact with Charlie. If there were any VC in front of us, they were able to stay far enough ahead to avoid a firefight. It is more likely Charlie was able to conceal himself, and we passed over him as we swept through the area. In any event, we were expending a lot of energy and not getting very good results. Finally, Captain K. called a halt, telling us we would be spending the next hour or so in our present position and to have the troops refill their canteens and find some shade.

After getting the platoon set up, I went to the company CP to see if Captain K. knew what was scheduled for the rest of the day. The first person I ran into was Sergeant Schwartz. He told me Captain K. was pretty torn up about Lieutenant Werner's death. We speculated on what happened earlier that morning.

Sergeant Schwartz commented, "We must have surprised Charlie, because they really let us get close to them before they started firing. It's my guess we walked up on top of them before they knew we were there."

I replied, "Maybe they just wanted to get us close in before they sprung the ambush like they did in Operation Union."

Sergeant Schwartz disagreed. "In Union, we were ambushed by an NVA regiment that continued to engage us for several days. From the looks of things this morning, there was only a handful of VC who took off running at the first opportunity. No, I think we surprised them, and they were damn lucky to get out of there alive."

"Well, Chuck Werner wasn't so lucky," I replied. "How is Rich Muler taking things?"

"He's pretty upset right now, but he is as tough as a boot, and he'll get through this. Besides, we have to keep on fighting this war. Charlie don't let you call time-out."

Captain K. walked up, and I asked if he knew how long we would stay in our present position. He said he didn't know. Apparently, Kilo Company had a heat casualty, and they were getting him cooled down.

A medevac had been called, and as soon as it picked up the casualty, we would probably move out. Our discussion turned to First Platoon, and Captain K. informed me Staff Sergeant Wood had taken over the platoon. Sergeant Wood had been the platoon sergeant for First Platoon for several months and was a very capable individual. They were lucky to have someone of his caliber to take over for Lieutenant Werner.

As I returned to Second Platoon, I thought about the irony of the situation in Lima Company. Two weeks earlier, we had too many officers, and I was relegated to the role of platoon commander of a nonexistent platoon. Now we were one officer short. Things can change pretty fast out in Vietnam, and change was probably the only constant.

As I arrived back at Second Platoon, word came down to move out, and we saddled up and resumed sweeping south. I assumed Charlie was pretty well aware of our presence by then and was either hauling ass out of the area or setting up one hell of an ambush. The former was probably the most likely.

It was getting close to 1500 hours, and the heat was becoming even more oppressive. As we were wading through the white sand and climbing up and down the dikes, the temperature reflecting off the sand had to be in excess of 125 degrees. Over the past several weeks, the heat had not been that much of a factor, because we were able to work around it. We ran our patrols in the mornings and late afternoons. In addition, we operated at our pace, giving ourselves plenty of time to complete the patrols. Even when we were involved in the company sweep of the TAOR, we could always find an excuse to slow things down in the middle of the day. The pace being set by Battalion didn't seem to be slacking up despite the heat casualty in Kilo Company. Humping in the excessive heat causes problems, in addition to the heat casualties. It is impossible to maintain tactical integrity under the conditions in which we were now operating. The troops were more concerned about surviving the heat than they were about getting shot by Charlie. How they were going to hump the next hundred yards was more important than who might be lying in ambush behind the next dike.

As we proceeded south, I started to become light headed, and my vision became blurred. I popped a couple of salt tablets and drank the water from one of my canteens. In a few minutes, my head cleared, but I was nauseous from the salt tablets. I drank some more water, which helped calm my stomach. All of the side effects from the heat made concentrating difficult, and it was all I could do to keep track of the platoon's location on the map. If Charlie were to spring an ambush now, we would have a difficult time fighting back. War was hard enough under the best of conditions; that day, it was impossible.

As I expected, we started taking more heat casualties. Lima Company had a man down in Third Platoon, and apparently Kilo Company had another man fall out. Captain K. instructed us to start looking for a location to spend the night. He informed us we would be setting up a company-size perimeter, and we might be joined by the battalion headquarters group. I checked the map, and there appeared to be a suitable location about two hundred meters ahead. We could anchor a portion of the perimeter on the riverbank, which would only require us to defend three-fourths of the perimeter. I radioed Captain K., asking his permission to take Second Platoon ahead and secure the perimeter. He told me to go ahead as soon as the platoon was sufficiently rested.

I gave everyone thirty minutes, and then we headed toward the proposed perimeter. We secured the area, and it appeared to be well suited to our needs. It was bordered on the east by the river and surrounded by large dikes. We could dig our fighting holes along the top of the dikes and have an almost impregnable fortress. I radioed back to Captain K. that the perimeter was secure, and it looked like a pretty good place to spend the night. An hour later, the rest of the company arrived along with the headquarters group from Battalion. Captain K. walked the perimeter along with the three platoon commanders of Lima Company. He assigned Second Platoon the southern end of the perimeter, and I gathered my three squad leaders, and we set up the location of each fighting position. I was taking extra care, because Colonel Brady would be spending the night, and I was sure he would take a look at the perimeter before turning in. I wanted things as squared away as possible to try to create a good impression with the battalion commander.

Later that evening, Sergeant Green and I were eating a meal of C rations when he brought up an unexpected subject. He wanted to know if we could obtain another radio so he could be in communication with the squad leaders and monitor the company net while we were on future operations.

I said, "I don't know where we would find another radio, and besides, none of the other platoon sergeants have radios."

He replied, "Well, Lieutenant, I really feel useless out here. I am usually in the thick of things when the shooting starts. Without a radio, I am just another trooper."

I told Sergeant Green we would discuss this after the operation, hoping he would forget about it.

I noticed Captain K. and Colonel Brady walking in the direction of Second Platoon's portion of the perimeter, and I grabbed my rifle to join them. When I caught up, they were walking along the perimeter observing the fighting positions we had set up. Colonel Brady seemed satisfied with things, and I left the tour when they departed the last of Second Platoon's positions. I returned to the area where Sergeant Green had set up Second Platoon's CP. Lance Corporal Moreno was manning the radio, and I noticed they had dug two large foxholes for our CP group. I told Doc Blake to make sure the men had plenty of salt tablets for the following day. He said he had made the rounds and instructed the men that he wanted them to take at least two tablets every hour during the hottest part of the day. Doc Blake was extremely competent and was one step ahead of me when it came to the health of Second Platoon.

As we sat around waiting for it to get dark, the discussion turned to the day's activities. Everyone was bummed out about Lieutenant Werner's death, and it was apparent he was well liked by the troops in our CP group. We also talked about the heat and the fact we would probably have to go through the same ordeal the next day.

Lance Corporal Moreno volunteered, "It's sure-as-shit certain that Colonel Brady ain't humping no radio. Man, that heat liked to have killed me today."

I suggested that my runner, Private First Class Wynn, carry the radio the following day. This brought an immediate response from Moreno.

"Over my dead body he will. As long as I'm the radioman, I carry the radio. Besides, he would fuck everything up, and I don't want no one to touch my radio."

Wynn joked, "I wouldn't touch your stinking radio. Besides, no one with half a brain would want to carry the damn thing. The first thing they teach Charlie is to shoot the dumb son of a bitch with an antenna growing out of his back. Anyway, Moreno, if you can't hack it, fall the fuck out."

The last expression is one I had heard on many occasions and would continue to hear in the future. Anytime someone complained about something, the response was "If you can't hack it, fall the fuck out." This pretty much expressed the philosophy of Second Platoon and all the grunts in Vietnam. The individual infantryman took pride in the fact that he could "hack it," no matter how difficult the situation became. The ability to persevere in spite of the difficulties was the mark of the grunt and is what distinguished us from the rest of the military. This is not to say those who served in other areas were not hackers; it's just they had never been put to the test. Many of them would measure up if given the opportunity, but for one reason or another, they never availed themselves of the chance to test themselves. They would never know for sure if they really could hack it. The battle-tested grunt never had a doubt about his abilities and knew for certain what he could endure and how far he could go. He would continue to hack it no matter what, and under no circumstances would he fall out.

The next morning, it was obvious that it would be another scorcher. We ate a meal of C rations, saddled up, and started moving west across Highway 1. After we crossed the highway, the companies got on line for the sweep back toward Hill 63. It was pretty obvious this would be a walk in the park. Every Vietcong within twenty klicks knew where we were and what we were up to. They were not about to take on three infantry companies in the open terrain where we were traversing.

Apparently, everyone but Colonel Brady thought this was going to be a cakewalk. The pace of the day before was maintained on our sweep back toward Hill 63. By noon, the walk in the park turned into another forced march, with heat casualties becoming a real concern. Colonel Brady finally called a halt at 1300 hours, and the men of Second Platoon sought out the shade and cooked a meal of C rations. We were only three klicks south of Hill 63, and after the break, we maintained a more leisurely pace back to the battalion perimeter. When we arrived at Hill 63, Lima Company went back to its position on the perimeter, and the routine of constructing defensive positions and patrolling the TAOR resumed.

First Operation

6

THE BATTLES CONTINUE

A WEEK LATER, I WAS at the company CP when Captain K. called me over and introduced me to Lieutenant Lee Gounds, who had just been assigned to Lima Company to replace Chuck Werner as commander of First Platoon. Lee and I graduated from the same class at Basic School, but I did not know him. He had just arrived in country after completing Marine Corps Reconnaissance School. Lee and I immediately hit it off. He was from Oklahoma, having graduated from the University of Oklahoma, where he played varsity football. In fact, he played on the offensive line next to Ralph Neely, who was from my hometown and who went on to play for the Dallas Cowboys. Since I had been in country for several weeks, I felt like an old salt and tried to give Lee the benefit of what little knowledge I had gained since arriving at Lima Company. Lee, Rich Muler, and I became very close friends in a short period of time.

After a couple of weeks of doing nothing but patrolling the TAOR, Captain K. called the three platoon commanders together to tell us that Battalion had scheduled another operation. We were going to sweep from Hill 63 to the village of Que Son, which was the headquarters of First Battalion, Fifth Marines (One-Five). We would be operating south of Route 535, which was the road that intersected Highway 1 at Hill 63 and ran almost due west to Que Son. Delta

Company of One-Five would be acting as a blocking force, hopefully allowing us to trap the enemy between the two companies. We were further informed that three tanks stationed at Hill 63 would be accompanying us on the operation. They would travel down Route 535 on our right flank and would be able to provide us with armored support in the event we were able to engage Charlie in a sustained firefight.

Since we would be operating in the heart of the Que Son Valley, there was a possibility we would come in contact with NVA forces. This increased the risk factor substantially, and Captain K. made us aware of the fact that this could be something other than a walk in the park. We were provided with maps of the area we would be traveling, and Captain K. informed us Second Platoon would be the lead platoon on this operation.

I contacted Second Platoon's squad leaders along with Sergeant Green and asked them if any of them were familiar with the area we would be operating in on our sweep toward Que Son. The platoon had never been through this area, and none of them were acquainted with the terrain we would encounter. This created additional problems in that I would be required to do all the navigating as the platoon commander of the lead platoon. If you were not familiar with the area you were operating in, it was substantially more difficult to keep track of your location on the maps. You must constantly check your position so you knew exactly where you were and where you were headed. This was further complicated by the fact that the platoon was expected to maintain a pace set by Battalion. I would not be afforded the luxury of stopping and reorientating myself in the event I became confused as to my location.

I checked the maps and noted several landmarks that would help me orientate myself as we crossed or passed near them. They were such things as hills, trails, streams, and other features that would be recognizable on the ground. As we traversed these features, I would be able to confirm I was navigating correctly and make adjustments for any errors in my calculations. Hopefully, this would prevent us from becoming lost on the way to Que Son.

Just as the rifle was the basic tool of the infantryman, the map and compass were the basic tools of the platoon commander. The job of the platoon commander was not to shoot the enemy but rather to navigate the platoon to a position where they could shoot the enemy. At the same time, it was essential the platoon commander knew where the platoon was at all times in the event he had to call in artillery or air strikes. The worst thing that could happen to a platoon was that it came into contact with the enemy and the platoon commander didn't know his location. Although this seemed pretty basic, I was always amazed at the number of times a platoon reported contact and couldn't get artillery support because the platoon commander didn't know where he was.

After reviewing the maps, I tended to the various details of getting the platoon ready for the operation. The next morning, we were assembled before dawn and began to maneuver into position at first light. On our way to the line of departure, we passed the three tanks that would be paralleling us along Route 535 during the operation. They would be accompanied by a squad from Third Platoon, which would provide ground cover for the tanks to make sure a VC hiding in the bushes didn't disable them with an RPG round.

As we began our sweep toward Que Son, it became immediately apparent we had problems with the operation. You could hear the tank's engines roaring as they traveled west along Route 535. We were about a klick south of the road, and it seemed like the tanks were right next to us. Every Vietcong in the vicinity had to know we had tanks moving west along Route 535. If they were smart, they would immediately clear out of the area, which was just as well for us. Hopefully, this would be another walk in the park.

We made good progress for the first three or four klicks, encountering nothing of any significance. The terrain consisted primarily of rice paddies and scattered villages with a few hills sprinkled here and there.

The farmers once again studiously ignored us as we moved across their fields and swept through their villages. They neither glanced in our direction nor acknowledged our presence in any way. It was as if we weren't there. Their attitude seemed to be "if we ignore these guys, maybe they will just go away." They continued to work their fields, and we continued to sweep toward Que Son.

Just as we were approaching a series of hills that would mark the halfway point to Que Son, Lance Corporal Moreno told me Corporal Hale, the Third Squad leader, wanted to talk to me. I got on the radio, and he informed me he had a man down and needed a medic right away. I sent Doc Blake in his direction and informed Captain K. we would be held up for a couple of minutes. I proceeded over to Third Squad's position and observed several marines gathered around a man lying on the ground. Doc Blake had the marine's shirt off and was pouring water over him. I recognized the prone marine as one who had joined the platoon the day before, having just arrived in country. Doc Blake told me the marine was suffering from heat prostration and we needed a medevac. I informed Lima Six of the situation, and he said they would get us one as quickly as possible. Apparently, the fallen marine had not had sufficient time to acclimate to the heat of Vietnam. Thirty minutes later, the medevac arrived to pick up the casualty. As soon as the medevac departed, we saddled up and continued sweeping west toward Que Son.

Around noon, we started picking up sniper fire from our left flank. Whoever was firing was several hundred meters away, and the firing was more disruptive than anything else. We returned fire with little chance of success. Although we were too far away to tell for sure, I assumed the VC who were shooting at us were concealed in trenches that ran everywhere in this area. Rifle fire had little or no chance of hitting a VC who was hiding in one of the trench lines. I called in artillery fire on the area where I thought the fire was coming from and asked Captain K. if he could get us a Blackcoat to fly along our left flank to discourage any more snipers. Captain K. called back on the radio, informing me Blackcoat was available, and we had to deal with the situation as best we could.

It was difficult to ignore the sniper fire for two reasons. First, nobody wanted to be the unlucky son of a bitch who got shot by a stray round. Second, by not responding to the fire, we would only encourage the VC to keep shooting at us. I decided to anticipate where the sniper fire would be coming from as we moved toward Que Son and registered these targets with the artillery fire control center. They informed me they would train their guns on a particular target as we moved west, and if we received fire from that area, they would immediately respond. I got lucky in that the next sniper rounds came from an area I had targeted for the artillery. As predicted, the artillery came raining in shortly after the snipers fired their first rounds. The VC stopped firing and apparently called it a day, because we didn't have any more problems from our left flank.

As we proceeded sweeping west, we encountered several huge rice paddies that extended some four to five hundred meters. Since we were in a company-size formation, it was conceivable the entire company would be in the rice paddy at the same time. The fact that we were in potential NVA country added to the problem. Getting caught in an open rice paddy by a company or battalion of NVA would spell disaster. The solution was to send a squad across the rice paddy to secure the other side before the company started across. If there was a company of NVA on the other side, the squad would get wiped out, but the rest of the company would be safe. It was my job to pick the squad that would cross the paddies ahead of the company. Needless to say, there was never a lot of enthusiasm by the chosen squad, but they always did what they were told. I tried to rotate this task so one squad didn't get stuck with the job too often.

This simple exercise of sending a squad across large rice paddies ahead of the company illustrated the sacrifices the grunts were willing to make in Vietnam. If we related the same situation to civilian life, it would illustrate and highlight these sacrifices. Assume that several hundred armed men were suspected of being entrenched outside of a small town in rural America for the purpose of killing anyone who might approach. Further assume the town fathers asked for several volunteers to go out and check to see if these armed men were really out there as suspected. How many men would be willing to volunteer for such a task? If you could find such volunteers, would they not become instant heroes within their communities as well as throughout the nation? This same situation faced the grunts of Second Platoon on numerous occasions this day. Their reward? A meal of C rations and the opportunity to saddle up and do the same thing the next day—all in the service of what later became an ungrateful nation.

The rest of the day turned out to be pretty uneventful—a walk in the park, as they say. We joined up with the blocking force of Delta One-Five, and I ran into Hank Pritchard, my old buddy from OCS. He was the platoon commander of First Platoon of Delta Company, and we had a chance to briefly exchange war stories. He told me things were pretty hairy around Que Son, and they were constantly anticipating being overrun by the NVA. Intelligence told them a regiment of NVA was operating less than two klicks from One-Five's perimeter. They never patrolled their TAOR with less than a platoon and were in almost constant contact with the enemy. Since Que Son was farther from the coast than Hill 63, the terrain favored the enemy in that it had less open area and more hills to provide cover and places for them to hide.

After a brief visit with Hank, we saddled up and proceeded to an area just outside of One-Five's lines to set up our nightly perimeter. This didn't make any sense, and I could not understand why we just didn't spend the night inside One-Five's firebase. The reason became obvious as soon as we set up for the night. We were the butt of what One-Five must have thought was a hilarious practical joke. Outside of every village is the communal toilet. Since there are no sewers in this part of Vietnam, everyone takes a shit wherever it is most convenient. Usually, there is an empty field next to a populated area that is designated for this purpose. Some joker in One-Five thought it would be funny if the area assigned to us to spend the night would be in the middle of this field. We didn't discover the joke until it was too late to change our positions. We spent the night wading through shit and cursing First Battalion. Hopefully, payback would be a motherfucker for them when we got our chance.

The next morning, we awoke to the smell of shit, ate our C rations, and saddled up to begin the day. We would return to Hill 63 along Route 535 with our primary mission to escort the tanks back to Hill 63. This would really be a walk in the park, because Charlie was not about to mess with a company of marines accompanied by three tanks. We proceeded east along Route 535, maintaining a tactical formation mostly out of habit. It would have been a lot easier to form up in a column formation for the walk back to Hill 63, but such was not to be.

Nothing much happened until we reached the halfway point between Que Son and Hill 63. A large explosion shattered the afternoon silence, and I initially thought we were being mortared. There was a lot of scrambling until we discovered that one of the tanks had hit a mine. It was obviously planted during the last twenty-four hours, because the tanks had traveled this same route the day before. Charlie had apparently figured out we would be returning to Hill 63 on the same road the tanks traversed down to Que Son. Captain K. informed us we would be held up for some time and to get the troops in a defensive position until we received further orders. After getting Second Platoon spread out into something resembling a perimeter, I went over to where the tank had struck the mine. The members of the tank crews were stripped to the waist repairing the tank. The only damage was that a portion of the tank's tread had been blown off. The tanks always carried an extra length of tread for just such an emergency, and the tank crews were removing the damaged tread and replacing it with the new tread.

After about an hour, the tread was replaced, and we were ready to renew our journey back to Hill 63. A couple of engineers with metal detectors had been brought in by chopper while we were waiting for the tank to be repaired, and they began sweeping the road ahead of the tank for any additional mines that might have been planted overnight. This slowed our progress considerably, and what started out as a walk in the park became a crawl in the park. We finally arrived back at Hill 63 just before dark and were assigned to several large tents that had been recently erected within the perimeter. This was a real luxury for Second Platoon. We would be sleeping on cots instead of the ground, with no responsibility for manning the perimeter or running ambushes. Captain K. decided a beer ration was in order, and the company spent the night getting drunk on warm beer. The next morning, we slept in, and when we awoke, we strolled over to the mess tent for a leisurely breakfast. This was too good to be true and surely wouldn't last.

After breakfast, I met one of my worst nightmares in Vietnam. The three Lima Company platoon commanders were sharing a tent with Sergeant Schwartz and a couple of the staff NCOs. We were lying around, writing letters and cleaning our gear when a major whom I had not seen before walked into the tent with the battalion sergeant major. He was dressed in stateside fatigues, which meant he had just arrived in country. Since military courtesy was pretty much ignored while we were in the field, no one bothered to stand up or even acknowledge his presence. He immediately asked, "Doesn't anyone here observe the basic rules of military courtesy? Isn't it appropriate to stand at attention when a superior officer enters the room?"

Lieutenant Muler immediately jumped to his feet, followed by Lee Gounds and myself. While we stood there, the major said, "My name is Major Franks, and I am your new executive officer. I'm inspecting the battalion, and this area is a mess and should be policed up immediately. As junior officers, you should be setting an example for the enlisted men, and having your gear scattered everywhere along with empty cans of beer is not a message we want to send."

Rich Muler had enough sense to keep his mouth shut, but Lee and I were not as wise. We tried to explain we had just occupied the tent the night before and had not had time to store our gear or square away the tent. Major Franks informed us he did not intend to debate this matter with junior officers and he would be back in one hour to complete his inspection. He further informed us, "In the future, I expect you to stand at attention when I enter the room."

He went on to explain that all military courtesy would be exercised henceforth. The sergeant major was standing behind the major rolling his eyes at each of his pronouncements.

After Major Franks exited the tent, I asked Rich Muler what the fuck that was all about. Rich told us Major Franks was what was known in the military as a flaming asshole whose sole purpose in life was to make our lives miserable. The job of a battalion executive officer (XO) is to kick ass and take names on behalf of the battalion commander, and I am sure that everyone familiar with the military is aware of this. There is a substantial difference between kicking ass and taking names and being a complete asshole like Major Franks. It would appear he intended to turn the battalion area into a stateside duty station. I would bet that while we would have to put up with him inside the perimeter, we would never see him outside the perimeter. Marines like Major Franks were generally able to avoid the inconvenience of humping the bush, preferring instead to make people's lives miserable within the safety of the battalion perimeter.

Officers like Major Franks were a day-and-night's difference from the likes of Captain K. and Colonel Brady. While Captain K. and Colonel Brady were concerned about the welfare of their men and recognized the sacrifices being made by the average grunt, officers like Major Franks were only concerned about their careers and how their performance would be judged by the officers writing their fitness reports. Unfortunately, for every Captain K. and Colonel Brady, there were several Major Frankses. I concluded it would be best to avoid Major Franks in the future.

We cleaned up the tent as best we could, throwing away the empty beer cans and stowing our gear under our cots. As promised, Major Franks returned and inspected the tent without comment. We made it a point to stand at attention during the inspection. When Major Franks satisfied himself everything was in order, he stalked off to make someone else's life miserable. Later, I hunted up Sergeant Schwartz to tell him about our adventure with Major Franks. I found him at the mess tent having a cup of coffee with the mess sergeant, Gunnery Sergeant Collins. I explained to him what happened earlier with the major. He answered, "I just heard about him myself from the sergeant major. He showed up yesterday and has been raising holy hell ever since. If he starts fucking with the troops, he could cause some problems."

Gunny Collins chimed in, "He came by yesterday to inspect the mess hall, and I had to clean it three times before he was satisfied. I just hope he stays off my ass."

Sergeant Schwartz joked, "Well, nobody ever accused you of running a clean mess hall. Maybe a little cleanliness is what this place needs."

Gunny Collins, feigning indignation, grabbed Sergeant Schwartz's cup of coffee and poured the contents on the ground, declaring, "The mess hall is now closed, and I would appreciate it if you fuckers would clear the area so that I can get back to my cleaning."

Sergeant Schwartz and I walked away laughing at the mess sergeant and went to the company CP where we found Captain K. He informed us Lima Company would take the day off and would start running platoon-size patrols in the battalion TAOR the following day. This would be the first day off since I joined the company several weeks earlier. Captain K. went on to tell us Battalion wanted to start running long-range patrols in an attempt to spread our influence farther from the perimeter. The patrols would last all day, and we were to extend our patrolling area. Since Charlie had pretty much abandoned the immediate area around the perimeter, it was hoped that by expanding the TAOR, we would have a better chance of engaging him with our extended patrols. Since we would be operating six or seven klicks from the perimeter, it was too risky for a single squad of marines, so we would go out in platoon-size strength. Captain K. ended the conversation by instructing us to prepare a patrol route for the next day. We would coordinate our routes to avoid unexpected contact between the platoons. We decided to divide the new TAOR into thirds, and each platoon would take a sector. That way, each platoon would be patrolling in the same area all the time and would become more familiar with the terrain in its sector. I chose the area north and west of Hill 63, which was generally the area that Second Platoon patrolled in the past. The only difference would be that we would be going farther out in larger numbers.

As we were finalizing our plans, who should walk up but our new buddy Major Franks on another one of his inspections. Of course, we immediately jumped to attention. Major Franks asked what we were doing, apparently concerned about the fact that we didn't appear to be engaged in some sort of constructive activity. Lieutenant Gounds explained we were planning the following day's patrols and invited him to join us on the patrols. I jumped in and said, "That would be a really good idea, Major. It would give you an opportunity to familiarize yourself with the TAOR, and we would be really glad to have you along."

Major Franks was somewhat taken aback by our suggestion and for a moment was speechless. The three of us were giving him shit-eating grins that read, "You don't have the balls to go out with us." Major Franks finally replied, "I really welcome the opportunity to go with you, but tomorrow is not a good time. Maybe some other time."

Rich Muler replied, "The invitation is always open. Just let us know when you can spare the time."

Major Franks stormed off, knowing full well we were playing mind games with him. Of course, it didn't bother him enough to take us up on our offer. It was apparent you couldn't pry Major Franks out of the safety of the battalion perimeter with a crowbar. He was a typical REMF, willing to fight this war to the last man, just so long as it didn't involve any undue risk to him.

I now had to come up with a plan for the following day's patrol. My first thought was we should initially run the patrols to get a feel for the lay of the land in the extended TAOR. After becoming familiar with the terrain and establishing some recognizable landmarks, we could become a little more creative in our planning and execution. At the same time, I felt we had the element of surprise on our side for at least the first couple of days of patrolling in the new area. Charlie was probably pretty complacent in the area we would be patrolling since there hadn't been any regular activity in that area in the past. Hopefully, we could catch him off guard on the initial patrols and maybe administer some payback.

I devised a plan that would give us the element of surprise and at the same time provide us with the opportunity to get a good look at the terrain we would be traversing in the future. I decided to leave the perimeter well before first light and travel due north on Highway 1 as quickly as possible to a point four klicks north of the perimeter. If everything went as planned, we would arrive at this location at first light and immediately start sweeping west in a large arc paralleling the perimeter. Optimistically, we would catch Charlie by surprise in the first couple of hours of the patrol. We would then continue to sweep west and south until we covered the entire length of our new TAOR, at which time we would return to the perimeter.

After setting forth the proposed route on a map, I coordinated this plan with India Company, who was now occupying the perimeter in our old area. While we would be running the long-range patrols, they would be patrolling closer to the perimeter. I didn't want to accidentally get into a firefight with one of their patrols while we were returning to the perimeter, and I wanted them to know where we would be in case one of their patrols spotted us in the distance.

I found Captain Frank Burke, the India Company commander, and explained the situation to him. He assured me all his men would be informed of our location and suggested we might coordinate our patrols in the future so his people could provide blocking positions for our sweeps. In addition, we devised a plan to let India Company know when we would be passing through their TAOR. I would simply come up on their radio net prior to entering their TAOR and talk directly to whatever patrols they had in the area. This way, we wouldn't have to worry about what time I was expected to enter their TAOR. After getting everything squared away, I left Captain Burke, assuring him I would get back in touch with him regarding some coordinated patrols.

The next morning, we were moving north on Highway 1 at 0400 hours. Since we weren't carrying backpacks and were walking on a straight road, we were able to move at a pretty good clip. I anticipated we could cover the four klicks in a little over an hour, which would put us in position to start patrolling west at 0530 hours.

The hump along Highway 1 was uneventful and somewhat pleasant in the cool of the night. When the sun came up, we would be fighting the oppressive heat and humidity, which was a daily occurrence.

At 0530, we were in position waiting for it to get light enough to begin our sweep. There was a rice paddy immediately in front of us and a small village on the other side of the paddy. I informed the squad leaders to get into the village before anyone knew we were there.

We quickly traversed the rice paddy and swept through the village without contact. As we exited the west side of the village, we came into heavy contact with the enemy from both our left and right fronts. We immediately returned fire, and I began calling in artillery on the VC positions. I could hear someone calling for a medic on my right side, and Doc Blake went running in that direction. It took about five minutes to get the first rounds on their way, and a few minutes later, I had the artillery on its target, which silenced the enemy fire. I got a report from First Squad that they had a wounded marine and would need a medevac. I told Sergeant Green to call in the medevac on my radio, and I went over to First Squad's position.

The wounded marine had been shot in the leg, and Doc Blake stated he would be okay and probably had a ticket home. I returned to Sergeant Green and could hear the *whump-whump-whump* of the medevac chopper.

Sergeant Duff of Second Squad informed me his men saw two VC running into the tree line in front of us just before the firing started. The VC were through the tree line before his men could get any rounds off, and immediately, the firefight started. I got the other two squad leaders on the radio and told them to be ready to move out and sweep the area where the artillery landed as soon as the medevac left. Ten minutes later, we were moving west toward the tree line from which we received the fire.

Luck was with us this day. As we entered the tree line, we discovered two dead VC, who apparently had been hit by the artillery rounds. There was another blood trail leading to the west. It looked like a third VC had been dragged from the scene either dead or badly wounded. The weapons of the dead VC had been retrieved by Charlie, but both of them had cartridge belts with hand grenades attached. We followed the blood trail, but it quickly petered out.

We continued our sweep when we came under attack again several hundred meters west of the first firefight. Once again, I called in artillery, but the VC broke off the assault before I could bring the first rounds in. After the fire mission, we once again moved to the west and south.

We continued to get sporadic resistance from the VC as the day progressed. Their brief assaults were effective in slowing our progress. As we came under attack, we would return small-arms fire, and I would attempt to call in artillery on the enemy positions. Usually, Charlie broke off contact and retreated before I could zero in the artillery. On each occasion, thirty minutes or more would pass before we were able to resume our sweep, and I decided to try a different tactic. While the rest of the platoon took a break, I identified several likely targets that lay ahead of us along the intended route of our sweep. When we resumed our march, I would call in fire missions on these targets as we approached them. The military term for this was "reconnaissance by fire." Rather than wait for sniper rounds from the enemy, I was laying down artillery fire ahead of us on potential targets.

Once again, luck was with us. Around noon, we entered a tree line and discovered a dead VC. This time, he had his weapon with him, which was an Sk-1 Soviet-made rifle. He also had about thirty rounds of ammunition and three hand grenades. After checking out the area, we decided to take a break and eat a lunch of C rations. As I confirmed our position on the map, it became apparent we were way behind schedule as a result of the hit-and-run activities of the VC. I wasn't overly concerned by this fact, but I would have liked to have gotten a look at the rest of the TAOR before the day was over.

After lunch, we resumed our sweep, calling in artillery in front of us. This strategy worked in that the enemy contact ceased, and we were able to make up for lost time.

Shortly after 1500 hours, the enemy changed their tactics and hit us from our right flank with a sustained barrage of fire. Since we were in a wedge formation, the platoon was able to quickly maneuver into a position to return fire on the attacking VC. I immediately called in an artillery fire mission on Charlie's position, and once again, I heard a cry for a medic coming from First Squad. The VC continued their attack as I attempted to bring in artillery fire on their position. Although it is hard to tell how many VC were actually firing at us, I felt it was at least a dozen and probably more. We were taking fire from a wide front, and even after the initial artillery rounds landed, Charlie continued the attack. I moved the artillery along the VC front and eventually silenced the enemy fire.

I went over to First Platoon and discovered we had one marine wounded. Doc Blake said the bullet was a flesh wound passing through the marine's shoulder, and he had the bleeding stopped. He assured me the marine could make it back to Hill 63, and we didn't need to call a medevac.

I debated on whether we should sweep the area from where we received the enemy fire but decided against it. It was getting late in the day, and Charlie could be trying to lure us into an even bigger ambush. I really wanted to continue moving west, but it was approaching 1600 hours. We were four klicks away from the perimeter, and it would take us at least two hours to get back home. I told the squad leaders we would turn south and head back to Hill 63.

As we started toward Hill 63, I called in another artillery strike on the area from which we had received the latest enemy fire. I then told the artillery to fire another mission on the same target in ten minutes to discourage Charlie from following us.

When I approached India Company's TAOR, I got on their radio net and raised the company radio operator. Our system worked well, and shortly, I was talking to a patrol from India Company. After informing them of our location, we proceeded to the perimeter. As expected, it took us a little over two hours to reach the perimeter of Hill 63.

I immediately went to Lima Company's CP to discuss the day's events with Captain K. He reminded me we were to go out again the next day, and I needed to have the platoon's patrol route determined so he could turn it in to Battalion. I grabbed a quick meal at the mess tent and set about planning the patrol. At that point, it struck me that our newest assignment was going to be a lot tougher than I had anticipated. The platoon was pretty worn out by the day's activities. We had humped over ten klicks that day and would have to hump another four klicks the following day just to get to a point where we could start sweeping the new TAOR. I decided we would use the same tactics we did earlier that day except we would start at the west side of the TAOR and sweep back to the east. Hopefully, we would traverse the area that we were unable to get to that day. I chose to leave the perimeter at first light and go due west to the railroad right-of-way. Once we got to the tracks, we would move due north along the right-of-way and sweep east back toward Highway 1. Our objective would be to get at least as far as the area in which we last had contact with the VC.

The next morning, we were exiting the west side of the perimeter at 0500 hours just as the sun was starting to come up. As planned, we made good time to the railroad bed and moved north to start our sweep. About five hundred meters from the point where we intended to turn east, we once again came under fire. The pattern was the same. Charlie hit us quickly and retreated before we could bring in artillery. Once again, I decided to plot targets along our intended route and employ the previous day's tactic of reconnaissance by fire. Our march was preceded by artillery barrages, and this discouraged Charlie's hit-and-run tactics. We made better time than we had the preceding day. By noon, we were well past the point where we had broken off contact with Charlie the previous day. I called a halt, and we set up a crude perimeter along a little stream that meandered through the area.

Since there were a number of trees along the bank of the stream, this appeared to be an ideal area in which to take a break, and I advised the squad leader to plan on being there for a while. It wasn't long before some of the troops wandered down to a little pool in the stream, took off their clothes, and jumped in the water. It was somewhat of an idyllic setting, and the troops splashing around in the water reminded me of a bunch of kids gathered at a swimming hole back in the world.

We lay around for a couple of hours when an idea struck me. It was apparent that we couldn't hump the new TAOR on a daily basis without collapsing from exhaustion. Why not use this location as a resting spot each day and ultimately shorten our patrols? While we could turn longer patrol routes in to Battalion, what they didn't know wouldn't hurt them and probably wouldn't dramatically affect the outcome of the war.

The next morning, we were headed back to the new TAOR along another major trail that ran north and south and which dumped us into the eastern edge of the new TAOR. The hump back and forth to the new TAOR was taxing on the men of Second Platoon. I had thought about suggesting to Captain K. that we establish a permanent platoon-size firebase in the new TAOR where the platoon could spend the nights. This would eliminate the four hours of humping each day to get back and forth to our new TAOR. The disadvantage would be the fact that we would have to construct a perimeter, which entailed a lot of work as well as requiring us to defend it each night. The way it was now, we were able to get hot chow and a good night's sleep inside the perimeter at Hill 63. The trade-off of humping back and forth each day was probably worth being able to go home to the security of Hill 63 at night.

The next day, I decided to change our route by beginning in the middle of the TAOR and patrolling east toward Highway 1. When we arrived at the TAOR, we once again came under enemy fire as we approached one of the small villages. Although Charlie broke off contact before I could adjust the artillery on his position, I decided to go ahead and fire the mission, anyway. The rounds landed in the village, doing a considerable amount of damage, which I hoped would send a message to both Charlie and the villagers: if you were going to fuck with us, you had better be ready to pay the price. We weren't winning the hearts and minds of these villagers, but at least they knew that if we received fire from their village, they had better get their asses in their bomb shelters.

After the fire mission, we searched the village to see what we could find. We went through it with a fine-tooth comb. As usual, there was a small Buddhist temple in the center of the village. Part of the floor of the temple was covered by tiles, and I took my knife and pried one of the tiles up. I then noticed that none of the pieces were cemented in place. We started removing the tiles and pretty soon had most of them dislodged and started probing the area with our K-bars. As I pushed my knife into the soft sand, I felt a clunk, which indicated I had hit something solid. As we carefully removed the sand, we discovered it was the top of a very large container. We removed the top by attaching a long cord, which we carried with us for just such occasions, to the top of the container and yanking the top off while standing some distance away. If the container was booby trapped, hopefully we would avoid any serious injury. In this case, the lid was not booby trapped, and after we removed it, we discovered the container was filled with rice.

We continued our probing and found two other similar containers, also filled with rice. The three containers held about four bushels of rice each, and we decided the rice should be destroyed in retribution for the rifle fire we received from the village. The fact the rice was probably the only food supply the villagers had never crossed our minds.

Our next problem was how to go about destroying several bushels of rice. We dumped the rice down the village water well, which probably contaminated the well and made it useless to the villagers. After dumping the rice, one of the members of First Squad suggested we make rice pudding by dropping a hand grenade in the well. Everybody thought this was a great idea, and when the grenade went off, it shot a geyser of rice and water several feet in the air. We found this hilarious and repeated it several times. We were like a bunch of little kids getting into mischief in the neighborhood. The only difference was there was no one there to scold us for our misdeeds.

Unfortunately, the villagers would pay dearly for our acts of vandalism and would probably go hungry until the next rice crop was harvested. This was of little concern to us. In our minds, the villagers were not human like us; they were slopes, gooks, and zipperheads. Surely they could not suffer the same emotions and feelings that we did. Anger, fear, joy, love, and sorrow were passions reserved for us and not something experienced by the subhumans who inhabited the Vietnamese countryside. War does funny things to people, and to us, it turned decent young men into individuals who on occasion had little concern for the suffering of their fellow man. We could always justify our acts by saying we deprived the VC of a source of supply.

After searching the village and finding nothing else of significance, we continued on to the east. Once again, we came under fire, and once again, I called in a fire mission on a target abandoned by the VC before the first rounds could land. I reverted back to the strategy of reconnaissance by fire, which once again stopped Charlie from his hit-and-run tactics. After searching several small villages, we finally arrived at Highway 1, where we got in column formation and returned to Hill 63.

While getting a meal at the battalion mess tent, I ran into Rich Muler and Lee Gounds. I discovered they weren't having any more success than Second Platoon in engaging Charlie. They were experiencing the same hit-and-run tactics with little chance of bringing firepower on the enemy. We didn't have a solution to the problem and decided to keep plugging away in hopes Charlie would get tired of the constant harassment and move on to someone else's TAOR.

The next morning, we repeated our pattern of the previous day by going immediately to the middle of the TAOR, except we swept to the west instead of east. I hoped to sweep to the railroad right-of-way and then return to Hill 63. By the end of the day, we would have swept the entire TAOR twice. We were becoming familiar with the terrain and the various landmarks that assisted us in locating our positions on the maps. In addition, I had requested artillery to record each target that we shot and to give it a target designation. I marked these target designations on my map, and in the future, we would be able to call in fire missions simply by giving the prerecorded target designations. We continued to get sniper fire on a regular basis, but it seemed that Charlie's enthusiasm was waning. He was firing fewer rounds on each encounter, and it had now dwindled to a point where we were receiving only one or two rounds on each encounter. We no longer attempted to call in artillery, and after returning token small-arms fire, we would continue on our way. We now had more time to spend searching the various villages that dotted the TAOR. The rest of the day was fairly uneventful, and we reached the railroad right-of-way with an hour to spare. We then turned south and returned home.

Early the next morning, I got with Doc Blake to discuss the physical well-being of the platoon. One of the continuing problems an infantry platoon faced was the physical condition of its members. Because of the constant heat and humidity, many of the troops suffered from skin conditions that could become debilitating if not treated. One of these conditions was known as "jungle rot," which could best be described as open sores that wouldn't heal. In addition, some of the troops suffered from a constant heat rash that on occasions would bleed. We were also faced with the problem of trench foot, which resulted from the feet being constantly wet. Add to this the constant exposure to dysentery from drinking untreated water and the threat of malaria from the mosquitoes and you can have a serious health problem within the platoon. The infantry platoon that is constantly on the go suffers even more from these problems. I would estimate that half of the members of Second Platoon would be declared unfit for duty if we had been stationed stateside.

I accompanied Doc Blake on a tour of the platoon so we could assess the health of each marine. I was somewhat taken aback by the results of our survey. Although I was aware of some of the health problems being experienced by the men, I didn't realize the full extent of the difficulties until we talked to each man.

Some of the men had jungle rot on large portions of their bodies, while one marine had heat rash covering most of his upper torso. In addition, a majority of the men had some sort of problem with their feet.

Another of the factors contributing to foot problems was the fact we seldom removed our boots. We slept with our boots on and probably changed our socks once a week if we had a clean pair to put on. Generally, we kept our boots on twenty-four hours a day. In addition, we seldom changed our jungle fatigues, because we didn't have a clean pair to put on. Usually we would wear our fatigues until they rotted away, at which time we would scrounge up a new pair. There was many a time I saw troopers walking around with their asses literally hanging out because the seams of their trousers had rotted away.

Doc Blake and I discussed the situation, and we agreed we needed to pay more attention to the problems observed in our survey of the platoon. Unfortunately, it was impossible to address these problems if the platoon was up at first light and spent the entire day patrolling the TAOR. The medical problems were exacerbated by the physical demands placed on the platoon as a result of the constant patrolling. Jungle sores got worse, feet stayed wet, and we were constantly exposed to the heat of the day. What Second Platoon needed was a couple of weeks off, but that just wasn't going to happen.

I also approached Sergeant Green about some problems I was having. One of the jobs of the platoon sergeant was to handle the administrative and logistical chores within the platoon. I had complaints from Sergeant Schwartz about the daily manpower reports he was receiving from Sergeant Green. In addition, there were some supply requests I sent to Sergeant Green that never seemed to get filled. While Sergeant Green was an excellent field marine, he was lacking in administrative skills. Another problem I was experiencing was his desire to play a larger role in the running of the platoon. As I stated earlier, I felt it was important that I deal directly with the squad leaders rather than go through the platoon sergeants. Sergeant Green obviously felt he was being left out of the chain of command, and in this regard, he was right. I had hoped this problem would resolve itself, but it had only gotten worse. I refused to get Sergeant Green a radio, and I noticed he was getting on the squad leaders' radios more and more.

I discussed the situation with Sergeant Green, and he assured me he would spend more time on the administrative and logistical aspects of his job. He was not as willing to compromise on his role within the command structure of the platoon. He told me, "Damn it, Lieutenant, I was a pretty good squad leader, and I feel left out when we are in the field."

I replied, "I know you did a hell of a job as a squad leader, but as a platoon sergeant, your job changes. I have to run the platoon my way, and that means I give the orders. I feel it's best I deal directly with the squad leaders, and that's how it's going to be."

It was clear Sergeant Green was not pleased with my response. There was an obvious solution to the problem, which was to return Sergeant Green to Third Squad and promote either Sergeant Presno or Sergeant Duff to platoon sergeant; both could handle the logistical and administrative duties better than Sergeant Green, and they wouldn't interfere with my running of the platoon. Although both of the other sergeants did an adequate job as squad leaders, they did not compare with Sergeant Green when it came to leading a squad when the rounds started flying. Unfortunately, returning Sergeant Green to Third Squad would be an admission I had made a mistake and, even worse, would reflect badly on Sergeant Green. It would appear to the troops that Sergeant Green couldn't handle his job and was being demoted as a result.

It wasn't Sergeant Green's fault that I made a mistake in selecting him as the platoon sergeant. He was still the best field marine in the platoon and did not deserve to be humiliated in front of the entire platoon. I told Sergeant Green to hang in there, and we would figure out something to resolve the problem. Unfortunately, I was not too optimistic that the problem would be resolved.

Over the next weeks, the pattern of enemy contact in the new TAOR mirrored the circumstances that we ran into in the original TAOR. As our patrolling continued, Charlie's attacks became less frequent. He found it easier to move on to greener pastures rather than put up with the continued harassment resulting from our presence in the TAOR. We were constantly patrolling, searching the villages for indications of his presence, and calling in artillery on his position if he chose to retaliate against us. We were fighting a war of attrition for this small piece of real estate, and he must have realized that it was a losing battle. In the parlance of those back in Da Nang, we had pretty much pacified the new TAOR, and the hearts and minds of its occupants would soon embrace the South Vietnamese government. Charlie knew this was just so much bullshit, and as soon as the Americans quit patrolling, he would move back in, and everything would be the same as before we began our patrols. The men of Second Platoon didn't give a shit one way or the other. As long as we weren't taking casualties, we couldn't care less what the peasants did or where their loyalties lay.

Standing in a marijuana field

7

A FRUSTRATING BATTLE
OVER NOTHING

AFTER ABOUT A MONTH OF patrolling, Captain K. called the platoon commanders together and told us we would be involved in a large-scale operation involving other elements of the Fifth Marine Regiment as well as ARVN troops. The operation was scheduled to kick off in two days. Lima Company would be acting as a blocking force along the north bank of the Song Ly River, while various units swept south on the south side of the river. In theory, we would intercept any VC trying to escape across the river. Captain K. further informed us Lima Company would start moving into position the next night at 2000 hours. We would be marching all night and hopefully be in our blocking position by first light.

I spent the next day escorting tanks down south of Hill 64. It took much longer than we thought, and we didn't get done until late dark thirty. I hustled the platoon over to Lima Company's area and found the rest of the company waiting for us. I asked Captain K. if we could go to the mess hall for a meal, but he said we didn't have time. Colonel Brady and the rest of the battalion CP group were at the company area apparently waiting for Second Platoon. I missed the briefing from Captain K. on the details of the operation, and it was all I could do to hurry my men to get their packs and C rations so we could depart with the rest of the company. Captain K. was obviously not happy about the situation, and he told me to fall in behind Third Platoon and try to keep up. He would brief me later as to what we were going to do.

I noticed that the battalion CP group was larger than usual. They had the battalion intelligence officer (S2) with them along with a team of ARVN interpreters, apparently to interrogate the civilians about the VC activities in the area. In addition, the battalion chaplain was going to accompany us—for what reason, I didn't know. There was also a propaganda team consisting of three ARVN soldiers and a portable loudspeaker. This had all the makings of a Chinese fire drill.

By the time we left the perimeter, I was dead tired and totally confused. I found Sergeant Green, and he told me he went to the company briefing and knew generally where we would be going. He pointed out an area on the map next to the Song Ly River where we would be setting up our blocking position. I asked him if he knew how to get there, and he laughed and said, "Sure. Just follow Third Platoon."

The night march turned into a nightmare. Second Platoon was worn out, and the pace of the march was slower than our hump to Que Son that morning. We were traveling through a series of flooded rice paddies, and whoever was navigating obviously had not been in that area before. We were constantly doubling back after wading into paddies too deep to cross. It seemed we stopped every few minutes and waited while the lead platoon tried to find a route that would get us to our destination without drowning half the company. Whenever we came to a halt, Second Platoon would lie down and immediately fall asleep. On one occasion, I fell asleep while standing up, only to be awakened when someone bumped into me in the dark. We finally reached our destination on the north bank of the Song Ly as the sun was starting to come up. Second Platoon had been humping for over twenty-four hours straight. All we wanted to do was get some shut-eye.

First and Third Platoons were strung out along the riverbank, and Second Platoon was responsible for providing security for their back side. Sergeant Green and I got the troops spread out on a line facing away from the Song Ly to defend against an enemy attack. I told everyone to get some sleep, and I headed for the platoon CP, which had been set up by Corporal Stang. Just as I was turning in, Lance Corporal Moreno told me Captain K. was on the radio and wanted me to report to his position for a briefing. Having no choice, I searched out the company CP and joined Lieutenants Muler and Gounds as they were being briefed by Captain K. We would be staying in this position for a couple of days, acting as a blocking force for the units operating across the river. They would be saturating the area with company- and battalion-size sweeps, making extensive searches of the local villages. Captain K. explained the entire area had been a VC stronghold, and we would be patrolling on the north side of the river trying to collect intelligence information as well as doing some propaganda work among the local villagers.

As the meeting broke up, I was passed by Captain King, the battalion S2, and his crew of interpreters with a couple of marines from the H&S company. Captain King informed me he was going to go out and round up a couple of the locals to see what they could tell him about VC activity in the area. *Lots of luck*, I thought. It had been our experience that the local villagers weren't going to tell you a fucking thing about the VC. I kept my thoughts to myself and wished them good luck.

I arrived at Second Platoon's CP, found a semicomfortable spot, rolled up in my poncho, and tried to get some much-needed sleep.

Before I could fall asleep, a firefight broke out just outside of our perimeter. I jumped to my feet and grabbed my M16, and along with Sergeant Green, I ran in the general direction of the rifle fire. When I got to our perimeter, we discovered the firing wasn't coming from Second Platoon. One of the squad leaders told us he didn't know what was going on but that Captain King had left in the direction of the firefight several minutes before. I got on a radio to see if I could find out what was happening. I contacted Lima Six, and they didn't know any more than I did. I told them I thought Captain King's group might be in a firefight and asked him if they could contact him on the battalion radio net. Captain K. contacted Battalion and discovered Captain King hadn't taken a radio when he left the perimeter.

I told Sergeant Green to get a squad saddled up and ready to go. Just then, one of the troopers from Captain King's group came running toward the perimeter yelling for help. He was out of breath and extremely excited. It took us several minutes to get him calmed down so he could explain what happened. He said they had been ambushed just outside of the perimeter and they had two men down, one of them in serious condition. We could still hear shooting outside the perimeter as Sergeant Green arrived with Third Squad. Lance Corporal Moreno showed up with the radio as we left the perimeter on the run toward the sound of the firefight. I had the marine from the H&S company with us so he could show us the exact location of Captain King and his group.

I had two concerns as we were maneuvering toward Captain King. One was whether or not Charlie was waiting to ambush us as we ran to the rescue of the trapped marines. Secondly, I was concerned about being mistakenly fired on by Captain King and his men when we approached their position. To make matters worse, the H&S company marine wasn't sure of his bearings and didn't know exactly where Captain King was. There hadn't been any firing for several minutes, and I couldn't tell where the trapped marines were.

I also began experiencing a new phenomenon that I had not dealt with before, and that was total exhaustion. It was now 1100 hours, and I had not slept for over thirty hours. During this time, Second Platoon had been constantly on the go, humping down to Que Son, riding the tanks back to Hill 63, and humping all night to our present location. Vince Lombardi, the famous football coach, once said, "Fatigue makes a coward of us all." He was referring to fatigue resulting from the expending of energy in an athletic competition. I was not only physically exhausted from the energy spent over the last day and a half but I was mentally exhausted from lack of sleep.

Because of the fatigue, my body wanted to shut down. The excitement of the moment causes your body to produce adrenaline, which will give you a rush of energy, but at some point, the adrenaline doesn't work anymore. I had arrived at that point. It had now become a supreme effort to force myself to think about what to do next. Third Squad was waiting for me to come up with a plan of attack, and I was having difficulty just focusing on where we were, let alone our next move.

Sergeant Green came to my rescue. He crawled over to my position and suggested we pop a smoke grenade and see if that would alert Captain West's group to our location. This seemed like a good idea, although any idea would have seemed like a good one so long as I didn't have to come up with it. We popped a yellow smoke, and pretty soon, we heard the shout of "Over here!" about fifty meters to our left front. We identified ourselves and began maneuvering toward Captain West and his stranded marines.

When we arrived at their position, they had two marines who were badly wounded, and Doc Blake immediately went to work on them. I called Lima Six on the radio, and he informed me that a medevac was on the way and should be arriving shortly. A few minutes later, I could hear the medevac approaching, and soon we had the marines on board the chopper and on their way to Da Nang. I left the job of directing the medevac to Sergeant Green, and he did his usual competent job. As the medevac left, Doc Blake told me he thought one of the marines was dead when they put him on the chopper.

I sat down next to Captain West, and he appeared to be devastated by the recent events. He said they had walked into an ambush, and he didn't have any idea how many VC there were. I asked him why they didn't have a radio with them, and he gave me a blank look and didn't answer the question. I now had to pull myself together enough to focus on the task of getting us back to Lima Company's position. I really didn't know our location on the map and estimated we were a couple of hundred meters from Lima Company's perimeter. I asked

Captain West if he knew where we were, and he wasn't much help. I knew the general direction of Lima Company, and I got the men on their feet and followed my instincts.

I called Lima Six and told them we were heading back toward the perimeter and requested they alert their units of our approach. We hadn't moved twenty meters when we started taking heavy fire from our right flank. We immediately returned the fire, and I got back on the radio. Captain K. wanted to know our location so he could get some artillery fire on the enemy position. I had to tell him I didn't know exactly where we were, which obviously wasn't the answer he wanted to hear. We continued taking fire, and I instructed the men to get ready to move out. We laid down a field of fire and began a tactical retreat back to the perimeter. We were able to break contact with the enemy almost immediately and within a short time were within sight of Second Platoon's position. We straggled into the perimeter, and Captain West and I went to the battalion CP, which was located next to Lima Company's CP.

Colonel Brady asked what the hell happened that morning. Captain West tried to explain the situation, and I was simply too tired to join in the conversation. I stood there saying nothing, and when Captain West was done, Colonel Brady pronounced that no unit was to leave the perimeter without a radio.

I thought, *What a brilliant idea.* The dumbest private in Second Platoon would have told you not to leave the perimeter without a radio when you were in enemy territory. Now that it had come from the lips of Colonel Brady, it was dogma that was to be strictly observed. Such is life in the Marine Corps. The only thing I wanted to do was get some sleep.

I left the battalion CP and headed back to Second Platoon. By this time, it was noon and hotter than hell with what felt like 100 percent humidity. I decided to eat a meal of C rations before I went to sleep, which was a mistake. Just as I was about to go to sleep, I became violently ill and puked up the C ration meal. Having done this, I was finally able to lie down and go to sleep.

I slept for a couple of hours when I was awakened by Sergeant Green, who told me Captain K. wanted to meet with the platoon commanders. I went to the company CP, where we were briefed. We were told Battalion wanted to expand the blocking force along the river. The units running the operation across the river had run into heavy resistance, and it was suspected Charlie would try to escape by crossing the Song Ly after dark. He ordered First and Third Platoons to spread out to the north along the riverbank while Second Platoon moved to the south and set up squad-size ambushes along the river. We were to cover at least five hundred meters of the riverfront.

I went back to the platoon, and I discussed the plan with Sergeant Green and the squad leaders. I selected three sites along the riverbank and assigned each of them to a squad. We would move into position after the sun went down in hopes Charlie would not detect our location. We were a long way from home, and getting a squad isolated and attacked by Charlie would be bad news.

At the briefing, Captain K. informed us we would be supported by a C-47 gunship, commonly referred to as "Puff, the Magic Dragon." Its call sign would be Spooky One-Three. The C-47s were World War II vintage fix-winged planes equipped with Gatling guns that could fire so many rounds it looked like a tongue of flames was licking down from the sky. In addition, they dropped large flares that lit up the night sky. They were a common sight in Vietnam, although this would be the first time I worked in proximity to one. They would be flying south of us and spraying the area across the river. Hopefully, they would be dropping enough flares so that we could see any enemy forces trying to cross the river.

Just before we left to move into our new positions, I gathered the squad leaders together for one last briefing. I told them, "We need to move into position quickly. We will wait as long as possible before we leave here, but I want to be in position before it gets completely dark. It should take us fifteen minutes to reach our ambush site, and we'll have plenty of time if everything goes well."

I also cautioned the squad leaders to make sure they kept enough men awake to provide security at all times. The men had only caught a couple of hours of sleep during the day, and they were still pretty tired. "We'll be running radio checks all night long, and I expect you to have someone on the radio who can stay awake."

With this said, it was time to move out, and the men of Second Platoon began stirring about. We moved rather quickly along the riverbank, and the squads were in position just before dark as planned. I left Sergeant Green with Third Squad, which was on the platoon's left flank. Second Squad was in the middle, and I accompanied Third Squad to the far end of the blocking position. It wasn't long before Spooky One-Three was flying over our position dropping flares and hosing down the countryside across the river with its Gatling guns.

The Gatling guns fired so many rounds so quickly it made a humming noise as it sprayed the area with .30-caliber bullets. The flares dropped from the C-47 added a surreal quality to the scene before us. The flares were very large and lit up an extensive area. As they floated down on their parachutes, they swung from side to side, causing the shadows cast by the flares to move eerily back and forth.

As we sat in our positions, mesmerized by the scene before us, things suddenly took a turn for the worse. We started receiving small-arms fire from our rear. The fire was not concentrated at any one squad but rather being indiscriminately fired in our direction. I got on the radio with the squad leaders and instructed them not to return the fire, because I didn't think Charlie knew exactly where we were. He was apparently shooting in our direction in hopes we would return fire so that he could pinpoint our location.

This went on for several minutes when I called Lima Six and asked for Captain K. He had heard the firing and had monitored the radio net when I instructed the squad leaders not to return the fire. I suggested we request the C-47 to make a few passes on this side of the river and hose down the gooks who were firing on our positions. Captain K. asked how far we were from the riverbank, and

I informed him we were on the edge of the river. If Spooky One-Three kept his fire at least one hundred meters north of the riverbank, we would all be safe. Captain K. acknowledged my request and told me to stand by.

Ten minutes later, Captain K. came back on the radio and said the gunship would shortly be making a couple of passes on our side of the river. True to his word, we could hear the C-47 moving across the river. Pretty soon, he was laying down fire to our rear. What had seemed like the hum coming from Spooky turned into a roar as it started working closer to our position. This was a devastating weapon, which obviously struck fear in the heart of anyone unlucky enough to be targeted by Puff, the Magic Dragon. After a couple of passes, the C-47 returned to the other side of the river to resume its original mission.

Things settled down for a while after Spooky left. Apparently, Charlie had his fill of the dragon from the sky. Around midnight, Second Squad was on the radio informing me they thought they saw movement on the far bank of the river. I was a little skeptical in that the flares made it appear that everything was moving across the river. I told Second Squad to hold their fire and called Lima Six to inform him of the situation. He said he would let Battalion know but instructed us not to fire unless we were sure of our targets. He called me back in a few minutes and said Spooky One-Three would be working the riverbank in a few minutes. It wasn't long before the C-47 was hosing down the area with a shower of .30-caliber rounds.

As Spooky One-Three was making a pass, we observed green tracer rounds being fired from the ground toward the C-47. Apparently, Charlie was firing back at the gunship. I excitedly reported this to Lima Six, but there wasn't much any of us could do since the firing was coming from across the river. We watched with focused intent until the early hours of the morning. Finally, the C-47 packed it in and left the area. Second Platoon settled down for the night and tried to catch up on its lost sleep.

The next morning, we returned to Lima Company's position, and after eating a breakfast of C rations, I went over to the company CP. I was told Battalion ordered us to begin patrolling in our immediate area. Captain K. instructed Second Platoon to accompany the interpreters from battalion intelligence to interrogate the local villagers regarding VC activities in the area. After pointing out the villages he wanted us to patrol on his map, Captain K. finished the briefing with "They also want you to take the propaganda team with you." I rolled my eyes but had no comment except to say, "Have them report to our area in thirty minutes."

When everything was ready, Second Platoon left the area looking like a traveling road show. We had three ARVN interpreters, a sergeant from S2, and a three-man propaganda team from God knows where accompanying us as we exited the perimeter. We arrived at the first village, and the propaganda team set up their loudspeakers and began blasting a message in Vietnamese. At the same time, the interpreters had rounded up several papa-sans in the village and were haranguing them about the activities of the VC. The villagers gathered around the scene, looking at us in amazement. The propaganda team had one guy who preached through the loudspeakers for several minutes and then played some gook music. This would be followed by another lecture. The ARVN interpreters were becoming more animated, and one of them was brandishing a pistol, trying to intimidate one of the papa-sans into telling him where the VC where.

The whole thing became a circus, and the villagers continued to stare in disbelief. The propaganda team was apparently trying to win the hearts and minds of the villagers while the interpreters were scaring the shit out of them. After an hour, everyone was done, and we moved on to the next village to repeat the sideshow. The troops of Second Platoon looked on with amusement as we went from village to village. After a while, they began laughing at the entire affair, mocking the activities of the propaganda team.

The S2 sergeant with the ARVN interrogators came over and suggested to me the men knock off their activities. I replied by telling him they meant no harm and were just having a little fun. He responded, "The ARVN are losing face among the villagers as a result of what your men are doing."

I replied, "Fuck the ARVNs. What have they done for us lately? If they could fight this war, we wouldn't be out here humping these rice paddies day in and day out."

"Lieutenant, I'm just trying to do my job, and your people are making it impossible."

I walked away thinking he could shove his job up his ass. After a few minutes, I cooled off and returned to the sergeant and apologized and told him I would take care of the matter. I found Sergeant Green and told him to tell the men to knock it off.

We went to the next villages, and the operation proceeded as intended with gook music and the interrogators scaring the shit out of villagers. I was pissed off at the ARVNs, and the men were pissed off at me. Was this a great war or what?

As the day was drawing to a close, we were approaching a large tree line when we started taking heavy small-arms fire from our right front. The platoon returned fire while I called in an artillery fire mission on the tree line. Once the artillery landed on target, I told the squad leaders to get their squads on line for an assault on the enemy positions. We were still taking sporadic fire as the squads maneuvered into position. I noticed the ARVNs, who were huddled down next to my position, were not moving as we began the assault on the tree line. I yelled to the S2 sergeant to get them on line, and he started screaming at them to no avail. The platoon continued moving toward the tree line without the ARVNs. The firing from the tree line ceased as we approached, and we took our objective without incident. We couldn't find any evidence of VC casualties as we swept through the area. After the tree line was secure, we were joined by our ARVN allies, who acted like nothing had happened.

I asked the S2 sergeant, "What the fuck happened to your men back there?"

He shrugged and said, "I guess they're not into assaulting tree lines."

I replied, "Well, at least they didn't lose face with the villagers."

The situation in Vietnam was hopeless. We were supposed to be fighting this war so the South Vietnamese government could retrain and refit its army. How could you retrain a bunch of cowards? All the training in the world wasn't going to make a fighting force out of these assholes. When we were in the villages, the ARVNs were the cock of the walk, bullying every poor son of a bitch they could get their hands on. When it came time to fight the VC, they hid like a bunch of yellow dogs.

We continued back to the company perimeter, and I reported to Captain K. I told him of the events of the day. When we discussed the incident about the ARVNs refusal to join the assault of the tree line, he just shook his head and said, "This is nothing new. The only thing you can count on is those bastards will let you down when you need them most."

Captain K. informed me we would probably move out the following morning. We would proceed west along the south bank of the Song Ly and join up with Delta One-Five, who was also in a blocking position farther up the river. After linking up, we would sweep north and then west back to Hill 63. I returned to Second Platoon and informed the squad leaders of the plan for the following day and turned in for the night.

I was awakened by the sounds of explosions and incoming small-arms fire. The explosions were going off behind Second Platoon's position in the area of the company CP, but the small-arms fire was coming directly into our position. I jumped into a foxhole and landed next to Lance Corporal Moreno, who had the radio with him. I got on the radio and informed Lima Six we were taking small-arms fire and discovered they were receiving mortar fire from across the river. By this time, Second Platoon was returning fire, and there was a heated exchange of gunfire for several minutes. I was able to get an artillery fire mission fired in front of our position, which quieted things down.

After everything was secure, I checked with the men on watch at the time the firing started, and they told me we started receiving small-arms fire at the same time that the mortars started landing behind us. This appeared to be a coordinated attack between the VC on our side of the river and whoever was firing the mortars from across the river. It is amazing to me how the VC could have organized such an attack in light of the fact that a large operation was being conducted across the river where the mortars were being fired. Charlie was sending us a message that we had better not underestimate their capabilities.

The next morning, the company saddled up and headed south to join up with Delta Company. It took us about an hour to reach their position. I once again sought out Hank Pritchard to see how he was getting along. He told me Delta Company had gotten in some deep shit on the edge of the Que Son Valley. They unknowingly walked into an NVA base camp and wound up in the middle of a battalion of NVA. He said he didn't know who was more surprised, the NVA or Delta Company. In any event, they had seven men killed and nineteen wounded before a reaction force could get to them and pull them out. After exchanging some additional war stories, it was time to move out toward Hill 63.

The two companies were to sweep adjacent to each other with Lima Company on the left side and Delta on the right. We would move northwest for three klicks and then turn west to Hill 63. I noticed a distinct difference between Delta Company and Lima Company in their methods of operation. Lima Company, along with the rest of Third Battalion, insisted its members wear a full set of jungle fatigues while in the field. In addition, all men were required to wear helmets and carry a backpack while on operation. Delta Company appeared just the opposite. Some of its men wore a full set of jungle fatigues while others wore T-shirts, and a few didn't wear any shirt at all. Also, there was no uniformity in their headgear. Some of them wore helmets, and others wore jungle hats referred to as "catch me, fuck me hats." While Lima Company looked raggedy ass as a result of the condition of their clothing, they couldn't hold a candle to Delta Company.

There was also a substantial difference in the way the two companies maneuvered through the bush. Lima Company moved at a deliberate pace in an effort to maintain tactical integrity. Intervals were maintained between each man, and we attempted to keep our formation as wide as it was long. We moved in wedge formation and kept the company spread out both horizontally and vertically. We weren't going to surprise too many VC as a result of our methodical approach. At the same time, we weren't going to get caught with our pants down. When we engaged the enemy, we were able to immediately deliver maximum firepower on their position. Our philosophy was based on caution rather than body count.

Delta Company took a different approach. They were as undisciplined as we were disciplined. There appeared to be little rhyme or reason attached to these movements. Some groups were spread out, while others were bunched up. One squad was in a wedge formation, while another was in column formation.

We continued sweeping northwest until we reached a point due east of Hill 63. We turned and began sweeping west toward our home base. If we stayed our course, we would cross Highway 1 about four hundred meters east of Hill 63. We reached a point about three hundred meters east of Highway 1 where the only obstacle between us and the highway was a large tree line. Delta Company was still on our right flank, and we heard them firing into the tree line that we were approaching. All of a sudden, we started receiving small-arms fire from the tree line. We had lucked onto the ideal situation. We had two infantry companies advancing on line and had Charlie trapped in a tree line. There was no place for the enemy to go. Behind him were some dry rice paddies, and if he tried to escape across them, he would run into Hill 63. We started laying down small-arms fire into the tree line. The incoming we received from the tree line escalated into a barrage of small-arms fire. Literally thousands of rounds came pouring at us from the tree line. I had never experienced anything like that, and I immediately concluded we must have walked into an NVA ambush.

I got on the radio in an attempt to call in an artillery fire mission and hopefully get some immediate air support. Lima Six came up on the radio yelling, "Cease fire, cease fire!" My immediate reaction was to conclude he had lost his mind. We were in a major firefight, and he wanted us to quit shooting. He once again demanded we quit firing and explained we had friendly forces out in front of us. I now had a serious problem. The din caused by the firing made it impossible to be heard, and I was unable to move in light of the deluge of small-arms fire being poured into our position. I had the squad leaders on the radio and instructed them to get their men to cease firing. I also started yelling to the men around me to stop firing, and those that heard me repeated the command.

After several minutes of the fiercest fighting imaginable, we were able to get the men to stop firing. The only problem was that incoming rounds kept on coming. After a minute or two, the men once again started firing back, and it took several minutes to get them to stop. The incoming fire finally ceased, and I lay there trying to figure out what the hell was going on.

The first order of business was to check and see if we had taken any casualties. After determining Second Platoon was still in one piece, I sought out the company command group to see if they knew any more than I did about what was going on. I found Captain K., who was on the radio to Battalion, obviously discussing the situation. I was joined by Rich Muler and Lee Gounds, who appeared as puzzled by the situation as I. Captain K. got off the radio and explained Charlie One-Five was on the other side of the tree line along Highway 1, acting as a blocking force for our sweep. For some reason, communications got screwed up, and they didn't know we were approaching their position. When the initial rounds fired by Delta Company came through the tree line, they thought they were taking incoming and returned fire. As the firing increased, they assumed they were under attack from the tree line and acted accordingly. I asked if anyone had taken casualties, and Captain K. said, "As near as I can tell, there were no injuries."

I walked away utterly amazed by the situation. At a minimum, a hundred thousand rounds had been fired, and no one had been scratched. It went to prove my theory that not many casualties could be inflicted by small-arms fire when the combatants had found shelter and kept their heads down. I returned to Second Platoon and explained the situation. It was apparent that we were all pretty shaken by the recent events, and it took us some time to gather ourselves. The order to move out was forthcoming, and we proceeded toward Hill 63. As we approached Highway 1, Charlie Company was strung out up and down Highway 1. Everyone appeared a little sheepish, and a lot of apologies were exchanged between the troops. Thank God there were no casualties, and the only consolation that could be offered was "All's well that ends well."

Sitting next to Father Capadono. A Catholic
Priest and a Medal of Honor recipient.

8

A VERY EFFECTIVE AMBUSH

When we arrived back at Hill 63, we were assigned to our old sector of the perimeter. It was like returning home. The bunkers that we had constructed weeks earlier were still there. We moved in with each squad knowing exactly which bunkers to occupy. Second Platoon continued to patrol its TAOR with sporadic contact with Charlie. Since we were running squad-size patrols, I usually didn't accompany them into the TAOR, which meant I had a lot of time on my hands. One morning, First Squad left the perimeter at 0600 hours for the morning patrol. A couple of hours later, we could hear a substantial amount of firing in the area where they were running the patrol. I got on the radio, and Sergeant Presno was very excited as he described to me what was happening. He had left behind a fire team in an ambush site along the patrol route, and they were now in heavy contact with the enemy. The rest of the squad was maneuvering back to their position. I asked if they needed an artillery fire mission, and he responded, "We probably will, but I'll have to get to the fire team first to give you a target."

Several minutes later, Sergeant Presno came back up on the radio and informed me Second Squad had three confirmed VC kills, and they had encountered at least a platoon of VC. He gave me a target for the artillery, and after calling in the fire mission, I had the rest of Second Platoon saddle up and headed for First Squad.

It took us about twenty minutes to arrive at First Squad's location, and we found them elated by what had happened that morning.

Every member of the squad wanted to tell what happened, and it took me several minutes to piece together the story. Sergeant Presno had decided to leave a fire team behind in an ambush site as he was patrolling along a major trail that bisected the TAOR. The fire team consisted of Corporal Murphy, who carried an M60 machine gun, and three other members of the machine gun crew. The ambush team wasn't in place for more than ten minutes when a hill, two hundred meters from them, started crawling with VC. Corporal Murphy estimated there were at least fifty of them. They were maneuvering along a route that would have taken them within sixty meters of the fire team. The strange thing about the VC was that their leaders had whistles and were guiding their men with blasts from the whistles. The fire team did not have a radio with them to call in artillery, so they decided to let the VC move into an open area in front of the ambush site and then open up on them with the machine gun. Their plans were dramatically interrupted.

As the fire team was watching the VC move toward the killing zone, they saw two figures dressed in black pajamas walking toward them from a different direction along the trail that ran directly in front of the ambush site. Both of these individuals were armed, and it became apparent that they would arrive at the ambush site before the platoon of VC got in the kill zone. The assistant gunner, Private Wilson, kept pointing to the two VC walking along the trail in order to alert Corporal Murphy of the fact that the fire team was about to be discovered. Corporal Murphy kept motioning to him to hold his fire until the VC platoon walked into the kill zone. The two VC arrived at the ambush site first, and as described by Private Wilson, "The first one walked past a tree and looked right at me. I damn near shit my pants. I fired my M16 and caught him right between the running lights [eyes]. The next gook kept on walking like nothing happened, and when he got to his buddy, he looked down at him and then looked at us. I shot him with several rounds on full automatic."

Corporal Murphy related the events surrounding the VC platoon. "Wilson kept jabbing me and pointing to the two VC walking down the trail, and I kept motioning for him to wait until the platoon of VC got into the open. The platoon was just starting to enter the kill zone when I heard Wilson fire the first round. This caused the VC in the platoon to look in our direction, and one of them that I hadn't seen before stood up and started walking right at me. When Wilson opened up on full auto, I nailed the guy walking in our direction. I then started spraying the area with my M60, and they hauled ass back up the hill. The funny thing was they never put up much of a fight. If they knew there was only four of us, we would have been fucked."

I examined the bodies, and the two dressed in the black pajamas were probably locals from one of the surrounding villages. One of them was carrying a World War II–vintage M1 rifle and the other a carbine. The VC from the platoon was a different story. He was dressed in a khaki-colored outfit and was carrying a Russian-made rifle fitted with a scope. He had about eighty rounds of ammunition, along with three hand grenades. He was also wearing a leather belt fastened by a buckle, which had an NVA star in the middle of it. My guess was this guy belonged to a large VC unit or could even have been an NVA regular, although I would have been surprised that the NVA were operating so close to a populated area.

We also searched the immediate area to see if we could locate any sign of other VC casualties. Finding none, I radioed Lima Six and informed him of the situation. He advised he wanted us to pursue the VC platoon and a Blackcoat was on its way. I wasn't too keen on this idea, because we could just as easily walk into an ambush as the VC platoon did earlier that morning, except it wouldn't be a fire team that was waiting for us. Hopefully, the Blackcoat would help even things out. Captain K. didn't ask me my opinion regarding the pursuit of the platoon, so I ordered the men to saddle up and move out.

As the men passed the bodies of the VC, I witnessed a phenomenon I would see repeated in the future. Each marine either kicked one of the bodies or jabbed it with his rifle or bayonet. This was neither a tradition nor an informal practice within the platoon but rather an individual reaction by each marine. It probably was a matter of instinct going back to the caveman days, an unconscious effort to desecrate the body of a fallen foe.

As we headed out in search of the VC platoon, the Blackcoat appeared overhead and started circling the area in front of the platoon. After several passes, the Blackcoat started taking fire from an area five hundred meters to our west, which was well into the foothills leading to the mountains. I informed Blackcoat he was taking ground fire and attempted to pinpoint the source of the fire. After observing green tracer rounds rising from the ground toward the airplane, I felt we had a pretty good fix on the enemy position. I assumed it was the VC platoon that First Squad had encountered earlier in the day. Blackcoat called in an artillery barrage on the target, and we started sweeping in that direction. I still wasn't very enthused about chasing the VC platoon. Now that they had moved up toward the mountains, I was even less excited about the prospect of engaging them. They could now pick the terrain and time of the encounter, and I was sure it wouldn't be to Second Platoon's advantage.

We swept through the area that we thought was the source of the ground fire and found nothing. The underbrush was getting thicker as we moved farther into the hills, and I started losing sight of some of the elements of Second Platoon. At 1500 hours, I contacted Lima Six and informed them of the situation and expressed my misgivings about proceeding farther. Captain K. came on the radio and advised us to return to Hill 63.

When we arrived back at the perimeter, the members of First Squad proudly displayed the captured weapons. There was a policy that provided that captured weapons were to be turned in to Division headquarters. If the weapon was not capable of firing on full automatic, then in theory, the weapon became the property of the marine who captured it. In reality, some REMF would appropriate it, and it was unlikely its rightful owner would ever see it again. In any event, we turned the weapons over to Battalion so they could be sent back to Da Nang.

Calling in Artillery

9

AN ABSOLUTE NIGHTMARE

THE NEXT COUPLE OF DAYS were uneventful, with sporadic enemy contact. One evening, I was on my way to the mess tent when I ran into Rich Muler. He asked me if I had heard the news, and I told him I hadn't.

"Lima Company's going to be moved north to occupy one of the Seventh Marines' perimeters while they're out on an operation."

The Seventh Marines were responsible for a TAOR west and south of Da Nang. They had firebases strung out for fifteen miles along Route 9, from just south of Da Nang to just north of An Hoa. Lieutenant Muler explained we would be occupying Hill 10, which was one of the northernmost firebases of the Seventh Marines. The best part of the move was we would be just south of Da Nang in an area that had been pacified by the marines for several years. As Rich explained, "This is going to be a real piece of cake."

I asked him when we would be moving north, and he told me he thought it would be either the next day or the following. I returned to Second Platoon with the news, and the men were elated. Corporal Hale explained we would be able to get to Da Nang on a regular basis, and that was the next best thing to being on R&R. He explained, "They have a huge PX next to China Beach. They even have round-eyed girls at some of the USO clubs. This is going to be great duty."

Sergeant Green agreed. "Charlie has long since abandoned that area. Hell, we won't get shot at all the time we're there. The only things you have to worry about are the rockets, and they shoot those things at Da Nang right over your head. Second Platoon finally got lucky."

The next morning, Captain K. officially gave us the word to be ready to move north the following day. He explained we would be loaded on six-bys (large open-bed trucks) the following morning at 0800 hours, and the men should prepare for an extended stay. What we didn't take with us should be stored in the company supply tent. I told the men to pack up everything we had and to be ready to move out first thing the next morning.

We spent the day getting ready for the move. It was really no big deal to move all our belongings, because we didn't have anything except what we could carry on our backs. Second Platoon had been living out of their backpacks for so long that moving to a new location was second nature. That evening, we called off the nightly ambush and issued a beer ration to the men.

The next morning, we slept in and were ready to go by 0800. The six-bys arrived at 0900, and we loaded the troops on board. Everyone was in a festive mood, and we were like a bunch of kids getting on a school bus for a field trip to Disneyland. There was a lot of laughing and joking, and everyone was making predictions about the great time they would have in Da Nang.

By 0930, we were on Highway 1, headed north toward Hill 10. After traveling several miles, we arrived at the village of Dien Ban, which housed the headquarters for Dien Ban District. The trucks came to a brief halt, and the troops piled out and descended on the street vendors set up along Highway 1. Most of the stands sold cold beer; some of it was made in America, but most of it was a Vietnamese beer called "panther piss" after the picture of a tiger on the bottle. The troops quickly bought all the beer available and clamored back aboard the trucks. This scene was repeated two more times as the trucks conveniently stopped in areas lined with the lean-tos of black market beer salesmen.

Just before noon, we turned off Highway 1 just south of Da Nang and headed west toward Route 9. By 1300 hours, we were pulling into the perimeter set up around Hill 10 feeling no pain. The troops were pretty boisterous as a result of the beer, and we quickly marched them to the mess hall, hoping a meal would sober them up. After lunch, we had an opportunity to inspect our new surroundings and were shocked by what we saw. The place looked like a pigsty. The firebase had been occupied for several years and was in a state of disrepair. In addition, the entire area was littered with trash. C ration boxes, both full and empty, were scattered everywhere—as were empty ammunition boxes and other assorted debris. The company that had previously occupied the area was departing on the same trucks that transported us there, and it was too late to protest the situation. The only alternative was to get to work and clean up the place.

That afternoon and the following day were spent trying to get things cleaned up. We were able to appropriate two six-bys, and we started filling the trucks up with trash to be transported to a dump site outside the compound. After innumerable trips and many hours of work, we had the perimeter clean enough to occupy. We then discovered, to our chagrin, another problem with our surroundings. The bunkers along the perimeter, which we were to occupy, were overrun with rats. We discovered this the first night when they came out for their evening meals. The troops of Second Platoon refused to sleep in the bunkers, and we constructed shelters with our ponchos and moved the folding cots out of the bunkers and under the shelters.

Captain K. was really pissed off about the condition of the firebase. After we cleaned things up, we had a pile of ordinance several feet high. There was enough ammunition and other ordinance scattered around the compound to keep Lima Company supplied for several months. The only problem was you couldn't tell how old most of it was, and it was too risky to hand out to the men. The only thing we could do was destroy it, and we found a group of engineers who were up to the task. We even found an extra barrel for an M60 machine gun being used as a tent stake.

After getting the place cleaned up, we were able to take stock of our situation. We had been briefed by one of the departing officers, and he explained our primary mission would be to prevent rocket attacks on Da Nang. The rockets fired at the giant military base were launched from a limited area surrounding Da Nang known as rocket alley. We were in the middle of rocket alley, and it would be our job to ambush the VC before they could launch their rockets. We asked about patrolling during the day and were told it was a waste of time. The briefing officer said, "You can run your daytime patrols, but you will find that they are fruitless. Charlie has long since learned not to fuck with us during the day. He is more likely to be the local barber than running around with a gun in his hand, shooting at our patrols. The only things you'll find are booby traps, and there are plenty of those. Tell your men to be careful when they move around, because every trail in the TAOR has been mined by the VC."

Since arriving in Vietnam, I had not had any experience with booby traps. The VC around Hill 63 had not deployed them against the marines operating within their TAOR. This pattern of not using booby traps in all areas illustrated the master plan of the enemy to win the war in Vietnam. The NVA operated in the unpopulated areas over terrain that was pretty much impassible to American forces. They existed in division-size force and were able to amass large armies in their efforts against us. In the more populated areas, which had not been "pacified" by the Americans, the VC operated in smaller numbers than the NVA but were still military-type forces willing to engage us in pitched battles. This was the situation in the TAOR around Hill 63.

At Hill 10, the American forces had pretty much driven the organized VC forces from the area, and Charlie's activities were reduced to inflicting casualties through the use of booby traps. As Second Platoon would learn, the VC were very effective in using this method, and it made little difference to the families back home how their loved ones were killed or wounded. A marine was just as dead if he was blown apart by a VC booby trap as he was if he were shot in the head by an NVA bullet.

The psychological effect of the enemy tactics on the Vietnamese peasant was also very effective. The enemy could point to the NVA and the main force Vietcong to demonstrate they had a real army in the field against the Americans. At the same time, they could show their resolve to fight by pointing to the local VC cadre who were engaging in firefights with the US forces on a local level. Finally, they could inflict casualties on us by the use of booby traps with little risk to the local VC.

Another beauty of the booby trap was that the troops who fell victim to them eventually vented their frustrations against the local villagers rather than against the VC. When we got fed up with the booby traps, villages got burned, and villagers were killed or wounded.

Second Platoon was now faced with the task of dealing with an entirely different situation than that which they encountered at Hill 63. We no longer had to concern ourselves with a daily encounter with the VC but rather must carefully avoid the hidden danger of the booby trap.

After getting the perimeter cleaned up, it was time to resume our war with Charlie. We didn't heed the advice of the officer who briefed us when we arrived at Hill 10 when he told us not to bother running daylight patrols. We were committed to a policy of aggressive patrolling, and we intended to continue that policy at Hill 10. What worked back at Hill 63 would surely work here. Captain K. instructed each platoon to plan on running two daylight patrols and a night ambush just as we had done back at Hill 63. Unbeknownst to us, this was a formula for disaster that would turn our stay at Hill 10 into a nightmare.

The nightmare started on the day we began our patrolling. That morning, a squad from First Platoon detonated a booby trap in a village just north of the perimeter, injuring two marines. When they attempted to bring in a medevac, they set off a second mine that severely injured a third marine. After getting their wounded on board the medevac chopper, the patrol returned to Hill 10. They had traveled less than three hundred meters, had not encountered any enemy fire, and had lost one-fourth of their patrol to the enemy mines. This incident was a precursor of things to come.

That afternoon, Second Platoon sent out its second patrol of the day, and on the way in, they tripped a booby trap along a main trail leading to Hill 10, injuring one marine. They had to hustle to get a medevac in before it got completely dark but were able to get the wounded marine on board and back to Da Nang before nightfall. Sergeant Presno told me the mine appeared to be a hand grenade attached to a trip wire that had been strung across the trail. He said First Squad had been as careful as possible during the patrol, but after leaving the last village, they thought they had a clear path back to Hill 10. They had traveled the same trail on their way out and assumed it would be free of mines on the way in. Somebody must have planted the booby trap after the squad passed through the area earlier in the afternoon. The wounded marine, who was not badly hurt, received shrapnel in his leg.

That night, the platoon leaders gathered with Captain K. in the command bunker to discuss the problem. To say we were shaken was an understatement. It was decided to issue flak jackets to each man. Captain K. said a six-by would be there first thing in the morning with a load of flak jackets, and he didn't want anyone leaving the perimeter without one. We then discussed what else we could do to reduce our casualties. Eliminating the patrols was never an option, because it was unthinkable that Lima Company would stop patrolling. We decided to give the squads more time to complete their patrols so they could take their time and search out the booby traps before they blundered into them. Captain K. told us to stress the importance of moving slowly while on patrol.

When the meeting ended, we left the command bunker, and I experienced something new in Vietnam—night blindness. Hill 10 had a generator, and the interior of the command bunker was fully lit by electric lights. When I walked out into the darkness, I was blinded and immediately tripped, falling flat on my face. I sat there in a daze, trying to get my bearings. The only thing lit up on our side of the perimeter was the inside of the command bunker. When you left the bunker, everything else was pitch black, and for several minutes, you couldn't see a thing. After recovering my vision, I got up and returned to Second Platoon.

The next morning, I had a meeting with the squad leaders and Sergeant Green to talk about ways we could avoid the booby traps. It was obvious the more time we spent patrolling the TAOR, the more we would be exposed to danger. If we limited the patrolling, we would obviously reduce the casualties, so I decided to shorten the routes of the patrols. Another proposal was to patrol in areas that were not likely to be mined. It seemed we encountered the booby traps next to the villages and along the trails. If we stayed away from the villages and off the trails, we should reduce our exposures to the mines. Finally, it was decided the troops had to be more careful. In the future, we would take our time and attempt to locate the trip wires before we set off the booby trap.

Shortly, we sent out a squad-size patrol decked out in their newly acquired flak jackets. Their patrol route was cut in half, and they were told to take as long as they needed to complete the patrol. In addition, they were admonished to stay off the trails as much as possible. There were a lot of flooded rice paddies in the area, and Sergeant Duff informed the squad they should be wading the paddies whenever possible. While it was a real pain in the ass to hump through water that was waist deep, it was impossible for the VC to mine the flooded paddies.

That night, I got an additional thrill when I was walking from the company CP bunker to Second Platoon. As usual, I had to sit down for several minutes to let my eyes adjust to the darkness after exiting the well-lit command bunker. When I finally could see well enough to make my way back to Second Platoon, I got up and started heading in that direction. About halfway down the hill, I heard a whooshing noise coming from an area south of Hill 10. Initially, I didn't know what the hell it was, but I finally realized Charlie was launching rockets toward Da Nang. I excitedly ran back to the command bunker to report my sightings. We radioed the information to higher authorities, and they immediately wanted to know the location of the launch site. I made a wild-ass guess as to where I thought the rockets were coming from, and we relayed that information on to headquarters. Pretty soon, a C-47 Spooky was hosing down the area south of our perimeter with fire from its Gatling guns. Second Platoon gathered to watch the C-47 doing its thing outside the perimeter. This lasted for about an hour until Spooky decided to take its business elsewhere.

The other platoon commanders voiced their frustrations with the patrolling in the populated areas around Hill 10. First Platoon took a casualty from a booby trap that afternoon, which brought our casualty count to seven since arriving at Hill 10. As yet, we had not fired a round at the enemy, and the prospects of engaging the enemy appeared to be slim. Everyone agreed we needed to change our tactics if we were going to experience any degree of success. Lee Gounds suggested we limit our daytime patrols and increase and extend our nightly ambushes to see if we could improve our luck. Captain K. agreed and decided we would start running larger and more extensive ambushes in the future. We also decided to once again change the routes of the daytime patrols so that we were staying on the roads and major trails to avoid the booby traps. It made little sense to patrol the back trails of the TAOR if we weren't able to generate contact with the VC.

I returned to Second Platoon and discussed the new strategy with Sergeant Green and the squad leaders. They were in favor of limiting the patrol routes to the roads and larger trails but were not thrilled about extending the night ambushes.

Sergeant Presno asked, "How far out do they want us to go?"

I answered, "I think we will take more men on the ambush and try to set up at least a klick and a half from the perimeter. Charlie has probably gotten used to our present ambushes, and he won't expect us to be that far away from Hill 10. Maybe we will get lucky, and he will stumble into one of our ambushes."

Sergeant Green asked, "How will we avoid the booby traps if we are moving around on the trails at night? They don't go away when it gets dark."

This raised an interesting question, and I was sure the troops would solve the problem by not going any farther beyond the perimeter than they had in the past despite the complexity of our proposed ambushes. We could make all the grandiose ambush plans we wanted. If the troops wouldn't execute the plans, they would not be successful. In general, the troops took a more practical approach to the ambushes than did the command.

I thought about this for a while and responded, "I'm sure you guys will figure out a way to avoid the booby traps."

That night, Lima Company's future took a dramatic turn. At about 0200 hours, I was awakened by Corporal Stang, who said Lima Six was calling a medevac into the perimeter. I asked him what happened, and he said, "I don't know. I heard a muffled shot about fifteen minutes ago, and then they were wanting a medevac."

I hustled over to the CP to see what was going on. The first person I ran into was Rich Muler, who said, "Captain K. has accidentally shot himself in the hand while cleaning his pistol."

"What the fuck is he doing cleaning his pistol in the middle of the night?" I asked.

"I don't know. He was apparently standing watch and decided to clean the pistol. It had a round in the chamber, and when he tried to clear the pistol, it went off."

I replied, "Is he hurt bad?"

"I don't think so. The bullet went clear through his hand and hit the wall in the bunker."

I could hear the medevac approaching and went to the LZ to see if I could assist with bringing the chopper in. The company radioman was there, and I took over the radio and guided the medevac in with the use of a strobe light placed in the middle of the LZ. As the chopper landed, Captain K. came walking to the LZ with the help of Rich Muler and Sergeant Schwartz. His hand was heavily bandaged, and as he boarded the medevac, he admonished us, "Take care of the company. I'll be back as quick as I can."

We returned to the CP, where Lee Gounds was on the radio trying to contact Third Battalion headquarters to let them know what happened. He was talking to someone in Da Nang who was relaying the message to Battalion headquarters. After he got off the radio, we sat down to try to figure out what the hell to do next. Rich had been through this before after Operation Union and told us, "Since I'm the senior officer in the company, I'll take over as company commander. Staff Sergeant Roy will take over First Platoon. Everything else will pretty much remain the same."

I felt confident with Rich Muler as company commander. He had plenty of experience and was even-tempered with a level head. Things wouldn't skip a beat, and I knew he would keep us out of trouble if it was at all possible. I returned to Second Platoon and went to sleep.

The next morning, I gathered everyone together and told them what happened the night before. I assured them everything would remain the same and we were in good hands. Everyone seemed to agree, and we broke up with everyone confident Lieutenant Muler would do a good job.

During the next few days, we ran patrols without incident. Since I had arrived in country, the weather had been hot and humid with little rain. I had heard the troops talk about the monsoon season, which started showing up in September and November. One afternoon, it started clouding up, and by nightfall, the rain came in buckets. I had never experienced rain like that. You were immediately soaking wet, and the visibility was limited. Despite the weather, we sent the ambushes out as usual, although it appeared to me to be an act in futility. No self-respecting VC would be out in that shit.

After dark, we were forced into the rat-infested bunkers; they were the only places to keep dry. Around 2300 hours, I went out for my nightly check of the perimeter. As I was hurrying from one bunker to the next, a firefight broke out right in front of the perimeter. I immediately hit the ground, trying to figure out what was going on. I concluded that Charlie was inside the wire, ready to overrun our position. I half ran and half crawled back to my command bunker to get to a radio. By the time I arrived, the firing had stopped. Lance Corporal Moreno was on the radio, talking to someone in an excited voice. He informed me our ambush made contact with the enemy, and they were headed back into the perimeter.

I commented, "It couldn't have been our ambush. The firing was just outside the wire, and the ambush site was supposed to be four hundred meters out."

Lance Corporal Moreno didn't respond, and pretty soon, the ambush team was back inside the perimeter and headed in my direction. I met them outside the bunker, and they were breathing hard from their run. Corporal Holland was in charge of the ambush, and he was trying to explain what happened while trying to catch his breath. I took him to the company command bunker, where we could get in out of the rain and have some light. When we arrived at the bunker, Rich Muler was there as curious as I was. Corporal Holland explained they had been in the ambush site for a couple of hours and couldn't see a thing because of the rain. He said, "A lightning bolt lit up the area, and we were surrounded by gooks. Each one of us emptied our clips, and we hauled ass back to the perimeter."

I asked, "Did you kill any of the VC?"

"I don't know. They were all around us, and we didn't have time to stop and check."

I was now very skeptical about the whole thing, and I pressed the point by asking, "Exactly where were you guys when all this happened?"

"I told you, we were in the ambush site when we saw the VC."

I said, "I was walking the perimeter when all this happened, and it looked to me like the firing was coming from just outside the wire."

Corporal Holland didn't respond, and I instructed him to go back to his squad and we would discuss it later. I told Rich I thought this whole thing was phony and the ambush team was probably tired of sitting out in the rain and wanted an excuse to come back into the perimeter. I concluded, "I'll check it out in the morning and let you know what I find out."

The next morning, I gathered the ambush team along with Sergeant Green to get to the bottom of what happened the night before. I instructed Corporal Holland to take us to the ambush site and show us where he made contact with the enemy. Apparently, he was aware of my skepticism, and he again insisted they had come in contact with the enemy. We proceeded outside the perimeter and walked along the wire to a point where I thought I heard the firing the night before. We then started walking away from the perimeter and came upon an amazing sight. Scattered everywhere were large rockets of a type that were fired at Da Nang from rocket alley. Each rocket weighed in excess of eighty pounds and was tied to a long piece of bamboo so that two men could carry it on their shoulders. We counted the rockets, and there were fifteen littering the open field. Apparently, Corporal Holland and his ambush team had been telling the truth about what happened the night before.

I called Lima Six and told Rich he had better get out here and take a look at what we found. While we were waiting for Rich, we looked around for signs of enemy casualties. Because of the rain, I doubted we would find any blood trails or other signs of VC dead or wounded. After a brief search, we were unable to come up with any evidence that the ambush had inflicted any casualties on the enemy.

I tried to piece together what happened the previous night. The VC probably took advantage of the rain to move their rockets. The visibility was so poor that it was unlikely they would be seen either from the ground or the air. Because of the poor visibility, they must have wandered off course. If they hadn't blundered into the ambush, they surely would have walked into the wire surrounding Hill 10.

It was also obvious that the ambush team was not in the location it was supposed to be. The rockets were lying at least three hundred meters from where the team was supposed to have set there ambush. I was certain the ambush team was lying just outside the wire of Hill 10, probably half-asleep. There had to have been at least thirty VC carrying the rockets if they were being carried two men to a rocket. I could understand why the team thought they were surrounded by VC when the lightning alerted them to Charlie's presence. I would also guess most of the VC were unarmed and were nothing more than porters carrying the rockets from one location to another. In all probability, they were local farmers recruited for the task by the local VC.

I could see Rich Muler approaching with Sergeant Schwartz and a radioman. After being briefed, he instructed us to gather the rockets into one location while he contacted the Seventh Marines' regimental headquarters and informed them of our success. They told us to stand by while they figured out what they wanted to do with the rockets. We piled up the rockets and waited until we heard the sound of an approaching helicopter. The chopper pilot contacted us on Rich's radio and, after ascertaining our location, set down about thirty meters away. A full colonel emerged from the chopper and introduced himself as the regimental commander of the Seventh Marines. Obviously, someone must have thought this was a pretty big deal. Shortly, we had another chopper approach from the north, which landed next to the first helicopter. Another bird colonel emerged along with a major and a captain, all of whom were from Division headquarters. After much posturing and examination of the rockets, we were congratulated on a job well done. One of the colonels even suggested the men on the ambush should be put in for some type of commendation, after which they all got in their helicopters and left the area.

What a crock of shit, I thought. The men in the ambush site were sleeping in the wire rather than doing what they were supposed to be doing. Those assholes from Da Nang didn't have enough sense or experience to even question the fact that there wasn't an ambush site within three hundred meters of the rockets. It never occurred to them that the VC blundered into the perimeter of Hill 10 rather than being surprised by a well-executed ambush. If they had known what had really happened, they would have wanted the men court-martialed instead of giving them medals. Oh well. All's well that ends well.

We waited for a third helicopter to come in and pick up the rockets. After loading them in, the chopper we headed back to Hill 10.

I decided to forgo patrolling for the rest of the day and instead run a squad-size ambush later that night along an intersection of two major trails about a thousand meters from the perimeter. Encouraged by the previous night's success, I was hoping we could back it up with another equally successful ambush. Only this time, I wanted a real ambush instead of what we had the night before. I contacted Sergeant Duff and explained the plan to him. I told him I wasn't going to put up with any more bullshit ambushes, and I wanted them to be at the ambush site and not lying in the wire. I further explained it would be his ass if I caught them doing something other than running the ambush. Sergeant Duff assured me the squad would make it to the right location. I felt comfortable with Sergeant Duff's response. As a career marine, he had too much to lose if he got caught disobeying a direct order.

The next day, I took the entire platoon out on a sweep of the east side of the TAOR. Because of the danger of booby traps, we stayed on the main roads and stopped at several villages to run "med caps." A med cap was a procedure designed to develop goodwill among the villagers. We brought an interpreter with us, and he informed the villagers we had a doctor from America with us, and he was there to provide free medical services for the village. Once we got all the villagers lined up, we turned loose our navy corpsman, Doc Blake, to do his healing. He listened to each person's heart with his stethoscope and prescribed medicine for each patient. The medicine turned out to be salt tablets, which he dispensed to each villager with a solemn air and instructions to take them once a day for the next week. The patients were mostly kids from the villages, and it turned into a fairly festive occasion. The salt tablets were probably the first "medicine" any of the kids had ever received. After everyone was examined, we dispersed treats to the kids in the form of cigarettes, which they eagerly accepted. As we left a village, all the kids had their cigarettes lit up and were passing them back and forth.

In addition to dispensing salt tablets, Doc Blake was able to help some of the kids in the villages. Many of them had open sores on their bodies that had become infected. He would clean these areas with peroxide and give their mothers extra peroxide with instructions on how to apply it in the future. In the worst cases, he would give the mothers penicillin tablets to be given to their child over the next several days. In one of the villages, he called me over to look at a wound one of the kids had in his scalp. It was a rather deep gash, and it was infested with maggots. He cleaned it out as best he could and tried to bandage it to keep the flies away from the lesion.

The physical condition of the villagers was almost impossible to describe. The constant heat and humidity took its toll on the villagers just as it did on the marines. The unsanitary conditions in which they lived compounded the problem, along with the lack of protein in their diets. The constant enemies of the villagers are hunger and disease, which exact a larger toll than the war. It was a common sight to see a young baby being held by its mother while flies were crawling over the baby's eyelids. The mother and baby ignored the flies as if they weren't there. The diseases experienced by the villagers were enough to shock the battle-hardened marines, who dealt with it by ignoring the plight of the villagers in most cases.

We were done with the patrol shortly after noon, and I went to the command bunker to see if anything new was happening. Rich Muler was there, and he informed me we might be heading back to Hill 63 in the next couple of days. He said, "The Fifth Marines are in major contact with the NVA in the Que Son Valley, and they want to move us back to Hill 63 as soon as possible."

I asked, "Is it pretty serious stuff?"

"From what they told me this morning, Delta One-Five walked into an ambush, taking heavy casualties, and they have sent in two more companies from First Battalion as well as three companies from Third Battalion. They've been able to link up with Delta Company, but everybody is getting the shit pounded out of them. Tell your men to get packed up, because we may have to move on a moment's notice."

I passed the word to Second Platoon and returned to the CP bunker for further news. Rich told me we would be picked up the following morning by helicopter to be moved back to Hill 63. I asked him if he wanted to cancel the ambushes for that night, and he decided to run them but to keep them pretty close to the perimeter. I returned to Second Platoon and informed the squad leaders to get everyone packed up and ready to go at first light. As an afterthought, I told Sergeant Green to send out an ambush next to Route 9, which was less than two hundred meters from the perimeter.

That evening, we were packing up to be airlifted back to Hill 63. As the sun was going down, we heard a loud explosion from outside the perimeter. A few seconds later, Lance Corporal Moreno called out, "Lieutenant, we've got a problem. The ambush team has just tripped a mine."

I ran to the radio, and a private was on the net calling for a medevac. I calmed him down, and he explained a booby trap had gone off, and he was the only man in the ambush who wasn't injured. He finished by saying, "If you don't get a medevac here in a hurry, Corporal Windsor isn't going to make it."

I yelled to Sergeant Presno to get First Squad saddled up and then called Lima Six for a medevac. They had been monitoring the radio net and informed me a medevac was on the way. I grabbed my cartridge belt and M16 and joined First Squad as they ran out the perimeter. Doc Blake caught up with us as we exited the perimeter, and pretty soon, we were at the site of the wounded marines. Things were a mess. Three of the men were on the ground, and blood was everywhere. Corporal Windsor was in the worst shape. It looked like his legs had been cut in half. The other two men were bleeding profusely from shrapnel wounds to their legs. Doc Blake started working on Corporal Windsor, and two other marines started applying compression bandages to the legs of the other two men.

I got on the radio to see what the word was from the medevac. Lima Six informed me it was five minutes out. In another minute, I could hear the medevac, and I attempted to pick it up on the radio. "Medevac, Medevac, this is Lima Two. Over."

"Lima Two, this is Medevac One-Six. I'm southbound to your location about half a klick north of Hill 10. Over."

"Roger, One-Six, I have you in sight. We're three hundred meters at your eleven o'clock. Over."

He came back, "Lima Two, when was the last time you took incoming? Over."

"Negative on the incoming, One-Six. We tripped a booby trap."

By this time, it was starting to get dark, and the medevac began circling our location. I called back to the medevac, "One-Six I'm ready to pop a smoke. The best approach would be from the north. I'll put the smoke in the middle of the LZ. Over."

The medevac called back, "Negative on the smoke, Lima Two. I'm not so sure it isn't getting too dark. Can you transport your casualties to your CP for pickup? Over."

"Negative on that, One-Six. They're in bad shape, and we need to get them out of here now, or we're going to lose them. Over."

"Lima Two, it's getting too dark to land this thing. I can hardly make you guys out down there. Over."

I was dumbstruck. I had never had a medevac refuse to come in before, and I didn't know what this guy's problem was. I yelled out asking if anyone had a flashlight, and one of the marines handed me one. I turned it on and discovered it had a red lens. I removed the lens cap, and the flashlight cast a strong beam out into the night. I got back on the radio and called the medevac.

"One-Six, you've got to come in. I've got a flashlight, and I'll talk you into the LZ. You're our only hope. If we don't get these guys out of here immediately, we're going to have dead marines on our hands. Over."

"Roger, Lima Two. I'll try to come in from the north. put the flashlight in the middle of the LZ, and I'll touch down right in front of it."

A few minutes later, the chopper was approaching from the north, and I had one of the men stand in the middle of the LZ pointing the flashlight at the helicopter.

I got back on the radio. "One-Six, you're fifty meters out and a little high. Over."

"I've got the flashlight in sight, Lima Two. I'll be on the ground in a second. Over."

The medevac landed, and we immediately had the wounded marines on board. The chopper lifted off, made a right turn, and headed for Da Nang.

I called to the departing helicopter, "Thanks a lot, One-Six. We really appreciate this. Over."

The medevac responded, "Roger. Out."

I was puzzled by the medevac pilot's reluctance to pick up our wounded. I knew a landing in the dark was risky business, but war involved a lot of risks. Maybe he was having a bad day, or maybe his nerves were shot. In any event, we had our three wounded marines headed for Da Nang. I talked to Doc Blake, and he thought Corporal Windsor would make it but didn't think they would be able to save his legs. The other two marines probably had tickets home. We headed back to the perimeter shocked and saddened by the turn of events.

When we arrived at the perimeter, the men of Second Platoon gathered around trying to find out what happened to the wounded marines. When the word went out about Corporal Windsor's condition, the men took it really hard. He was very popular with the troops, and the reports of his condition cast a pall over the platoon.

I overheard Private Jones, who was on the patrol that captured the weapons back at Hill 63, say to one of his companions, "I told Windsor just before they put him on the medevac that he could have that Russian rifle that I took off that dead gook."

I was really touched be this act of kindness by Private Jones. He, like most of the men in Second Platoon, didn't have a worldly possession to his name. The most valuable thing he owned was that beat-up old rifle that he hoped to take home as a souvenir of this lousy war. It may not seem like much of a gift, but it was all that he had to give.

Private Jones reflected the type of young men who were out there fighting for their country. The Vietnam grunts have one thing in common, and that is their lack of worldly goods. Very few of them come from affluent backgrounds. The sons of the rich and, in most cases, the sons of the middle class never made it to the rice paddies of Vietnam. They were able to successfully avoid the draft or find military assignments that kept them from Vietnam. Most of those who did make it to Vietnam were able to stay out of the infantry for cushier jobs in the rear. The average grunt was from the streets rather than the country club. He was more likely a high school dropout than a college graduate. His parents were working men and women rather than doctors and lawyers. Many times, the color of his skin was brown, black, or red. His parents may not have lived the American Dream, and he might not, either. When this war was over, he would go back home with limited job skills to a family that might not be able to support him. On the other hand, I wouldn't have traded that ragtag bunch of marines in Second Platoon for an army full of draft-dodging sons of bitches from the States no matter how fancy their pedigree. They may have been smarter, better educated, richer, and prettier, but they damn sure weren't the fighters that these men were. I could stake my life on the men of Second Platoon and did so on a daily basis. They never let me down, not once, not ever.

That night, we sat around swapping stories about Corporal Windsor and the other two marines who were wounded by the booby trap. Corporal Windsor was on his second extension and had been with the platoon for almost two years. He was one of those marines you felt was invincible. There were some marines you immediately sensed weren't going to make it back to the States in one piece, while there were others that had an aura about them that led you to believe they were bulletproof. Corporal Windsor was one of those individuals. He exuded confidence and was never reluctant to take on any task assigned to him. When someone like that gets badly wounded, you feel like you've been kicked in the gut. Unfortunately, the war keeps on going, and I didn't have much time to sit around and mope about the turn of events.

Looking for a hand out

10

TRAVELING TO A LIVING HELL

THE NEXT MORNING, WE WERE packed and ready to be airlifted back to Hill 63. I had all I wanted of Hill 10. What was supposed to be R&R for Lima Company turned into a nightmare. We lost Captain K., who, for a lifer, was a really great guy. With Captain K., the men always came first, and you couldn't find a fairer man. In addition, I lost four men during our brief stay, and I was now returning to Hill 63 a fire team short. Third Squad only had ten men instead of the normal fourteen. Since Second Platoon took a major hit the night before, we were in a somber mood when we boarded the choppers for Hill 63. What had taken us several hours by truck on our way to Hill 10 turned out to be a thirty-minute helicopter ride back.

When we landed at Hill 63, I was shocked by the fact that the firebase appeared to be deserted. What was normally an area filled with the hustle and bustle of marines was now empty. Rich Muler reported to the battalion CP and shortly returned, informing us we would be occupying our old area on the perimeter for the time being. We humped over the top of the hill to take over our old bunkers when we discovered why the compound appeared deserted. The perimeter was being guarded by members of the H&S company. The clerks, cooks, and other administrative and logistical personnel were sitting in the bunkers in full battle gear.

They had hair-raising tales to pass on to us about what was happening in the Que Son Valley. The Fifth Marines were locked in a major battle with the NVA. The other three line companies of Third Battalion were committed to the battle along with two companies from First Battalion, Fifth Marines and one company from First Battalion, First Marines.

After getting my men set up on the perimeter, I humped back to the battalion CP and found a captain who was able to give me a detailed description of what was happening in the Que Son Valley.

The operation began innocently enough two days earlier when Delta One-Five was patrolling in the middle of the Que Son Valley. Just before dawn, they began taking incoming small-arms and sporadic mortar fire. They returned fire and immediately called for air support from Battalion headquarters. Within minutes, Delta Company had enemy contact on at least two sides, and a Blackcoat along with a Huey gunship were dispatched to their aid. When Delta Company attempted to identify its position for the air support using a strobe light, the NVA were able to pinpoint their exact location, and the enemy attack increased. Within the hour, the NVA were infiltrating Delta Company's lines, pinning them down with mortar and small-arms fire. By 0600 hours, they had one marine killed and ten wounded.

Delta Company, assisted by the Blackcoat, was able to bring in artillery on the NVA position and temporarily suppressed the enemy fire. They then consolidated their position and attempted to clear a small village to their west. As the swept through the village, they were ambushed by a company of NVA, wounding the Delta Company CO and inflicting other serious casualties. Delta Company once again attempted to consolidate their position in order to medevac their dead and wounded. As the medevacs were headed for Delta Company's position, the NVA popped colored-smoke grenades, confusing the helicopters, resulting in two medevac helicopters being shot down.

This forced Delta Company to move its perimeter to encircle the downed helicopters, and the NVA once again launched a massive assault on the marine positions.

At 0700 hours, Bravo Company, First Battalion, Fifth Marines was dispatched from the base at Que Son to go to the aid of Delta Company. The NVA were up to their old tricks. They ambushed Bravo Company as they approached Delta Company's perimeter. The two companies were three hundred meters apart, both of them under heavy attack and pinned down by small-arms and mortar fire. The Blackcoat was able to call in Huey helicopters armed with tear gas (CS), which they proceeded to drop on the NVA positions, causing the NVA to disengage from the battle. By 0930 hours, the combined casualties of the two companies were twenty-six marines killed and thirty-three wounded. The two companies then attempted to consolidate their positions and police the battlefield.

Shortly before noon, Bravo Company was once again attacked by an undetermined number of NVA. This time, the NVA were firing from fortified positions. The Blackcoat was able to bring in air strikes on the enemy position, which was followed by a ground assault by Bravo Company. The battle lasted well into the afternoon, and before it was over, Bravo Company incurred five more marines killed and eight wounded. Both Bravo and Delta Companies were having a difficult time getting their dead and wounded evacuated as a result of a lack of available helicopters. This severely hindered the two companies' ability to tactically respond to the NVA attacks.

Shortly after noon, Kilo and Mike Companies, Third Battalion, Fifth Marines along with the battalion command group of First Battalion, Fifth Marines were airlifted into an LZ four klicks northeast of Delta and Bravo Companies. By 1230 hours, both Kilo and Mike Companies were moving southwest in an attempt to relieve the pressure on the embattled companies while the battalion command group followed in trace. As the two companies moved east, they observed signs of recent NVA occupation, including abandoned weapons, uniforms, and ammunition.

At 1300 hours, Kilo Company came under heavy attack by at least a company of NVA as they progressed toward Delta and Bravo Companies' position. Once again, the NVA repeated their strategy of ambushing relief forces as they attempted to rescue their trapped comrades. The attack on Kilo Company lasted the rest of the day, with Kilo Company attempting to maneuver against their attackers and the NVA continuing to pour on small-arms and mortar fire. Mike Company endeavored to move in to support Kilo Company, and at 1630 hours, they were ambushed by a battalion-size force. The NVA attacked with ground assaults on the marine positions. They were able to close with the forward elements of Mike Company, infiltrating their front lines, and the battle was reduced to hand-to-hand combat. Again, CS gas, along with napalm, was dropped in an attempt to force the NVA to disengage from Mike Company. This strategy was partially successful, and by nightfall, Mike and Kilo Company were able to link up and consolidate their positions along with the command group from One-Five. Kilo Company had one marine killed and thirteen wounded, while Mike Company had seventeen marines killed and thirty-eight wounded. By the end of the day, the combined units had 54 marines killed and 104 wounded.

That evening, two more companies of marines, along with the Third Battalion, Fifth Marines command group, were thrown into the fray. The Third Battalion command group—led by Colonel Brady—was joined by Delta Company, First Battalion, First Marines at Hill 63 and were heli-lifted to the firebase at Que Son. From there, they humped all night into the battlefield, joining Bravo One-Five and Delta One-Five at 0720 hours the next day. At the same time, India Company, Third Battalion, Fifth Marines left Hill 63 and walked west along Route 534S to join up with Kilo Three-Five, Mike Three-Five, and First Battalion, Fifth Marines headquarters group. India Company arrived at 0430 hours the next day and set up a perimeter adjacent to Kilo Three-Five. There were now two distinct marine units in the Que Son Valley: Bravo One-Five, Delta One-Five, and Delta

One-One under the command of Colonel Brady; and India Three-Five, Kilo Three-Five, and Mike Three-Five under the command of the battalion commander of First Battalion, Fifth Marines, Lieutenant Colonel P. L. Hilgartener.

The following day, which was yesterday, the NVA broke off all contact, and the marine units continued to consolidate their positions as well as police up the battlefield. Patrols were run by both marine units, and various NVA weapons and equipment were recovered along with several NVA prisoners. In addition, numerous freshly dug graves were uncovered, exposing bodies of dead NVA regulars. Mysteriously, there was no contact whatsoever with the enemy forces; it seemed the NVA vanished into thin air. Presumably, the NVA were in full retreat and had abandoned the battlefield. Things remained quiet for the rest of the day and through the night with no further enemy contact.

That morning, the Fifth Marines decided they would go hunting for their vanished foe. The first order of business was the exchange of commands. Colonel Brady took charge of the three companies from Third Battalion, Fifth Marines while Colonel Hilgartner took charge of the two companies from First Battalion, Fifth Marines as well as Delta One-One. It was decided to attack to the southeast, and the two groups moved abreast with Third Battalion on the left flank (north) of First Battalion. The two battalions had been receiving sporadic sniper fire as they swept to the southeast.

After receiving a blow-by-blow account of Operation Swift, I returned to my platoon. Hopefully, the NVA had permanently withdrawn from the battlefield; if not, it seemed inevitable that Lima Company would be committed to the operation. Unfortunately, the NVA were still around. Shortly after 1600 hours, Rich Muler sent word down that there was to be an immediate meeting of the platoon commanders at the company CP. I hustled over to the CP, along with Sergeant Green. Rich confirmed the report I received from the captain from Battalion and then reported the latest developments from Operation Swift.

At 1530 hours that day, both battalions had been attacked by a regiment of NVA. They were now surrounded and taking heavy casualties as a result of the attack. The decision had been made to commit Lima Company to the operation. We were going to escort the tank platoon stationed at Hill 63 into the battle area. We would leave right after dark aboard six-bys, which would transport us south on Highway 1 to Route 534S, which ran west from Highway 1 to the District headquarters of Hiep Duc. Route 534S should take us to within 1,500 meters of the battle, and once there, we could sweep south with the tanks and hopefully kick some NVA ass—that is, if we could get the tanks to the battlefield.

Rich explained Route 534S wasn't much of a highway, and most of the bridges had been long since destroyed. The tanks had been attempting to move to the battle site all day, but one of them had struck a mine, completely disabling it. We would join up with the tanks and attempt to escort them into the battle site. If the tanks could get around the fallen bridges, they would have a chance at getting into the battle. If they couldn't, we would proceed without them and attempt to link up with the other units who were engaging the NVA.

I spent the next couple of hours getting Second Platoon ready to head out that evening. We tried to carry the maximum amount of ammo possible, with each man packing several hundred rounds for his M16. Just before dark, we assembled at the mess tent for a meal and then boarded the six-bys for our trip to the south and west. I had some qualms about traveling in the trucks at night through what was known enemy territory. One RPG rocket could wipe out a truck and all the marines in it. I was in the front seat of the lead truck, and there was the added danger of striking a mine, which would also destroy the six-by and its occupants.

We made it to the turn off to route 534S without incident. As we turned and headed west, the road changed dramatically. We were no longer on a maintained road but rather on what could best be described as a very wide trail. The driver of the truck had to pick his way around barricades as well as huge potholes. After traveling along Route 534S for three klicks, we finally linked up with the tanks, which had been waiting for us for several hours. We gladly dismounted the trucks, which turned around and headed back to Hill 63. I really admired the bravery of those truck drivers. On the way down there, each truck was occupied by a squad of marines. On the way back, they were empty and sitting ducks for any type of ambush the VC could put together. The only thing they could rely on was sheer luck in getting back to Hill 63.

Rich Muler found the commander of the tank platoon and met with him and the three platoon commanders of Lima Company. We were to proceed west along 534S for another three klicks where we would set up an LZ. Apparently, we would then be joined by Alpha Company from First Battalion, Fifth Marines who would be choppered in. We headed for our rendezvous site with Second Platoon on the point. The tanks were strung out along the route at intervals of fifty meters with members of Lima Company between each tank. We made pretty good time and had the LZ set up by midnight. I instructed my men to get some sleep until the choppers arrived with the company from One-Five.

To our west, we could see what appeared to be a major battle taking place several klicks away. There were two C-47 Spookys working the area, along with several Huey gunships. We could not hear the fighting, but the tracers from the C-47s and the gunships were everywhere. In addition, the night sky was lit up with flares dropped from the Spookys. What was most significant was the steady stream of green tracers that were being fired from the ground at the gunships. Whoever was being fired upon by the gunships was fighting back with antiaircraft fire of their own. I had never witnessed anything like this, and it was apparent we were heading into a major confrontation.

As we waited for the choppers to arrive, Rich filled us in on the latest developments in the battle. That afternoon, as the two battalion groups were approaching their respective objectives, they were attacked by two NVA regiments, presumably the same ones they had been fighting with the last couple of days. First Battalion was hit first at approximately 1515 hours. Shortly after First Battalion was hit, Third Battalion was also attacked in what appeared to be a coordinated effort by the NVA. Although the two battalions were operating independently from each other, they were simultaneously engaged by the enemy. After several hours of fierce fighting, the two battalions were able to consolidate their positions, and by 2200 hours, the enemy decreased their attack after the Huey gunships employed CS gas. Once again, the marines were required to use riot-control gas to pull the enemy forces off their backs. The NVA were still harassing the marines with sporadic small-arms fire, which dramatically increased every time the medevac helicopters attempted to land to pick up the dead and wounded.

The results of the day's activities were devastating to the marine units. By the end of the day, First Battalion had an additional thirty-five marines killed and ninety-five wounded, while Third Battalion had an additional thirty-four marines killed and eighty-eight wounded. After the day's activities, almost one-third of the marines participating in Operation Swift were either killed or wounded. The two battalions were now trying to evacuate their most seriously wounded, and we could see the lights of the medevacs as they were flying in and out of the marine positions. Every time one of them approached the battlefield, it was met by streams of green tracers.

Shortly after 0100 hours, we could hear the choppers approaching from the north. The CH-53 Sea Stallion helicopters landed and unloaded their cargo of about two hundred marines. I accompanied Rich Muler and the other two platoon commanders to meet with what would become our nemesis during the next two days. I first observed a major dressed in stateside fatigues, along with a captain who was dressed the same way. It was obvious they hadn't been in country very long. I then noticed they were wearing their rank insignias, and they would become prime targets for any enemy in the vicinity.

The major identified himself and informed us he would be in charge of our group until further ordered. Rich briefed him on our situation, including the number of tanks and men we had. The major immediately started in with some gung ho bullshit about how we were going to get in there and whip some ass. I was dumbstruck by the ridiculous bravado displayed by the major. He sounded like someone making a halftime speech to a high school football team. Lima Company knew what they had to do and were willing to go out there and fight like hell. We didn't need a pep talk from some gung ho major who was brand-new to Vietnam. Unfortunately, things would only get worse.

The major informed us Alpha Company would take the point, and Lima Company would provide security on the flanks and rear. I should have kept my mouth shut, but I didn't. I asked, "How are we going to provide security for the flanks?"

He responded, "I want a squad of marines a hundred meters out on each side of the column."

I replied, "Sir, that ain't going to work. If you send out flank security, there is no way they can keep up. They are going to be wading through all kinds of shit while the rest of us will be walking down the road. It will be impossible for them to keep up, let alone maintain any type of security."

The major was somewhat taken aback by my response and said, "Lieutenant, I'm giving you an order, and I expect it to be obeyed."

I changed the subject and replied, "Who's going to do the navigating?"

The captain who had arrived with the major spoke up for the first time. "I'll do the navigating. Your people just need to maintain security for the march."

The major concluded the meeting by saying, "I expect this operation to go smoothly. I want maximum effort from your men, and we will maintain tactical integrity at all times. I can't believe you people brought these tanks down this far without having your flanks protected. This bullshit is about to stop, and you will start acting like marines. Get your men ready to move out in five minutes."

I had already said too much to this idiot and kept my mouth shut as we walked away from the meeting. Rich Muler was obviously not happy about the situation, but he knew enough not to argue with a superior officer. He told me, "Since you've already pissed the major off, why don't you provide the two squads for flank security?"

I replied, "Rich, you know this isn't going to work."

"Yeah, I know, but what the hell are we going to do? It won't do any good to argue with him. Just do what he tells you."

I returned to Second Platoon and told them the good news. They were astounded by the major's orders, and I explained I did everything I could do to try to talk some sense into him. I told First Squad to take the left flank and Third Squad to cover the right. I instructed them to stay about fifty meters out and to try to pick their route as best they could. I finished with "Do your best to keep up. If you start to fall behind, let me know. You should be able to guide off the sounds of the tanks. I will be right behind Alpha Company if you need to find me."

With these instructions given, I headed for the Alpha Company captain to see if I could reason with him. I found him just as he was getting ready to head out. I brought up the subject of flank security, and I said, "Sir, my men are going to have a hard time keeping up out there on the flanks. Could you tell your point man to try to slow down the pace?"

He replied, "Lieutenant, I'm tired of listening to your bellyaching. You tell your men it's their job to keep up."

Now I was really pissed off but maintained my composure and replied, "We'll do our best. You're going to do the navigating, right?"

He replied in the affirmative and walked off to join his men as they were moving out. This was going to turn into a Chinese fire drill. It is fundamental that when a military unit moves, it maintains security on its flanks. The plan the major proposed came right out of the book. Unfortunately, the book wasn't written to cover the situation in Vietnam. We were moving into a major battle in the dark of night across terrain that was barely passable during the day.

At night, it was impossible to traverse that country except on the roads and major trails. If you got off the roads, you would constantly blunder into areas that were impassible. There were hedgerows that simply couldn't be penetrated unless there was an opening. In the dark, this was impossible. In addition, you were walking off into rice paddies where the water was waist deep. In order to move through that terrain, you had to carefully pick your way and constantly double back when you picked the wrong route. Unfortunately, there wasn't enough time to do that if we expected to be at our destination by first light.

As we started out, I suspected the captain wasn't up to navigating our route down to the battle site. It was hard enough to navigate during the day; at night, it was almost impossible. The fact we were on a major road helped substantially. You always knew you were on the road. Exactly how far down the road you were was another matter. I decided I would keep track of our location just in case the captain screwed up.

We hadn't gone three hundred meters when Lima Two-One came up on the radio telling me they were in the rice paddies and couldn't find a way across. The water was waist deep and getting deeper. They were going to backtrack and return to the road so they could move around the water. Rich was monitoring the net, and he told me he would request we stop the march until Second Squad got caught up.

The pace continued for the next couple of klicks, with constant halts so the squads on the flanks could catch up with the main body. Finally, the major came storming up to my position wanting to know what the hell was going on. By this time, I no longer gave a shit. I was tired and frustrated by this idiot major who didn't have a clue about what he was doing. I explained to him, "What is happening is exactly what I told you was going to happen. The flanks can't keep up."

"Lieutenant, I'm getting tired of your bullshit."

"Sir, you can do anything you want to me, but my men still can't keep up out there on the flanks. Why don't you send some of your men out there and see if they can do a better job?"

By this time, the Alpha Company captain came walking back to our position. The major turned to him and said, "Captain, can your men handle the flank positions?"

I could tell by the look on the captain's face that he didn't like the way the situation was developing. It was one thing to insist that Second Platoon's men keep up the pace; it was another thing to send his men out there. There wasn't much he could do except say, "Yes, sir. I think my men can handle the job."

The major turned to me and said, "Lieutenant, call your men in. I'm going to replace them with Alpha Company. I'll deal with you later. Can your men at least handle the job of walking point?"

Handling the point was fine with me, but I had a suspicion the captain hadn't done much of a job navigating. I replied, "Yes, sir. We can handle that if the captain can tell me our location."

I knew exactly where we were, but I didn't think the captain did. I had guessed right. The captain called to his radioman and asked, "How many paces are we from the LZ where we started?"

The radioman replied, "I don't know, sir. I lost count."

At this point, I went berserk. "You're telling me you tried to navigate your way down here by counting paces? Hansel and fucking Gretel had a better plan than that!"

The major spoke up. "Lieutenant, that's enough out of you. We'll figure out our location when we come to a bridge over one of these streams."

I wouldn't leave it alone. "In the meantime, Major, we could get ambushed, and we wouldn't have any fucking idea where we are."

"I said that's enough, Lieutenant. Get your ass up to the front of the column so we can move out."

As I proceeded toward the front of the column, I radioed the two squads who had been out on the flanks and instructed them to come on in. As I was passing the men from Alpha Company, I noticed some of them had on stateside fatigues. At that point, it occurred to me they were new replacements who had just shown up in country like their major and captain. This was going to be a real introduction to Vietnam when they tried to slog through the shit out there on the flanks.

When everyone was in position, the major gave the order to move out, and we headed west. I instructed my point man to slow it down, because I knew there was no way those poor sons of bitches out on the flanks were going to keep up. We hadn't gone three hundred meters when Lance Corporal Moreno, who was monitoring the radio net, told me the marines out on the flanks were calling in asking the column to slow down. I then began monitoring the radio net, and it wasn't long before the major once again called a halt. Only this time, he got me on the radio and ate my ass out for moving too fast. I again told my men to slow things down, and soon, we were barely moving. Even at this pace, the marines out on the flanks couldn't keep up.

Every time we stopped, it gave me an opportunity to check my location. It was so damn dark that you couldn't see a thing except the outline of hills to our north, and I was using these hills to navigate by. When we stopped, I would crawl under a poncho with a flashlight to try to reorientate our position on the map. I felt pretty comfortable using this method, and most of the time, I knew where we were to within fifty meters. Even though the major and captain from One-Five didn't appreciate the importance of knowing exactly where we were at all times, I was well aware of the pitfalls of being lost.

After we stopped for the umpteenth time to wait for the flanking squads to catch up, the major decided to call them in and proceed without security on the flanks. It took him a while, but he finally figured out what I was trying to tell him. This was one more example of the problem with this war. I didn't know the major's background, but it was apparent he had little or no combat experience in Vietnam. He was going by the book, and the book said a unit must always provide security on its flanks while moving through enemy territory. What the major didn't take in to consideration was this was Vietnam, and sometimes you have to throw the book away. If we were going to be at our destination by first light, we had to do it without security on the flanks. In this case, we had to trade security for mobility. Unfortunately, we were provided with a major who had little or no experience, and the only thing that qualified him to lead was his rank. We wasted valuable time trying to educate someone who had no business leading us into battle in the first place. The worst thing about the situation was the fact that it was beneath the major to heed the advice of a second lieutenant.

Of course, the major didn't bother to admit he was wrong. As a matter of fact, when I walked back to his position, he completely ignored me. It was just as well, because I was still steaming from our previous encounter, and I am sure I would have smarted off to him about his lack of experience. While I was at the major's position, he and his captain were huddled over a map trying to figure out where the hell we were. I didn't bother to help them, and I was sure if they wanted my advice, they would have asked for it.

As we moved west, closer to the battle, it became apparent things had settled down. There was the occasional exchange of rifle fire, but in general, the intensity of the battle had abated. The only real action occurred as the medevac helicopters attempted to evacuate the wounded. They were still drawing fire as they entered and exited the perimeters.

As we arrived at a major stream crossing, it was apparent the bridge spanning it was not strong enough to hold the tanks. I radioed this information back to the major, and shortly, he and his captain were surveying the stream and arrived at the same conclusion. Only this time, the determination had been made by a major rather than a second lieutenant and carried substantially more weight. The bank leading down to the stream was straight up and down and far too steep to allow the tanks to traverse it. The major instructed me to send patrols in both directions along the stream bank to see if we could find a place for the tanks to cross. I sent First and Third Squads, and they proceeded a couple of hundred meters in each direction without finding a suitable crossing point.

The major decided to leave the tanks behind and to proceed to our destination without them.

We made good time, and by 0400 hours, our forward elements were approaching an area along Route 534S due north of the battlefield. I radioed back to the major we were about as close to our objective as we could get without leaving the road. The major called a halt and came forward to my position, accompanied by his captain and Rich Muler. He decided we should set up a defensive perimeter and wait for first light before moving south toward the positions of the stranded marines. That was fine with me. My men were worn out from humping all night, and the one thing they needed was some sleep. The major pronounced we would dig in and stay on 100 percent alert until first light. I could agree with the digging in part, but the 100 percent alert was another asinine decision by an inexperienced commander.

We got the perimeter set up, and I instructed my men to dig in as quickly as possible. I also instructed them to put one man on watch for every fighting hole that was dug; the rest of the men could get some sleep. This was in direct violation of the major's order, but I no longer gave a shit. One of the foremost enemies of men engaged in combat is fatigue. The exhausted grunt is not going to perform as well as the rested one. This is a simple rule based on common sense and experience rather than from some book at the war college. A couple of hours of sleep would do wonders for the men of Second Platoon. The major and his captain buddy weren't going to let that happen. They started patrolling the perimeter to make sure everyone stayed awake. The first time around, they rousted me out and demanded to know why some of my men were asleep. I responded we needed to get the men some rest and showed them the clear fields of fire out in front of our position. I explained, "Sir, the enemy can't sneak up on us, we have nothing but rice paddies around us, and the NVA are smart enough not to try to attack across that open ground. If they launched an attack, I am sure everyone would wake up in time to slaughter them out in the paddies. We're safe here, and we need the rest."

I had still not learned my lesson about arguing with a superior officer, and once again, I was fighting a losing battle. The major responded, "Lieutenant, I have given you an order. Are you refusing to obey it?"

"No, sir. I'll make sure the men stay awake."

As he walked away, I went back to my CP to try to get some sleep. I did not rescind my instructions to the troops of Second Platoon. Fuck the major. What was he going to do, court-martial me and send me to Vietnam? We were able to catch less than an hour of shut-eye before it was time to move out and join up with the beleaguered elements of Third Battalion. The troops were still exhausted from humping all night, but the hour of sleep helped a little.

Lance Corporal Moreno told me the major wanted to meet with the platoon commanders before we started moving south. I went to the center of the perimeter, where I joined Rich Muler and the other platoon commanders, conferring with the major and his captain. They were discussing the route we would take to attempt to link up with the troops to the south. There was an obvious route that would lead us directly to the previous night's battle site. It was fairly flat and provided adequate cover in case of attack. More importantly, it was flanked on both sides by rice paddies, which meant the only way we could be attacked by the NVA was from our direct front. If we did engage the enemy, our flanks would be protected by the open rice paddies. Of course, the major did not choose this option. Instead, he decided we would take a circuitous route traversing several hills on our way in to join the rest of the battalion. The hills were heavily overgrown, providing an ideal ambush site for the NVA.

Having said enough, I had no comment on the inane choice of routes by which we would be moving south. The next orders from the major placed the icing on the cake. He set forth the order to march for our attempt to link up with the surrounded marines to the south. He wanted Lima Company to lead the way, with his men from Alpha Company bringing up the rear. His headquarters group would remain with Alpha Company. This was fine and dandy; our fearless leader would be leading his troops from the rear of the column. I was about to say something when I got a look from Rich Muler, which could only be interpreted as "Hynes, keep your fucking mouth shut!" I bit my tongue and said nothing in deference to Rich. He knew how screwed things were but understood we would never get anywhere arguing with our superior officer. We were going to do things their way, regardless of the outcome, and little was gained by arguing the point. I chalked this up to just one more example of how messed up the military bureaucracy could be and how poorly this war was being managed.

It was bad enough we were being led into a critical battle by a major who didn't know his ass from third base about fighting a guerilla war in Southeast Asia, but now he was going to lead us from the rear element of the tactical column. What happened to the gung ho major that gave us the pep talk the night before back on Route 534S? When he said we were going to kick some NVA ass, he apparently wasn't including himself or the rest of his men from One-Five. There were a lot of senior officers in the Marine Corps who led their men by example, with courage and valor. Unfortunately, there were others, like our major, who were all smoke and no fire. I am sure in his own mind he was a hard-charging marine; in reality, he was a blowhard phony, who, when the chips were down, chose to lead the charge from the rear.

After the meeting broke up, Rich Muler gave us the order for the company to march. He said, "We will move with two up and one back. I want First and Second Platoons abreast as we sweep south. The headquarters group will be behind them followed by Third Platoon."

This order made sense. We would have the two lead platoons side by side, providing mutual support for each other. Rich would be in the best position to lead the company, and Third Platoon would be covering our rear. Rich concluded our meeting with

"We're about to walk into some deep shit. The men are tired, and you need to stay on their asses. Take your time, and try to keep everyone spread out as much as possible. We'll get through this if everyone does their job."

Let's figure this thing out

11

ARRIVING INTO A LIVING HELL

WITH THAT, WE SADDLED UP and headed south. I had Second Platoon in a wedge formation with Second Squad on point, First Squad trailing on the left, and Third Squad trailing on the right. I was positioned behind Second Squad and between First and Third Squads. As we left Route 534S, we negotiated a small hill. As Second Squad topped the hill and started down the other side, they radioed back they observed three heavily camouflaged NVA run from the base of the hill, across a dry rice paddy, and into the tree line at the bottom of the next hill in our line of march. Rich called a halt and requested the platoon commanders rendezvous with him. When I got to his position, he was on the radio with the major, explaining the situation. Shortly thereafter, the major arrived, and Rich explained he thought we needed the next hill prepped with artillery before we proceeded. The major wasn't buying it and wanted to continue on.

Rich attempted to explain, "Major, if we see three of them, that means there are a hundred of them that we don't see. They're lying up on that hill waiting for us. If we soften them up with the artillery it's going to make our job a lot easier."

The major said, "I'm not going to call in a fire mission simply because we saw a couple of NVA. Unless you can give me an exact target, we're going to move on."

Rich obviously didn't have a precise location of the three NVA that fled the area, so we once again headed south. By this time, we had a Blackcoat on station, and Rich was able to raise him on Lima Company's radio net. Rich alerted him to the sighting, and he was circling the area to our immediate front looking for any sign of the NVA. We crossed the dry rice paddy where the NVA were observed and started up the next hill. Unlike the previous hill, this one was heavily overgrown with bamboo, tree lines, and underbrush. It wasn't long before Second Platoon lost visual contact with First Platoon on its right flank. I radioed this information to Lima Six, and Lee Gounds also confirmed the fact that First Platoon could no longer see Second Platoon. Rich told us to keep moving and hopefully things would thin out and we could reestablish contact.

At this point, I made what could be the biggest mistake of my short Marine Corps career. I let the terrain dictate our course of march. Instead of keeping the men spread out perpendicular to our line of march, I allowed them to narrow our column to a point where it was less than thirty meters wide. I no longer had a wedge formation. We were strung out horizontally, trying to pick our way through the thick underbrush. I will never understand why I let this happen. Perhaps it was fatigue. Maybe I was just careless. Regardless of why, Second Platoon's left flank was exposed to attack.

I radioed to Rich I still had not regained visual contact with First Platoon, and the cover was still as thick as ever. He told me to keep moving until we reached the top of the hill and we would reestablish contact at that point. I rogered his order, and we continued our advance. I estimated we were within a hundred meters of the crest of the hill. When we topped out, I could not only link back up with First Platoon but could also get Second Platoon formed back into a wedge formation.

The lead element of Second Platoon was about to reach the top of the hill when small-arms fire broke out to my front and left flank. This was followed immediately by several explosions throughout Second Platoon. I was initially confused and thought we were tripping booby traps, causing the explosions. Then someone shouted, "Incoming!" and I realized we were being mortared. As the mortar rounds continued to land, the incoming small-arms fire increased to a point where we were being engulfed by a lead curtain. The firing was coming from several directions, and it was so intense that anyone who stood up would surely be struck by ground fire. Second Platoon was screwed. We couldn't maneuver, and the NVA continued to rain down mortars on our positions.

I was lying in a small indentation on the ground with my radioman next to me. The one thing in the world I wanted to do most was to stay where I was and hope the shooting would stop. I began to hear the cries of "Corpsman!" and I realized we were taking casualties. It took all the willpower I had to force myself to begin crawling forward to the lead elements of Second Platoon. I was able to reach a tree line about twenty meters in front of my original position. I started through the tree line when a marine to my left said, "Lieutenant, don't go through there. I don't know whether we have anyone left alive in front of us or not."

I stopped crawling and looked around to figure out what the hell we were going to do. The mortaring had stopped, but we were still being raked by small-arms fire. It was obvious we had to do something to consolidate our position. We were extremely vulnerable to being overrun. Unfortunately, Lance Corporal Moreno had stayed where he was when I crawled forward, and I was now without a radio. I began yelling directions for men to start moving out on our left flanks and for others to move up to my position to start forming a defensive perimeter. At the same time, I noticed men were filtering back from the forward positions, either wounded or assisting wounded marines. My main concern was to try to get the platoon in a defensive position; the wounded would have to take care of themselves for the time being.

Just then, Lance Corporal Moreno was next to me with the radio. I got on the horn trying to raise the squad leaders. I instructed Sergeant Presno to try to move his squad forward on our left flank to protect us from being overrun from that direction. At the same time, I instructed Corporal Hale to move Third Squad forward to reinforce Second Squad. I was not too concerned about our right flank, because I knew First Platoon was out there somewhere and would be covering for us. I also knew Third Platoon was covering our rear. I got Sergeant Duff on the radio. He appeared to be incoherent. I instructed him to get his men to fall back into the defensive position I was trying to set up.

He replied, "I don't have a squad. They're all gone. They're all gone."

I then realized Sergeant Duff was only several meters to my right, talking into his radio. I crawled over to his position and tried to figure out where Second Squad was. He again repeated that his squad was gone. I couldn't figure out where they had gone, and I asked Sergeant Duff's radioman where Second Squad was. He said, "Most of them are wounded or dead."

I yelled at him, "Where are they? I need to know where they're at!"

He pointed behind me. I rolled over and observed several marines lying on the ground being administered to by Doc Blake and a couple of other marines. By this time, the small-arms fire was abating, but we were still receiving sporadic incoming. You could now move about, half walking or half crawling without getting your head blown off. I ran over to Doc Blake and asked him how many wounded we had, and he said he thought we had eight or nine men down. I asked if we had any KIAs, and he replied, "A couple."

I returned to Sergeant Duff's radio and got on the horn with Lima Six. Rich wanted to know what the situation was, and I explained it as best I could. He asked me if I had all men accounted for, and I realized I didn't. I told him I would get on that right away. He said, "We're setting up a LZ at the base of the hill, and I have medevacs on the way. As soon as we get the LZ secured, you can start sending you casualties back down to us."

I acknowledged his transmission and set about trying to account for all the men of Second Platoon. I contacted Sergeant Presno and Corporal Hale, and they told me all their men were present, and they didn't have any casualties. This left Second Squad. Sergeant Duff was still out of control, so I asked his radioman if everyone from Second Squad was back in our perimeter. He said he thought so but couldn't say for sure. I sent him over to the wounded marines and told him to find out whether we had anyone missing from Second Squad. As he scurried off, Lee Gounds came half running and half crawling over to my position with several of his men.

Lee told me when the firefight started, First Platoon was a little behind us and about fifty meters to our right. He pushed his platoon forward so they were now on our right flank. His right flank was secured by the dry rice paddy at the base of the hill. Only Second Platoon's left flank was exposed. I found Sergeant Green and sent him in that direction with orders to assist Sergeant Presno in consolidating our position on that side. I was then approached by the Second Squad's radioman, who told me we had all of Second Squad accounted for. I asked him how many casualties we had, and he told me we had six men wounded and three KIAs. I got on the radio with Lima Six and informed him of our casualties and said we would be sending them back as soon as he gave us the word. With that, I sat down next to Lee Gounds and smoked a cigarette.

I had completely lost track of time, looked at my watch, and discovered it was 1030 hours. Once again, I was taken aback by the passage of time. I would have bet the farm we had only been at it for a couple of hours. Four and a half hours had passed since we departed our positions that morning. I asked Lee Gounds what he thought would happen once we got the wounded evacuated. He replied, "I don't know. The shooting has let up, but we're still taking some incoming. If we try to move ahead, our left flank will be exposed. I'm surprised they didn't try to hit us from that side when they sprung the ambush."

Lance Corporal Moreno told me Lima Six was on the radio and wanted to talk to me. When I picked up the handset, Rich told me to start sending the wounded back; the medevacs would be there in a few minutes. I found Doc Blake, and as usual, he had things under control. Three of the wounded marines could walk back down the hill to the LZ, leaving three wounded and three dead marines who had to be carried. Doc Blake had already lined up the marines to assist him, and I told him to start moving them down the hill.

I returned to where Lee Gounds was sitting and realized I was completely exhausted. As I sat there, my mind started to drift off, and I was starting to fall asleep. Unfortunately, the day was not done.

I could hear the medevac chopper approaching. As they came in, all hell broke loose. The incoming small-arms fire began again, only this time with more intensity, if that was possible. All of Second Platoon was pretty much protected from the small-arms fire, but I could hear the NVA mortars leaving their tubes to our southeast. Once again, the mortar rounds started landing among us, all we could do was to hunker down as best we could. After several mortar rounds landed on our position, the NVA started walking the rounds down to the LZ, which took some of the pressure off us. All the while, the small-arms barrage continued over our heads, forcing us to hug the ground. I didn't know if the enemy was trying to keep us pinned down or if they were firing at the helicopters. It didn't make any difference, because they were scaring the shit out of me either way.

The small-arms and mortar fire would intensify as each medevac landed to pick up our wounded and dead marines. I was on the radio with the Blackcoat, trying to direct him to the mortar tubes, which sounded like they were less than three hundred meters away. I shot an azimuth to their location and estimated their position and gave this information to the Blackcoat. Despite my assistance, he could not locate the rounds coming out of the tubes, which seemed strange to me. The Blackcoat had been directing artillery on what he thought were likely NVA positions, but he couldn't call it in on the NVA who were directing small-arms fire at us. They were way too close to our perimeter. I estimated they were at the top of the hill that was less than fifty meters from our front lines.

After the last medevac lifted off, Blackcoat informed us he had air on station and wanted to drop some napalm as close as possible to our position. He wanted us to put out air panels (small fluorescent-colored cloth panels) to mark the front of our lines. We couldn't find our panels, so we decided to do the next best thing and use smoke grenades to mark our position. As we popped our smoke, Blackcoat told us he had us spotted and wanted to know how close we wanted the napalm. I told him to bring it in as close as he could, because Charlie was right on top of us. He acknowledged my transmission and informed me the fixed wing would make an initial pass without dropping any ordinance, and we should expect the napalm the second time around. I radioed this information to the squad leaders, and within minutes, two F-4 Phantoms, one behind the other, made their initial passes from right to left in front of our positions. They were less than one hundred meters off the deck, and the roar was deafening as they passed by. Blackcoat came over the radio, asking if the jets were on target. I asked if he could bring them in closer, and he replied he couldn't without endangering the lives of our men.

On the second pass, both planes dropped their loads, and we could feel the heat from the bombs as we lay there hugging the ground. In response to the bombing run, the NVA unleashed another barrage of small-arms fire as if to say, "You didn't get us that time."

I again contacted Blackcoat and informed him the napalm didn't solve our problem, and we were still pinned down. He replied he would have some more air on station shortly, and he would get back to us. This still left us with the dilemma of what to do next. I discussed this with Lee Gounds, and we both agreed that trying to advance would be suicide in light of the fact that our left flank was completely exposed. Lee and I got on the radio to discuss the situation with Lima Six. We all agreed that the exposed left flank presented a serious problem. Lee suggested Third Platoon advance even with the left flank of Second Platoon, which would give us three platoons abreast, and the unit from First Battalion could move forward to take Third Platoon's position to provide security to our rear. The problem was we would still have an exposed left flank, only it would be Third Platoon's flank instead of Second Platoon's. As we sat there contemplating our next move, we received word from Blackcoat that he had more air on station.

The decision as to what we were going to do next was not left up to Lima Company. Rich came over the radio telling us we had gotten orders to get ready to retreat from our present position and for everyone to get their gas masks on. The fixed wings were armed with tear gas canisters and were prepared to drop them in front of our lines. The entire area would be blanketed in tear gas, which should blind the enemy and allow us to get our people off the hill. Rich told us once the gas deployed, we should start backing down the hill passing through Third Platoon's position. Once we reached the base of the hill, Third Platoon would abandon its position, and we would establish a defensive perimeter in the area of the LZ, now protected by the marines from First Battalion.

The F-4s dropped the tear gas, and the entire area was engulfed in the blinding and choking gas. Unfortunately, all our gas masks didn't work, and I could hear some of the troops coughing and gasping for air. As soon as I felt the gas had enveloped the entire area, I gave the word to move out. The tear gas must have impaired the NVA, because we didn't receive any small-arms fire as we walked off the hill and down to the LZ.

We set up a perimeter at the LZ and were joined by First and Third Platoons. Although we were still in range of the NVA mortars, I felt a lot more secure in our present location. We had good fields of fire and could see any enemy who tried to approach our position. I ordered the platoon to dig. I didn't know how long we would be there, and the NVA might renew their mortar attacks.

I then mentally reviewed the events of the morning. We had obviously blundered into an NVA ambush, and it was clear we were helpless. Fortunately, the NVA did not fully exploit the advantage they had gained in springing the ambush. For whatever reason, they were unable to isolate and cut off any of our units. The fact that

Second Squad, although decimated by mortar and small-arms fire, was able to extricate itself back into our lines probably saved the day. If they had been trapped out in front of the platoon, we would have still been up on the hill trying to rescue them. The NVA would have used this to their advantage with deadly results.

A second factor that helped was that we had two platoons abreast as we proceeded up the hill. If we had our platoons in column formation, the NVA would have driven a wedge through Second Platoon, isolating part of the platoon and again forcing Lima Company to stay on the hill attempting to rescue the survivors of the cut-off unit. Since First and Second Platoons were side by side, the NVA could not split Second Platoon without running into First Platoon.

A third factor that may have entered into the equation was sheer luck. It is possible we walked into the ambush before it was fully set up. The NVA did not let the forward elements of Second Platoon pass through their lines before springing the ambush. If they had done that, we would have been decimated. There was no way Second Squad would have been able to get back to our lines if they had ventured another fifty meters into the NVA positions.

It was also possible the NVA were trying to conserve ammunition after they sprang the ambush. While the NVA had us pinned down with small-arms fire, they could have continued their mortar attack and inflicted heavy casualties as we helplessly lay there, unable to move. I estimated they dropped at least fifty mortar rounds on our position. Additional rounds would obviously have increased our casualties. The fact that the NVA had expended substantial munitions while heavily engaged with the Fifth Marines for three days prior to our entering the battle may have saved some lives in Lima Company. Taking nine casualties was a calamity, but it could have been a lot worse. We were lucky to be off the hill and in our present condition.

My reverie was interrupted by Doc Blake, who came over to report on the casualties. Of the six wounded marines, we had four with shrapnel wounds from the mortars and two with gunshot wounds. Doc Blake said he thought they would all survive, but most of them had tickets back to the world.

Unfortunately, the three dead marines would also be going back to the world—to their mothers and fathers, brothers and sisters, and maybe to their wives and kids. Their families would grieve, surrounded by extended family and friends. Within a couple of weeks, they would be nothing more than statistics of a war that involved the killing of young Americans in remote places like the Que Son Valley, for what purpose I knew not.

Doc Blake also admonished me to look at Sergeant Duff. He said, "I don't think he is in any condition to remain out here and should be medevaced."

I had forgotten about Sergeant Duff's peculiar behavior up on the hill, and I found him sitting by himself near First Squad. I asked him if he was all right, and he didn't respond. He just gave me a blank stare. After asking him again and getting no response, I returned to Doc Blake and told him to get Sergeant Duff out on the next chopper.

Exhaustion continued to plague us. Although humping all night didn't help, the stress and strain of the previous five hours completely drained our energy. While adrenaline can act as a stimulant, when it quits flowing, you come down totally exhausted. I was getting to the point where I no longer gave a shit about what happened. I was running on empty, and my ability to function as an effective platoon commander was coming into question. I noticed the same thing happening with the men of Second Platoon; they were starting to get a faraway look in their eyes. Hopefully, we would be getting some rest soon.

As a result of our casualties and the fatigue of the men, the effectiveness of Second Platoon as a fighting force was rapidly deteriorating. We were down to thirty-three men, just two squads, and a headquarters group. Hopefully, we would not be called upon to do much fighting until we got some rest.

Lance Corporal Moreno told me Lima Six wanted me over at the company CP. When I arrived, the other platoon commanders were approaching. The major and his captain were also there waiting for us to arrive. The major started the meeting without any comment about what happened that morning. In fact, he appeared to be shaken by the events of the day and had lost most of the braggadocio he exhibited earlier. He informed us we had been ordered to attempt to reengage the enemy forces from which we had just retreated. We would head back to the north away from the morning's battle for two hundred meters, swing east, and then back south to try to encircle the enemy's position, which we encountered that morning. He said the contingent from First Battalion would lead the way, followed by Lima Company.

When the major left, Rich briefed the Lima Company platoon commanders. He wanted First and Third Platoons abreast directly behind the majors group. Second Platoon would bring up the rear, which was fine with me. I had all I wanted of the NVA for one day.

We saddled up and headed north back toward Route 534S for a couple of hundred meters and then swung east for another three hundred meters. The lead element of our group swung south and started moving parallel to our route of the march earlier that morning. They hadn't gone two hundred meters when small-arms fire began to ring out at the head of the column. At the same time, I could hear rounds coming out of the NVA mortar tubes farther to the south. Someone yelled, "Incoming!" and the men of Second Platoon hit the ground. We were in an open area, and we scrambled to find what little cover was available to protect us from the mortar rounds. Luckily for us, the rounds landed at the head of the column in the area of the firefight. I hastily set up a small perimeter, and we waited to see what would develop. The men of Second Platoon showed little interest in what was happening in the firefight being waged at the head of the column. Most lay behind whatever cover was available with vacant stares waiting for whatever would come our way.

I was monitoring the radio, and I could hear the traffic coming over the net. The captain and the major were excitedly talking back and forth, making little sense. I could hear the small-arms fire and could distinguish the sound of what I thought was a .50-caliber machine gun. Since we weren't carrying a weapon that large, I could only assume that it belonged to the NVA. The battle raged on for several minutes, with the NVA continuing to lob mortar rounds on top of the marines at the head of the column. My hope was the battle stayed up there and the NVA left Second Platoon alone.

Lima Six came over the radio and asked if we had an available site for an LZ. I informed him we had set up a perimeter on what could serve as an LZ, and he told me to stand by for a medevac. They were sending back casualties to our position. I acknowledged his transmission and informed the squad leaders a chopper was headed our way.

There was a small hill between Second Platoon and the existing firefight. As a result, we were not taking any direct small-arms fire. I was concerned the medevac would draw mortar fire, and I radioed the squad leaders to have the men find as much cover as possible before the medevac arrived. The men of Second Platoon did not respond to those orders, and most of them were pretty well exposed to incoming mortar rounds. It was my job to get up and kick some ass and force the men to take cover, but I found myself with no enthusiasm for the task. The lack of sleep and the unbearable heat were about to get the best of me and the men of Second Platoon. I finally forced myself to my feet, and I started around the perimeter, directing the men to defensive positions from which they could better protect the perimeter as well as shelter themselves from incoming mortar rounds.

A few minutes later, several dead and wounded marines filtered back from the front. Some of them were able to walk, while the remaining were carried. Doc Blake immediately located a pickup spot in the lone shady area within the perimeter. I got on the radio and asked Lima Six if there were any more casualties. They informed me those were it, and the medevac would be arriving shortly. I told Doc Blake to make sure Sergeant Duff got on the medevac chopper, as well.

A few minutes later, I could hear the approaching medevac. The chopper pilot came up on the company radio net. I gave him our location and told him we were at his eleven o'clock about three hundred meters out. I also informed him I didn't want to pop a smoke, because it would pinpoint our position for the NVA mortars. The chopper pilot wanted the smoke, but I was able to convince him we were out in the open, and he wouldn't have any trouble finding us. He came right to our location, made a tight 360, and dropped into the middle of our perimeter. As soon as the medevac's wheels touched down, the casualties along with Sergeant Duff were loaded into the CH-46, and it immediately lifted off. I could hear the NVA mortar rounds leave the tube as the medevac was making its approach. Fortunately, they were off target and landed a hundred meters to our south. Maybe the NVA gunners weren't invincible, after all.

We lay there for several minutes while the NVA continued to drop mortars harmlessly off target to our south. I assumed they would start walking the mortars in our direction, but that never happened. Lima Six came over the net and informed the company to get ready to move. We would backtrack out of our present location and move north toward Route 534. The order of march would remain the same, except everything would be reversed. Second Platoon would be on point, followed by First and Third Platoons moving abreast, and the group from the First Marines would bring up the rear.

We got the orders to move out, and I put First Squad on point with Third Squad trailing. I was between the two squads as we moved northeast toward the site we left that morning at first light. It seemed like days had passed since we hooked up with the major and his contingent from First Marines. In reality, it was 1800 hours, and we had been together for less than a day.

As we approached Route 534S, I radioed back to Rich and asked him what he wanted us to do next. After conferring with the major, he instructed me to locate a site for a perimeter where we would spend the night. I found a large, open area that would give us good fields of fire in all directions, and we began setting up a perimeter.

We were still digging in for the night as darkness set in. I checked Second Platoon's fighting holes and had to jump on the men for not digging them deep enough. I was operating on autopilot along with the rest of the men from Second Platoon, and it was difficult to do even the simplest of tasks as a result of our state of total exhaustion. After I satisfied myself the perimeter was as secure as it was going to get, we were ready to collapse in our fighting holes. I got a call on the radio telling me there was going to be a meeting with the major in five minutes. I dragged myself over to the company CP, wondering what the major had in store for us.

As the meeting progressed, it became apparent the major had undergone a transformation in the last twenty-four hours. He was no longer the gung ho senior officer who was going to lead us to glory on the battlefield. He had apparently gotten a taste of reality and discovered this war was not all that it was cracked up to be. He also learned the NVA were a formidable opponent who made you fight them on their terrain and under conditions of their choosing. Although I wouldn't describe the major as a beaten man, he certainly was subdued from what we had encountered the night before.

He told us he thought we had fought well, and the troops should be commended for the day's action. I thought we had gotten our asses kicked but kept that to myself. He also stressed the fact the NVA were still out there, and we might come under a night attack, emphasizing the importance of maintaining security and keeping people awake on watch. I knew keeping people awake was going to be a difficult task and planned to have the squad leaders and myself constantly walking the lines.

The meeting broke up, and I gathered Sergeant Green, Corporal Hall, and Sergeant Presno together and assigned two-hour shifts to walk the lines and make sure we had one man awake in each fighting position at all times. I took the midnight-to-0200 shift and immediately fell into a deep sleep.

I awoke with a start. I was standing in a field all by myself. I immediately hit the deck and discovered I was unarmed. My mind started racing. Where was I, and how had I gotten there? I was paralyzed with fear as I heard sounds off to my left and hugged the ground. I discovered that whoever was off to my left was speaking

English, and I began crawling in that direction. As I approached the voices, I realized I was coming upon the company CP. I stood up trying to look as casual as possible and approached a marine who was manning the company's radios. I asked him how everything was, and he told me everything was fine while looking at me as if I had lost my mind. I then told him I was just checking and turned around and proceeded back to Second Platoon. I realized I must have been sleepwalking when I awoke in the middle of the field. Thank God I was still inside of the perimeter. When I arrived at Second Platoon's CP, I asked Lance Corporal Moreno, who was monitoring the radio, why he let me walk off like I did. He said, "I thought you were going to take a shit. Where the hell did you go?"

I replied, "Never mind," and I went back to sleep.

The next time I awoke, it was starting to get light, and I couldn't remember whether I had walked the lines or not. Doc Blake was manning the radio, and I asked him if I had made the rounds that night. He told me he didn't know, and I decided to leave it at that. No use dwelling on what might have happened.

The night's sleep did wonders for Second Platoon. Although we were still physically worn out from the previous day's encounter, mentally we were more alert, which was far more important.

As the sun was coming up, I could hear helicopters approaching from the north. They circled once and set down in the middle of the perimeter, unloading two companies of marines. I got on the horn with Lima Six and discovered we were being reinforced with two additional companies—one from Second Battalion, Fifth Marines and the other from Third Battalion, First Marines. I didn't give it much thought until Lieutenant Roy Norman, the lieutenant I replaced as platoon commander of Second Platoon, walked over to our position. He was now the platoon commander of one of the incoming platoons from Hotel Company Two-Five. He circulated among Second Platoon, renewing old acquaintances among the troops. He studiously avoided me, which was just as well, given our previous encounters. After a breakfast of C rations, it was time to meet with the major for our morning briefing.

The night's sleep had done wonders for the major, as well. He was now back to his old hard-charging self, ready to once again kick some NVA ass. He explained it was vital that we link up with the stranded marines to our south, and this time, he chose the most direct route to their position. This was the protected route, which was would've obviously been the best choice the previous morning. Unfortunately, his failure to recognize this was costly to Second Platoon. Once again, he put Lima Company on point with the troops from the remaining companies following behind. He must still have felt more comfortable being with his own men, because he placed his headquarters group in the rear with Alpha Company.

Rich placed Lima Company in a wedge formation with one platoon up and two platoons back. First Platoon had the point, with Second Platoon trailing on the left and Third Platoon on the right. This formation made the most sense. We had both flanks protected by open rice paddies. If the NVA attacked, they would have to do it from our front, and we could immediately maneuver the two trailing platoons abreast of Third Platoon. We would then have a three-platoon front with both flanks covered by the open rice paddies, which would be the ideal tactical situation. At 0630 hours, we headed south toward the rest of the Fifth Marines.

The route was substantially easier to negotiate than that which we had taken the previous day. Although we still had sufficient cover, it was not as thick as it had been the day before, and we were able to maintain visual contact between the three platoons. We were making good time as we headed south when we once again came under mortar and small-arms fire—only this time, we were being fired at from a tree line on our right flank, which was more than three hundred meters from our location. There was a rice paddy between us and the tree line, which prevented the NVA from maneuvering toward our position. The mortar rounds came pounding in, but the NVA barrage was less than a dozen rounds causing no casualties. The Blackcoat, which was escorting us south, immediately called in artillery on the tree line, which squelched the small-arms fire. The

Blackcoat must have spotted something in the tree line, because he had air on station immediately after the artillery barrage lifted. He brought in several air strikes using a combination of napalm and snake-eye bombs.

The snake eye was a large, high-explosive bomb that was identifiable by its huge tail fins, which opened up as the bomb was released, causing a substantial amount of drag on the bomb. This slowed down the speed of the bomb, allowing the jets to make lower passes over the target without being blown out of the sky by the explosion of the bomb. Fixed-wing aircraft, armed with snake eyes, were a lot more accurate than those with conventional bombs.

As the air strikes continued, our contingent of marines was once again treated to an impressive show of US military might. The tree line was alternately rocked by five hundred–pound bombs and scorched by napalm. Although we had stopped receiving fire, there still must have been enemy activity in the area, because the bombardment continued on for well over an hour. After the Blackcoat was satisfied he had unleashed sufficient armament on the hapless NVA, we were ordered to sweep the tree line to assess the damage. Rich placed First and Third Platoons on line with Second Platoon following, and we swung west toward the tree line.

As we approached the tree line, I was concerned about being lured into another ambush. We were leaving the safe haven of our intended route and now sweeping toward a tree line that could still be inhabited by the NVA, despite the massive pounding from the air and artillery. If the NVA were still in the tree line, they could pin us down in the open rice paddies and pound us with their mortars. Fortunately, the NVA had abandoned the tree line, and we safely cleared the paddies. Once in the tree line, we began a search for signs of enemy casualties. After sweeping the area twice, we were unable to come up with any positive signs that the air strikes had done any damage. We did discover two unexploded snake eyes, which we turned over to the engineers for destruction. The bombs looked substantially larger up close than they appeared when they were being dropped from the fixed wing.

After clearing the area, we once again swung south to join the rest of the battalion. We finally linked up with India Company, Third Battalion, Fifth Marines at 1500 hours. They had established a perimeter on top of a small hill, and needless to say, they were glad to see us. They had been in the fray for three days and had taken substantial casualties. The troops from India Company were filled with stories about their adventures over the previous couple of days. They told us hair-raising tales of being overrun by the NVA and engaging in hand-to-hand combat with the enemy.

After listening to the varied tales, I was summoned to a meeting by Rich Muler. I found the combined Lima and India Companies CP, and when I arrived, the mood was somber. Captain Frank Burke, the India Company commander, was doing most of the talking. He related the events of the previous three days and how the NVA nearly annihilated India Company. He was concerned Colonel Brady was going to be relieved of command for failing to link up the battalion headquarters group with Mike Company before he sent them to the aid of Kilo and India Companies.

Captain Burke concluded by saying, "I don't care what Regiment thinks; I'm going to put Colonel Brady in for the Navy Cross. His actions saved the lives of lots of marines over the last couple of days. We were just trying to survive, and if Mike Company had not arrived when they did, we might have been wiped out. How Regiment can fight this war from their secure firebase beats the shit out me. Colonel Brady was a hero of this operation, and I'm not sure he will be around tomorrow as our commander."

Captain Burke had good reason to be pissed off. First and Third Battalions had taken the brunt of the NVA attacks and had suffered dearly. Unless you were on the ground experiencing the fury of the NVA onslaught, it was impossible to appreciate the intensity of their attacks. They were masters at picking the right terrain and minimizing the effectiveness of the air and artillery support available to the American ground forces. They were also fighting for a cause in which they truly believed, and they were willing to sacrifice the lives of their men to obtain their goals. When they attacked, they attacked with a ferocity unknown to the American soldier and beyond the comprehension of someone sitting safely inside of a secure firebase.

While the marines were more than willing to engage the NVA, they didn't hold a candle to the NVA when it came to making extreme sacrifices in order to inflict casualties on the enemy. The NVA had a cause to fight for, and the marines did not. We had been fed the nonsense about stopping Communism and how the domino effect would lead to a takeover of the world by the Communist regime. Once in Vietnam, it didn't take us long to realize that we were there to support a corrupt South Vietnamese government and their gutless army. The NVA were fighting to unite their two countries against what they viewed as an attempt by the United States to make South Vietnam an American colony. They fought with the fervor of all people who believe their cause to be just.

The meeting broke up, and the morale of the officers of Lima Company was at an all-time low. It was incomprehensible that Regimental headquarters would consider replacing Colonel Brady. He had led us ever since Operation Union, and his concern for the welfare of his men was unquestioned. You couldn't ask for a better leader, and the officers of Third Battalion had total confidence in his ability to lead us into battle. Hopefully, the information Captain Burke had was untrue and Colonel Brady would not be replaced.

We remained in position with India Company for the rest of the day. I did not have to jump on the men to get dug in; they were well aware of the dangers we faced. That night, we braced ourselves for an NVA attack that never came. As far as we could tell, the NVA had left the valley, as none of the units involved in Operation Swift had reported any contact during the night.

The next morning, Lima Company saddled up for a company-size sweep to the east of our present position. At last, we were on our own, free of the major and his sidekick captain. We could operate at our tempo, picking our route and choosing the tactical formation that best suited the conditions. Most importantly, we were well rested and ready to face the enemy.

We stayed in a wedge formation for most of the day, rotating the point platoon every couple of hours. We swept the area where the previous day's battles had been fought. The countryside was littered with fresh bomb craters and tree lines scorched by napalm. Shortly after 1300 hours, we came across a recently abandoned NVA base camp, which was expertly hidden from aerial observation beneath a stand of trees. We searched the area, discovering well-concealed bunkers with mutually supporting fields of fire. After our search was completed, we continued our sweep, circling back to a rendezvous site, which was west of the hill where we had spent the previous night. At the site, we joined up with the battalion headquarters group and then moved west to set in for the night.

As predicted, we had a new battalion commander. Rich Muler came back from a meeting at the battalion CP with the news. He said, "Colonel Brady is gone. He's been replaced by a Lieutenant Colonel Turner. I don't know anything about him, but he seems squared away."

Where the hell are we

12

THE FIGHT GOES ON WITH MORE TRAGEDY

WE ESTABLISHED A PERIMETER AROUND a fairly large village in the middle of where the action had been occurring since Operation Swift began. Rich told us we would be patrolling the area, trying to reestablish contact with the NVA. Battalion wanted Lima Company to send out a platoon-size ambush about six hundred meters south of the perimeter. Rich chose Third Platoon, which was all right with me. I didn't want to spend the night isolated from the rest of the company, waiting to be overrun by a battalion of NVA.

After our company meeting, we set about establishing the perimeter. There was a tree line surrounding the village, and we pretty much followed it as we positioned the fighting holes. There was a slight problem in the sector of the perimeter assigned to Second Platoon. The tree line took a ninety-degree turn back toward the village and then another ninety-degree turn heading back along its original course. The tree line essentially made a zigzag right in the middle of Second Platoon's lines. This left me with a problem of where to place my fighting holes. I put one of the fighting positions in the level field in front of the tree line, which straightened out the zigzag. The problem was that the fighting position was isolated in the field with no cover for anyone trying to approach the hole from inside the perimeter. The advantage was I needed fewer fighting holes to cover my area of the perimeter because we eliminated the zigzag. I decided to stay with my plan, because I was short of men, and Second Platoon's lines were already spread thin. This decision would have tragic consequences.

The next day, Rich called a meeting of the Lima Company platoon commanders and assigned patrol routes. Because of the previous enemy contacts, we were running platoon-size patrols around the perimeter. Second Platoon was assigned the area east of the perimeter. Battalion wanted us to go out two klicks, sweep parallel to the perimeter for a couple of klicks, and then return to the perimeter. Rich described our mission as an attempt to reestablish contact with the enemy. I knew better than that; we were being used as bait for the NVA. Sending a platoon-size patrol out was no different from dangling a piece of cheese in front of a hungry rat. If the NVA could isolate the platoon, the carnage would begin anew. Since Rich didn't take a vote as to whether or not we should send out the patrols, I resigned myself to the fact that Second Platoon was going to be used to try to lure the NVA into another battle.

The next morning, Second Platoon set out at 0600 hours to find the NVA. We passed Third Platoon as they were returning from their ambush. Fortunately, everything went well, but they looked like they had put in a long night. I asked Sergeant Wood how it went, and he said it had gotten pretty hairy out there.

"We kept hearing movement, but it was nothing we could identify or pinpoint. I think Charlie is still out there, and I damn sure don't want to spend another night like that one."

I had no voice in the decision to send Third Platoon on the ambush or Second Platoon out on this patrol. Fortunately, I could control the actions of Second Platoon once we left the perimeter, and I was determined we would not walk into an ambush. I chose a route that kept us as far away as possible from ground cover that could conceal a large enemy force. I was fortunate to be assigned a sector that consisted primarily of rice paddies and small villages. Although

Battalion wanted us to go out two klicks, we probably didn't make it that far; it was more like 1,500 meters. In addition, we took our time, spending lots of time in areas providing cover and dashing across open areas where we would be exposed to enemy fire.

I was most concerned about the size of Second Platoon. We were down to two squads, which was less than a full platoon. Getting surrounded by the NVA a thousand meters from the company perimeter meant annihilation. I didn't care how much Battalion wanted to reestablish contact with the NVA; I wasn't going to sacrifice the lives of the men of Second Platoon so we could increase the enemy body count in Operation Swift.

Although we passed through several villages, most of them were deserted. In addition, we didn't see farmers out working their fields, which was always a bad sign. There was no doubt we were being watched by the NVA, who were waiting for us to make a mistake. Make the wrong turn and we would be standing in the middle of a battalion-size ambush.

We finally came upon an isolated hooch occupied by a Vietnamese family. We tried to interrogate them using our limited Vietnamese language skills. Despite the battles being waged in the surrounding area, they assured us they hadn't seen the NVA and were unaware of where they might be. After leaving the family, we started to swing back toward the company perimeter. We were supposed to sweep parallel to the perimeter, but I didn't like this idea in that it would have placed a small hill between us and the rest of the company—an ideal location for an NVA ambush.

As we moved back toward the company CP, we began traveling along a ridgeline, which was an ideal route for Second Platoon. We could see for several hundred meters on our right flank, and if taken under attack from our left flank, we could drop below the ridgeline for protection. It was obvious the NVA liked this ridgeline, as well. It was laced with bunkers that had been recently camouflaged. There were also signs of recent excavation around the bunkers, which led me to believe the NVA had intended to use the ridgeline in as a defensive position. We also came across an antiaircraft position that had been recently camouflaged, which further convinced me we were in prime NVA country.

In examining the NVA positions, it became apparent why they liked the ridgeline and why they were so successful in battling the American forces. The bunkers were well concealed and offered mutually supporting fields of fire. From the ridgeline, they could wreak havoc on enemy forces approaching them across the open terrain; when things got too hot for them, there were convenient escape routes that they could use to melt back into the hills. This was the ideal ambush site, and pity the poor marines who walked into this fortress while the NVA were waiting. I radioed the location of the bunker complex back to Lima Six, and they assured me they would take appropriate action.

After leaving the bunkers, we continued on down the ridgeline, encountering various signs of recent NVA occupation. We stopped frequently, visually checking the route ahead of us, making sure we weren't walking into a potential ambush site. Because of the frequent stops, the patrol lasted several hours. As we approached the company perimeter, we came upon a teenage boy dressed only in a pair of underpants. He was obviously watching our perimeter, and we immediately took him in custody. After trying to interrogate him, we concluded he was mentally retarded and let him go.

I reported the results of our patrol to Rich Muler, explaining we were unable to generate any enemy contact despite our best effort. He was interested in the bunker complex, and he decided to send out Third Platoon with a group of engineers to destroy the bunkers. With our patrolling done, I had the rest of the day off to catch up on my sleep.

Shortly after 1500 hours, a large battle broke out to the north of our perimeter. We could hear the small-arms fire as well as the artillery and air strikes. The battle raged on for a couple of hours, and I went to the battalion CP to see what I could find out. The new battalion commander was monitoring the radios and giving orders to whomever was on the other end of the line. I asked the battalion sergeant major what was going on, and he said Hotel Company, Second Battalion, Fifth Marines had made contact with the NVA and were locked up with them about four klicks to the north.

Upon leaving the battalion CP, I came across the eighty-one-millimeter mortar section, which was firing in support of Hotel Company. They were dropping round after round through their mortar tubes, and as a result, the mortars were sinking down into the muddy ground. By the time I left, you could barely see the top of the mortar tubes sticking out of the ground. I had never before witnessed this phenomenon and wondered how they could still aim the mortars, given the fact that 90 percent of the mortar tube was below the ground. After the firing stopped, I returned to the mortar site, and the crews were trying to dig the mortars out and move them to a location were the ground was a little firmer.

I returned to Lima Company's CP just as Third Platoon was returning from its patrol. They had in tow the crazy teenager whom we had encountered earlier in the day. Sergeant Wood told us they caught him spying on the perimeter, and I added we had observed him doing the same thing that morning. Rich Muler instructed Third Platoon to take him over to the S2 and let them decide what to do with him.

Rich then dropped a small bomb when he informed me Second Platoon should get ready to move out for the night. Battalion wanted Lima Company to send a platoon to occupy Mike Company's position, which was some four hundred meters to our northeast on a rocky outcropping. Mike Company would be moving to set up a perimeter near the bunker complex that we had discovered earlier that morning. We would move over to their vacated position as soon as they left.

I really didn't like this assignment in that Second Platoon was down to two squads. Trying to occupy a company-size perimeter with less than three dozen men was going to be a difficult task. In addition, the NVA would like nothing more than to cut off Second

Platoon from the rest of the battalion and grind us into hamburger. Since Third Platoon had been out on the ambush the previous night, it did little good to complain. I asked Rich what time he wanted us to move out, and he replied, "Mike Company is leaving in an hour. They have an undetonated 750-pound bomb in the perimeter, which they have rigged to explode after they leave. As soon as the bomb goes off, you can move over to their position. In the meantime, you need to coordinate with Sergeant Wood to place his men in Second Platoon's position along the perimeter."

After telling Sergeant Green and the two squad leaders the bad news, I got with Sergeant Wood, and we walked Second Platoon's lines. I pointed out Second Platoon's fighting positions and directed Sergeant Wood's attention to the zigzag in the tree line and the isolated foxhole out in front of the tree line. I said, "Last night when I was checking the lines, I really didn't like walking out to that position. It is sticking out there like a sore thumb."

"Since I have more men than Second Platoon, I'm going to eliminate that foxhole and set up along the tree line instead," replied Sergeant Hall. I agreed with his decision, and after walking the rest of the lines with him, I returned to Second Platoon's CP, which was directly behind the zigzag in the tree line, to check on the platoon's progress. Everyone was getting saddled up and ready to move out. We walked over to the north edge of the perimeter, and I could observe the forward elements of Mike Company moving off the rocky hill.

Sergeant Green was standing next to me and said, "Lieutenant, I really don't like this. Our ass will really be hanging out when we get over to that hill. The worst part is we will be walking over there while it is still light, and Charlie can see just how many of us there really are. If he wants to take us out, we won't have enough men to stop him."

I assured Sergeant Green I was aware of the problem, but there wasn't anything I could do about it. "Third Platoon was out on ambush all last night, and Lieutenant Muler couldn't ask them to go out again. It's just our turn, and we will have to make the best of it. As soon as we get over there, I will register artillery targets around the perimeter, and you make sure that the men get dug in as quickly as possible."

By now, the rear element of Mike Company was exiting the hill, and it looked like an army of ants was attacking the vacated outcropping. The local villagers were swarming over the area scavenging whatever the troops from Mike Company left behind. Primarily, they were looking for cans of unused C rations and cigarettes but would certainly latch on to any munitions carelessly discarded by the marines. We waited for the bomb to detonate and speculated about what would happen to the villagers once it went off. Mike Company had obviously used a delayed fuse on the bomb, and we expected it to go off shortly after they exited the area. Such was not the case. We waited and then waited some more, and nothing happened. I became concerned and started to conclude that the villagers may have disconnected the denoting device from the bomb. Finally, after twenty minutes of waiting, the bomb exploded, followed by a mass exodus from the hill by the villagers. They were running full tilt away from the explosion, and the troops of Second Platoon found this hilarious.

After the bomb exploded, Second Platoon headed out to meet their fate on the isolated hill in the middle of the Que Son Valley. I was convinced we were walking into a death trap and we would spend the night fighting for our lives. I moved the troops as quickly as possible in that the sun was going down, and we needed as much time as possible to get set in for the night.

When we arrived at the hill, the conditions were worse than I had thought. The hill was small enough to allow Mike Company to set up around the base of it but too large to allow Second Platoon to do the same. We were forced to set our perimeter around the top of the hill. The problem was the hill was nothing but a mass of rock, with some of the boulders standing several feet tall. The troops could not scrape anything resembling fighting holes out of the hardpan of the hillside.

I discussed the problem with Sergeant Green, and we came up with what we thought would be the best solution under the circumstances. We formed a crude perimeter around the top of the hill and then had each fire team select a sheltered position among the huge boulders that dotted the area. If we were attacked, the men were not to leave their position under any circumstances. We would shoot at anything that moved on the hill. Normally, you wanted your men to be aggressive when they came under attack, and staying in a hole in the rocks was contrary to that theory, but I could not come up with a better alternative. We were finally set in as it started getting dark, and I feared it was going to be a long night for Second Platoon.

I was awakened at midnight by the sound of explosions and small-arms fire. I thought we were under attack but soon realized the firing was coming from the battalion perimeter that we had left earlier in the evening. The fighting was furious and lasted for several minutes. We could see explosions and small-arms fire, most of which was being fired on the south side of the perimeter. I was monitoring the radio and could hear Lima Six calling for a medevac, which meant they had taken casualties. After the fighting stopped, I expected to see a chopper come into the battalion perimeter, but when none showed up, I went out and checked the lines. Everyone was awake and wanted to know what was going on back at the Lima Company CP. I told them I didn't know, and they needed to stay alert, because we might be next. With that, I went back to sleep, expecting the worse.

When I next awoke, it was just starting to get light. We had made it through another night, and the troops were starting to go about fixing their breakfast of C rations. I called Lima Six, and they told me to hold my position until a medevac chopper came into their perimeter for a pickup, and then we were free to return. I passed the word we would be moving out shortly. As soon as the medevac made its run, we saddled up and headed back to the perimeter.

When we arrived at the Lima Company CP, everyone was in a somber mood. I discovered Third Platoon had three KIAs, including Sergeant Wood, the acting platoon commander. I was flabbergasted. The fighting lasted for less than fifteen minutes, and I couldn't understand how we could have taken that many casualties in such a short period of time. I approached Sergeant Schwartz and asked him what the hell happened. He explained, "I can't figure it out. Somehow, a gook slipped into our lines and threw a hand grenade into the fighting hole Sergeant Wood was sleeping in, killing him and his radio operator. We had mass confusion for several minutes. Three NVA were in the foxhole that you guys had dug out in front of the tree line, and we had a hell of a time getting them out of there. They killed another marine from Third Platoon. We finally killed them, along with the gook that got Sergeant Wood."

I examined the bodies of the dead NVA. Three of them were lying beside the fighting position that we had dug to straighten out the zigzag in the tree line. The fourth one was lying next to a trench inside the perimeter. Obviously, Third Platoon had not filled in the fighting hole they abandoned, and the NVA used it to their advantage. I talked to the machine gun crew that was set up at one of the corners of the zigzag and asked them what happened. The machine gunner said, "I don't know how the hell them fuckers were able to get so close to our perimeter. The first thing I know, a grenade goes off, and the shit hits the fan. I could see the firing coming from the foxhole out in the field, but I couldn't figure out who was doing the firing. We were finally able to throw some grenades in the hole and get those motherfuckers. I don't know who got the gook inside the perimeter."

I returned to the company CP, and Rich was really torn up. Sergeant Wood had been his platoon sergeant since he took over Third Platoon several months prior, and they were really close. The loss was heartbreaking to him and especially to Third Platoon. Rich moved Staff Sergeant Williamson, Lee Gounds's platoon sergeant, from First Platoon over to Third Platoon to take Sergeant Wood's place. Sergeant Williamson was very capable and would do an excellent job with Third Platoon, but it was always disruptive when a platoon suddenly lost its leader.

In my mind, I attempted to reconstruct what happened the previous night. By rights, Second Platoon should have been wiped out in their precarious position on the rocky hilltop. Instead, Sergeant Wood and two other marines were killed in what was a secure position inside the battalion perimeter. Sergeant Wood was sleeping in the same foxhole I would have been in if Second Platoon had not been moved off the perimeter. Those of us who had their asses hanging out woke up safe and sound while the platoon who was given the night off took three KIAs. It didn't make any sense, and they wondered why we became so fatalistic out there in the bush. When your number came up, you were gone.

It was also puzzling how the NVA got so close to the perimeter without being detected. It is possible they were on a suicide mission, crawling across the open rice paddies up to our lines and into our perimeter. I find this theory hard to accept. It wasn't like the NVA to do something that desperate. They didn't have much to gain and were damn lucky they didn't get detected sooner. A more likely explanation is that the four NVA mistakenly blundered into the perimeter without being detected. They may have been lost or were new replacements trying to find their assigned unit. That still leaves the question of why someone didn't see them approaching the perimeter. People could have been asleep or just not paying attention. We will never know the truth, but three marines were dead.

Later that morning, we got more bad news. Lieutenant Norman was killed in the firefight the day before between the NVA and Hotel Two-Five. Apparently, his platoon sergeant was shot and lying out in the middle of a rice paddy. Lieutenant Norman went to his rescue and was killed by an enemy bullet. For all his faults, Lieutenant Norman died a hero, sacrificing his life in an attempt to save a fellow marine. The previous three days had been disastrous for Lima Company and the marines on Operation Swift. Payback was a motherfucker, and we were getting paid back big-time.

Shortly, we had another company meeting, and Rich informed us that Battalion requested we send out two platoon-size patrols, one to the north and one to the south. Once again, we were to attempt to reestablish contact with the enemy, and once again, I interpreted this to mean we were going to be used as bait. Rich assigned Second Platoon to the southern patrol, and I began platting a patrol route on my map. My goal was not to find a route that would reestablish contact with the enemy but rather one that would prevent annihilation of Second Platoon. I tried to avoid any obvious ambush sites and picked a course that would allow us an escape path if we made contact with the NVA. The goal of the Marine Corps may have been to continue the carnage of Operation Swift, but my goal was to get what was left of Second Platoon the hell out of the Que Son Valley in one piece.

At 1300 hours, we saddled up and headed south along our designated patrol route. We continually came across signs of recent NVA activity, including another base camp that had been recently abandoned. We also discovered several unexploded bombs that we detonated using plastic explosives, which we carried for just such purpose. As the patrol progressed, we were moving farther away from the battalion perimeter and thus becoming more vulnerable to enemy attack and isolation from our base camp. Sergeant Presno radioed that the forward elements of First Squad spotted three NVA running into a tree line four hundred meters to our southwest. I called in a Blackcoat to fly over the area to see if he could spot anything. He reported a negative result, and I continued along our designated route. I failed report the sighting to Lima Six, because they would report it to Battalion, who would want us to check it out. I did not want to be lured into an ambush, especially this far from the battalion perimeter. We continued on with the patrol, arriving back at the perimeter at 1700 hours.

I reported to the Lima Company CP and once again discovered things in a state of turmoil. It seemed some villagers inside of our perimeter got roughed up pretty good, allegedly by some of the members of Third Platoon. There were three or four papa-sans with knots on their head being administered to by a navy corpsman, and Sergeant Schwartz was questioning a group of marines from Third Platoon. This was none of my business, but I stuck around to see what would develop. The villagers had obviously been beaten, probably in retaliation for the casualties taken by Third Platoon the night before. It was a senseless act of violence on the part of whoever mistreated the villagers; it was also an attempt to vent frustrations by eighteen- and nineteen-year-old marines in the only way they knew how. It was finally decided the villagers couldn't or wouldn't identify their attackers, and the matter was dropped. Shortly thereafter, there was a lecture from Lieutenant Muler to Third Platoon about the serious nature of what had been done, and if the offenders were ever discovered, they would be dealt with harshly.

Once again, the problems with this war manifested themselves through the retribution taken against the helpless villagers. Sure, the villagers probably fed the NVA over the last several months, and none of them stepped forward to show us where the NVA were hiding, but they were still unwilling participants in this war. The peasants could no more stand up to the NVA than they could to the marines. They tended their crops and tried to provide for their families. They did not want to feed the NVA, and they did not want to house the marines now occupying their villages. For them, life went on, innocent victims of a war that was not of their making.

As the resupply choppers came in for their evening run, we were introduced to a new phenomenon: news reporters. The word must have gotten out regarding the number of casualties being taken on Operation Swift, and the news media desired firsthand coverage. They were decked out in jungle fatigues, cameras, and flak jackets. The flak jackets caused them to stand out from the marines, who had long ago abandoned such protective devices as being too cumbersome. That night, Second Platoon occupied the perimeter vacated by First Platoon, who would run an ambush east of the perimeter.

The next morning, we got the word to saddle up and move out. The entire battalion was going to move east. I had Second Platoon ready to go by 0600, and Rich informed me we would be walking point, with First and Third Platoon behind us in a wedge formation. He gave us a general route of march and said we would be joined by the battalion headquarters group, including Colonel Turner, the new battalion commander. I had seen him on several occasions since he had taken over for Colonel Brady, but he never stopped to talk to anyone. Mostly, he just walked around, followed by the battalion sergeant major.

At 0630, we got the word to move out. I put my two squads abreast, and we began moving east. After a couple of hundred meters, we were told to hold our position. Mike Company was going to join up with our contingent, and it would be some time before they reached our position. We took off our packs and settled in to wait for someone to make up his mind as to what the hell we were going to do. All the while, the news reporters were running about taking pictures of pretty much nothing. Every time we turned around, they had cameras in our faces or were asking questions about the operation.

After about an hour, Colonel Turner came striding up with the battalion sergeant major in tow. I jumped to my feet but was ignored. He hurried past me to our forward position and started walking out past our position in search of God knows what. I yelled at Sergeant Presno to saddle up First Squad, and I started running after our fearless leader, who by now was a quarter of the way across a small rice paddy, headed toward the far tree line. In my mind, I couldn't figure out what the hell he was doing. One NVA sniper in the tree line, and he was dead meat. I caught up with him in the middle of the rice paddy, and when he turned around to face me, all he could see was First Squad running after him at full tilt.

I said, "Colonel, you had better let us go with you. There's no telling what's out there."

He looked at me somewhat perplexed and said, "I'm just doing a little reconnoitering of the terrain out in front of us."

"We'll follow you, just in case," I replied.

I could see a look of relief come over the face of the sergeant major whose eyes were as big as saucers when I first came upon him and the colonel.

The colonel said, "All right. Come along," and he stepped out toward the tree line.

I tried to get first squad in some sort of tactical formation as they were running up to our position, but this was complicated by the fact that the colonel was almost to the tree line by the time all of First Squad was assembled in the rice paddy. We spent the next thirty minutes following the colonel as he conducted his inspection of the terrain. I still had no idea what he was looking for. All the tree lines in the area look pretty much the same—if you'd seen one of them, you'd seen them all. The colonel evidently satisfied himself, because we returned to Second Platoon's position, at which time he strode off toward the battalion CP without a "Thank you" or "Kiss my ass."

Finally, we got word to move out and once again started working our way to the east. A new problem immediately arose. Instead of having two squads out in front of me, I now had three. The extra squad consisted of the news media that had latched on to Operation Swift. In their eagerness to get a story, they decided the best place to be was in the middle of the lead platoon. I immediately called a halt and informed the reporters that they had to stay behind me if they were going to accompany Second Platoon. They looked at me as if I were crazy. One of them informed me they were not part of the military, did not take orders from me, and could go anywhere they damn well pleased. I was somewhat taken aback by this reply. Surely, the reporter realized it wasn't wise to talk like that to someone who was carrying an M16 rifle. Being an officer and a gentleman, I did not wish to abuse the news media, so I told Private Driscol, "Get these motherfuckers out of here."

Driscol was more than happy to oblige, and he walked up to the reporter who had mouthed off and stuck his rifle in the startled newsman's face. He said, "The lieutenant wants you all to move to the rear, and he wants you to do it right now."

Private Driscol was able to command substantially more respect than I, and the press corps beat a hasty retreat toward the rear of the column. Having resolved our problems with the press, Second

Platoon once again started sweeping east. We were making good progress when once again the column was halted. Second Platoon dropped their packs, waiting for someone to make up his mind as to when and where we were going. We really had no complaints about the stop-and-go tactics being employed by Battalion. It beat the shit out of humping all day in the miserable heat.

As we were waiting for something to happen, the battalion S5 officer, Captain Watson, walked up to our position, followed by several of the news reporters who had recently abandoned Second Platoon at the urging of Private Driscol. The captain approached me and said in a voice loud enough to be heard by the reporters, "I've received a report that you and your men threatened some of the reporters."

"Sir, I don't know what you're talking about," I replied, trying to stall for enough time to come up with an excuse for what we did.

"They've told me that one of your men pointed a rifle at them and demanded that they move to the rear."

"No, sir. I didn't see anyone point a rifle. I told the reporters they had to stay behind Second Platoon. If we were to engage Charlie, half of them would be shot by friendly fire. I can't have them out in front of my men interfering with our movement and endangering their lives."

Captain Watson turned around and returned to the reporters huddled in a group a short distance away. After a brief discussion, he returned and said, "Lieutenant, we don't need to piss these guys off. Can't we reach a compromise with them?"

"Captain, I don't give a fuck where they go or what they do. I just don't want them out on point where they're in our way. I have enough trouble keeping track of where my men are without having these assholes walking around in front of us."

We finally compromised by agreeing the press corps would stay behind my headquarters group. It was time to move out, and we again started heading along our original route. As the platoon got into position, I intentionally fell back so my headquarters group was trailing Second Platoon even farther. This kept the reporters well behind the rest of the platoon. I would have liked to think I did this for tactical reasons, but mostly I did it out of spite.

By 1600 hours, we had made no contact with the enemy and were looking for a place to set in for the night. Rich Muler directed me to a small hill to our southeast as a likely location to set up a perimeter. We moved in that direction and shortly reached the hill. As the forward elements of Second Platoon reached the top of the hill, someone yelled, "Freeze!" I immediately dropped to the ground, thinking somebody had spotted enemy movement.

Sergeant Presno yelled out, "The hill is covered with butterfly bombs!"

I looked around and discovered I was standing almost on top of one of the bombs. A butterfly bomb is an explosive device dropped from an aircraft. It gets its name from a set of wings attached to the small bomb that cause it to land gently on the ground. The bomb itself is the size of a hand grenade and does not detonate when it hits the ground. Instead, it is designed to go off when someone steps on it. At that moment, I was standing near one of one of them, and as I looked around, they were scattered everywhere on the hillside. The first thing I did was move away from the one I was standing close to, expecting it to go off at any second. Needless to say, I was scared shitless.

I contacted Lima Six and informed them of our problem and then instructed Second Platoon to start backing off the hill as carefully as possible. Since none of the bombs exploded, I assumed they had a short life span and were designed to defuse themselves after a set period of time. I had no way of knowing this for sure, and we spent a scary twenty minutes trying to get off the hill. Lima Six selected another hill a short distance away, and we headed in that direction to set in for the night.

We reached the adjacent hill and were preparing the perimeter for the night when a huge firefight broke out some ten klicks to our northwest. Although the battle was being waged several miles away, we had a ringside seat perched on the hilltop. We stopped what we were doing and watched the battle develop. Initially, the fighting was limited to small-arms fire with an occasional blast from mortar rounds being fired by both sides. Eventually, a Blackcoat showed up and called in artillery rounds on the enemy lines. This was followed by fixed-wing aircraft, which began making bombing runs around 1730 hours. The NVA were back to their old tricks. They had antiaircraft guns set up, and green tracers were following the jets as they dropped their bombs on the enemy positions. The fighting was every bit as furious as that which we observed when we were humping into the Que Son Valley. So much for my hope that the NVA had left the valley.

Word filtered down that the battle was being fought by an ARVN ranger battalion who had been hit just as they were setting in for the night. The fighting was taking place just south of Route 534S in the area where we entered the fray several days prior. Worse yet, we were told to get ready to move out and that we were going to the aid of the embattled battalion. I couldn't imagine worse news. The sun was starting to set, and it was getting dark. It looked like we were in for a long night.

The platoon commanders were summoned to the CP set up by Battalion. When I arrived, the company commander for Mike Company and his platoon commanders were already at the CP. Colonel Watson informed us we were going to be picked up by helicopters and airlifted to the ensuing battle. I returned to Second Platoon to brief them on the plan and get them ready to move out toward the LZ to be picked up by the choppers. Instead of the logical choice of placing the LZ on the top of the hill, someone decided to put it at the base of the hill in a small rice paddy bordering our perimeter.

We moved over to the LZ and lined up in single file, waiting our turn to board the incoming helicopters. By now, it was completely dark, and it became apparent getting us on the helicopters was not going to be an easy task. The LZ was too small, and it was so dark you couldn't see your hand in front of your face. To add to our problems, some of the elements of Mike Company were coming to the LZ from the opposite side of the hill. No one alerted Lima Company of this fact, and a brief firefight broke out between the two units, wounding two marines. It was now apparent our evacuation by helicopter wasn't going to work. As soon as we got the two marines medevaced, it was decided we would abandon the airlift and hump to Hill 35 instead. Hill 35 was a secure firebase several klicks away.

Mike Company took the lead and started moving southeast. The battalion headquarters group was behind Mike Company, followed by Lima Company. Second Platoon was the last platoon in line and was providing rear security for the column, which wasn't so bad, because we were a lot less likely to get ambushed at the rear of the column than in the front. Unbeknownst to us, being Tail-End Charlie was going to result in a long and exhausting night.

The marines that entered the firebase at Hill 35 were the most bedraggled lot imaginable. We had been in the bush for several days, and we were caked with mud and filth. The jungle fatigues of some of the men were coming apart, and their asses were literally hanging out. I was included in this group.

Accompanying Second Platoon's headquarters group was a Private First Class Miller, who had joined us within the previous couple of days. He had been originally assigned to Second Platoon several months prior, but I requested he be transferred to the company supply unit, because he was just not cut out to be a grunt. He was a nice kid but was extremely nervous and convinced he would be blown away if he stayed in the field. After several requests, I finally convinced Sergeant Schwartz he would be better off in the rear, guarding the company's gear.

Because of the casualties taken by Second Platoon, he had been reassigned to us to try to bolster our ranks. I made him my assistant radioman so I could keep an eye on him and hopefully keep him out of harm's way.

After entering the perimeter of the firebase, we passed a group of army personnel. They were intently observing us, and when they saw us struggling to carry the injured marine from Mike Company, one of them said, "I don't think I could have done that."

Private First Class Miller calmly looked at them and said, "You could have if you were a marine."

I was too tired to react on the outside, but on the inside, I was busting a gut. The biggest shit bird in the platoon came up with one of the all-time great lines. After taking several steps, I turned to Miller and said, "I guess you told his sorry ass."

We followed the rest of the column over to the LZ, which was in the middle of the perimeter to await further orders. I sought out Rich Muler to find out what we would be doing next. It was obvious he was still upset with me about what happened the previous night, and I avoided bringing up the subject of Second Platoon having to carry the injured marine well over half the distance of the march. Rich informed the platoon commanders to get everyone fed, and at 0800 hours, the choppers would be there to lift us back into the Que Son Valley as a relief force for the ARVNs engaging the NVA. I returned to Second Platoon to get them ready for the airlift. No one offered us a hot meal, so we resorted to our old standby—a C ration meal cooked over a heat tab.

As Second Platoon rested next to the LZ eating their C rations and getting ready to be airlifted back into the battle, a somber mood set in. The platoon was on the verge of exhaustion. The hump into this unknown base camp had sapped its strength, and the night without sleep had dulled its senses.

Despite their fatigued condition, they were more concerned about the events that were about to unfold than their physical and mental states. The one thing the marines of Second Platoon hated the most was to be airlifted into a potentially hot LZ. It was not that the marines were concerned about the prospect of employing helicopters to increase their mobility; it was the way the Marine Corps went about it. The Marine Corps' approach to the air mobile concept was similar to a child's approach to driving a car. They had observed others do it, but they had neither the experience nor equipment to pull it off. The Marine Corps still had the frontal-assault mentality: what worked on the beaches of the South Pacific would damn sure work in South Vietnam.

The next morning, everyone was in a lot better shape than the day before. We even got some good news. Operation Swift was officially declared over, and we would be airlifted back to Hill 63 later in the day.

The official version of Operation Swift would be written at a later date. The casualties suffered by the marines came to 138 killed and 398 wounded. At the same time, we were credited with inflicting 540 KIAs on the enemy.

I later read the after-action report on the operation, and it was my opinion the official version of Operation Swift was suspect. In order to create the illusion that the Americans were winning the war, the military had to leave the impression we won every major battle in which we engaged the NVA. Unfortunately, we could not use the old standby of how much enemy territory we captured, so we were left with body count as the barometer by which success was measured. If we killed more NVA than they did Americans, then the operation was deemed a success by the military and hopefully in the eyes of the American people. It would simply not be acceptable to have more American casualties than NVA casualties.

It was also unfortunate for the American fighting man—as well as the American people—that the enemy body count could not be verified with any kind of certainty. No military commander was going to allow a low enemy body count go into the record. If we had two confirmed enemy kills, that easily became four and then eight when the final figures were tallied. As a result, we had no verifiable method to gauge the success of the American forces.

From my perspective, Operation Swift was at best a draw for the marines, and in reality, I think we got our asses kicked. Neither I nor anyone else could determine the number of casualties received by the NVA as a result of air and artillery strikes. Surely the NVA took substantial casualties from these sources, but there was no way to verify the numbers. From what I observed on the ground, there were a lot more dead and wounded marines than there were NVA casualties. Tactically, the NVA had us on the run during the entire operation. Most of the time, we were in a defensive posture, reacting to the attacks of the NVA, fighting on terrain chosen by them under conditions selected by them. To say Operation Swift was a victory for the marines was a real stretch. Sure, we were left standing on the battlefield, and arguably, we had driven the enemy from its lair. In reality, the enemy had chosen to withdraw to fight again another day. The Marine Corps could ill afford many more "victories" like that.

Another yardstick by which to measure the success of the marines in Operation Swift was the use of CS gas to force the NVA to disengage from the pitched battles. If the mission of the infantry was to close with and destroy the enemy, then why were we using CS gas to get the NVA off our backs? It would appear the NVA were closing with and attempting to destroy us. We were employing CS gas as a defensive measure to force the NVA to disengage from the fight. This certainly is contrary to everything I was taught at the Basic School and did not portray the marines as the aggressor.

In any event, we were headed back to Hill 63, and as far as I was concerned, the NVA could have that piece of real estate. If I never saw the Que Son Valley again, it would be too soon.

We once again moved north across Route 534S and then turned west toward the district headquarters at Que Son. After traveling several klicks, it was decided we had put enough distance between us and the NVA, and an LZ was set up. Shortly, three CH-53 helicopters came to ferry us to Hill 63. We were back at our home base by 1100 hours for some well-deserved rest. The rest was well deserved; it just wasn't going to happen.

13

NO DAY ON THE BEACH WHILE ON THE GO NOI ISLANDS

RICH CAME BACK FROM BATTALION with the bad news. One of the reasons Operation Swift ended so quickly was that Third Battalion was scheduled to begin another operation the next night. It was a joint operation with the First Marine Regiment, designed to attack another enemy hot spot known as the Go Noi Islands. The term *islands* is a misnomer, as the area in question consisted primarily of coastal plain bordered on the north by the Thu Bon River and on the south by the Than Quat River, which flowed from west to east, dumping into the Song Ly north of Hill 63. The "islands" were also bordered on the east by Highway 1 and on the west by the abandoned railroad right-of-way. The entire area consisted of about ten square miles and was being used by the VC as a safe haven from enemy attack as well as a major food source. The "islands" were twenty miles south of Da Nang, lying just south of the TAOR of the First Marine Regiment and just north of Third Battalion's TAOR at Hill 63. We were about to become well acquainted with what had been for years an enemy sanctuary.

The plan of battle was relatively simple. The First Marines would sweep east from the railroad right-of-way toward Highway 1. Units from the Fifth Marines would block their southern flanks along the banks of the Than Quat while ARVN units blocked the northern flank along the Thu Bon. Two companies from First Battalion, Fifth Marines would be waiting along Highway 1 if the VC attempted to escape in that direction. It sounded like a walk in the park. We would be sitting in a blocking position, fighting the VC instead of the NVA. The only ballbuster should be the all-night hump into the blocking position. Of course, I was wrong in my prediction.

As we were picking our way toward the Than Quat, the sun was beginning to rise. All of a sudden, gunshots rang out at the front of the column. Word came back that Third Platoon had surprised three VC suspects on the riverbank and had killed all three of them as they attempted to escape across the river. We also discovered we were two hundred meters east of our assigned blocking position, and we began moving west along the riverbank. We moved through head-high elephant grass and large bamboo thickets until we finally reached our assigned location. By 0600 hours, we were in position just as the operation kicked off.

We established a company-size perimeter on the southern bank of the Than Quat. The battalion headquarters group, along with Colonel Turner, was with us, so the perimeter was a little larger than usual. The only problem we faced was the elephant grass that surrounded us. We had a clear view to the north across the Than Quat, but the rest of the perimeter was blinded by the six-foot-high grass. We tried to cut fields of fire, but it was a futile task. There was simply too much grass to cut, and we could barely see ten feet in front of the perimeter on our south side. After digging in, we had hoped we would get some rest during the remainder of the day. Unfortunately, Battalion had other ideas.

Lima Company was instructed to run patrols both east and west of our perimeter along the bank of the Than Quat to try to catch anyone attempting to cross the river. We could track the progress of the First Marines across the river as they swept east from the railroad right-of-way by the sound of their gunfire as they engaged the VC. They were making repeated contact as they swept toward Highway

1. They had a Blackcoat on station, and he was calling in repeated air strikes on Charlie's positions as the day progressed. Because of the heat and patrolling, Second Platoon got little rest during the day. At 1500 hours, we got one more ill-conceived order.

Lima Company, along with the battalion headquarters group, was dug in along a portion of the Than Quat that bowed out to the north. It was an ideal location, because we could observe not only to the north but both east and west up and down the river. Instead of being limited to observing the area of our immediate front, we could see three to four hundred meters of river on either side. Unfortunately, someone higher up must have noticed Lima Company was not on line with the other two companies blocking to our east. The order was passed down that Lima Company should move back south, away from the riverbank some two hundred meters, so all three companies would be in a straight line. This was ludicrous. If we moved away from the riverbank, we would be unable to see anything and therefore would be useless as a blocking force. Apparently, someone pointed this out to the powers that be, because they came down with an order to leave a platoon on the riverbank and move the rest of the company to the south. As a result, only two-thirds of the company would be useless instead of the entire company.

Rich chose First Platoon to stay on the riverbank, and the rest of us picked up and moved to the south. The elephant grass ended after about a hundred meters, and we moved into a small village to set up a perimeter. As predicted, we couldn't see more than twenty meters outside our lines, and we were totally ineffectual as a blocking force. An entire division of NVA could have passed within fifty meters of our present position without being detected. No one asked my opinion about the situation, and we set about digging in for the night.

After giving the platoon their defensive positions, I returned to my CP. I had a new guy, who had showed up the day before, traveling with my headquarters group. I had not had an opportunity to assign him to a squad before we left the night before, and he was tagging along with us until I gave him his assignment. As we were preparing our C rations, he left to fill some canteens. Shortly, we heard an explosion and went running in that direction. We discovered the new guy had tripped a booby trap, and he lay on the ground withering in pain. Doc Blake went to his assistance while I looked around for a location for an LZ to land a medevac. Within thirty minutes, we had him headed to Da Nang and, according to Doc Blake, on his way back to the world. It was an apparent tragedy—here was a guy who had been with us for a little over twenty-four hours and was headed home. On the other hand, maybe he was the lucky one.

Just as it was getting dark, gunfire erupted in the area where we left First Platoon on the riverbank. I grabbed the radio and could hear one of the squad leaders from First Platoon excitedly calling in a situation report to Lee Gounds.

"Lima One, we just walked head-on into a bunch of VC. We're coming back into the perimeter."

Lee responded, "Get back in on the double. We'll hold our fire."

Another squad leader from First Platoon joined in. "Lima One, I've got movement across our left front; I can't see them, but we can damn sure hear them."

"Roger, Lima One-Three. Hold your fire until Second Squad gets back into the perimeter. It might be them that you're hearing. Over."

Seconds later, Lee came back over the radio. "Lima One-Three, I've got Second Squad back in. Are you still hearing the movement? Over."

"Everything's quiet right now. Over."

Lee then informed First Platoon, "Everyone's inside the perimeter. If you detect any movement, you're free to blast away."

He then called Lima Six. "Lima Six, this is Lima One. I've got a casualty. Over."

Rich Muler responded, "Lima One, this is Six. Do you need a medevac? Over."

"Negative, Lima Six. We've got a man down with a twisted knee. He should be all right until morning. Right now, he's in a lot of pain."

Shortly, rifle fire once again broke out near the riverbank. Lee Gounds came back on the radio. "Lima Six, this is Lima One. We're getting a lot of movement down here. They just set off a trip flare outside our perimeter. I think they're all around us. Over."

"Roger, Lima One. I copy that you have VC all around you. I'll see if I can get you some help. Over."

By this time, I had made my way over to the company CP, where Rich was talking to Battalion on the radio. After a few minutes, he said to me, "Battalion said they are trying to bring in a 'basketball' for First Platoon."

"What the fuck is a 'basketball'?" I replied.

"I'm not sure. It's some kind of Air Force gunship team. Let's go over to the battalion CP to find out what's going on."

Rich and I walked over to the battalion CP, and the battalion air liaison officer was on the radio talking to someone about our situation. After several minutes, he told everyone a basketball was on its way. I once again asked what a basketball was and was told it consisted of four Huey gunships along with a C-47 fixed-wing aircraft, which was used to drop flares to light up the night sky.

We could still hear rifle fire coming from the area of First Platoon, and Rich got on the horn to inform them help was on the way. Rich then told me we may have to go to First Platoon's assistance. I headed back to Second Platoon to brief the squad leaders on the situation and to get the platoon ready to move out if we had to rescue First Platoon. Once again, fatigue was becoming a factor. We did not get a chance to sleep during the day, and we had now been awake for over forty hours. In addition, we'd only had one night's sleep in the previous three days. The troops were beat, and the prospect of organizing a reaction force to go to the aid of First Platoon was not something we looked forward to.

I continued to monitor the company net to find out what was happening with First Platoon. They were still exchanging sporadic fire with the VC, and Charlie appeared to be right outside their perimeter. All of a sudden, the night sky was lit up by a flare dropped from the C-47 attached to the basketball team, followed by Huey gunships passing over our position. The gunships were on Lima

Company's radio net, and I could monitor the exchange between Lee Gounds and the gunships.

The first order of business was the location of the exact position of First Platoon by the gunships. After the gunships pinpointed the location of First Platoon, they started making runs over the enemy positions, firing the miniguns mounted on their skids as well as rockets from the pods attached to both sides of their fuselage. I could hear the Huey pilots informing Rich they could detect movement outside of his perimeter, and they continued to blast away at the VC.

After thirty minutes, one of the pilots came over the radio and asked Rich if any of his men had set off green flares. Rich responded in the negative, and the choppers started strafing an area of the riverbank west of First Platoon's perimeter. Apparently, a group of VC had set off handheld flares trying to convince the gunships there were friendlies in the area. Although we couldn't see the action, it was obvious the gunships were finding plenty of targets. Lee reported the Hueys were taking ground fire from several locations around his perimeter. The battle intensified as the Hueys continued their passes along the riverbank.

We could see the Hueys as they passed over our perimeter, but the battle was being waged near the riverbank, and we were unable to observe the actual firing by the gunships. The Hueys stayed on station for over an hour when they informed First Platoon they were running low on fuel and ammo and had to return to Da Nang. They assured First Platoon they would be back as soon as possible.

After the choppers left, First Platoon once again started taking incoming from outside their perimeter. Further problems developed when Lee Gounds informed Lima Six he was having trouble with the marine who had twisted his knee. Apparently, he was going into shock, and the corpsman was becoming concerned about his welfare. The injured marine had stopped breathing on two occasions and had to be resuscitated. Rich again asked First Platoon if they needed a medevac, and Lee replied they would try to hang on without one.

Thirty minutes later, the gunships returned and once again began firing on the VC surrounding First Platoon. As the night progressed, the situation became even more complicated; one of the Hueys passed over our perimeter with sparks flying from the area of its rotors. I could hear the pilot on the radio reporting he had lost power and was being forced down. He called to First Platoon, "Lima One, this is Basketball One-Four. I am going to put this thing down just east of your perimeter."

Immediately, Lee Gounds replied, "Roger, Basketball One-Four. I've got you marked down about 150 meters to our east. We're coming out to get you. Over."

Lee Gounds informed Lima Six he was taking a squad out to retrieve the helicopter crew. The leader of the basketball team wanted us to move the entire platoon over to the downed helicopter to set up a perimeter and protect it for the night. After several minutes of debate between Battalion and the basketball team, it was decided the crew would be rescued and brought back to First Platoon's position. The helicopter would have to take care of itself.

As I monitored the radio net, I could hear the conversation between Lee Gounds and the downed crew. It was evident the chopper pilot was in a new environment with his gunship on the ground. He was no longer the calm-and-collected commander of a Huey gunship flying over the treetops, dispensing death and destruction. He was now on the ground with us, and from the tone of his voice, he was extremely uncomfortable. He demanded to know when the patrol was going to reach his position and how far away they were. I could also hear indiscriminate gunfire coming from the area of the downed helicopter. The door gunners on the chopper were apparently spraying the area with fire from their M60 machine guns. The machine-gun fire was a threat to the rescue squad from First Platoon, and Lee Gounds tried to reason with the chopper crew.

"Basketball One-Four, we can't come any closer to your position until you stop firing those machine guns. Over."

The pilot answered, "Lima One, we keep hearing movement in the grass. Over."

"Well, just keep on firing. When you get done, we'll come get you," Lee replied.

The firing from the Huey kept up for several minutes, and the pilot came back over the radio. "Lima One, are you about to reach our location? Over."

"Negative, Basketball. We're not moving until you quit firing."

"Okay, Lima One. We'll stop firing. How long will it take you to get here? Over."

Lee Gounds replied, "We can be there in a couple of minutes. We just don't want to get shot when we arrive. Over."

"Roger, Lima One. We'll hold our fire."

Everything was quiet for several minutes, and Lima One finally confirmed they had the helicopter crew back inside their perimeter. The gunships continued to fly over the area, but they were now focusing on the downed helicopter rather than the stranded platoon. They proceeded to make pass after pass over the Huey, spraying everything in sight with machine-gun fire. Two of the gunships stayed on station while the other two returned to Da Nang for fuel and ammunition. The strafing continued for the rest of the night, and it was difficult to get any sleep despite the fact we were dead tired. At first light, the Hueys were still hovering overhead, shooting at anything that resembled an enemy position.

By sunup, Lima Company was moving toward the downed chopper, and thirty minutes later, we had established a perimeter around the helicopter. I was pretty happy about the situation. I assumed the air force would fly in some mechanics to work on the chopper, and we would be there for the rest of the day catching up on our sleep. No such luck. At 0700 hours, a flying crane was approaching our position along with three other Huey Slicks. We now had gunships hovering overhead, Huey Slicks on the ground picking up the stranded crew, as well as an air force squad hooking up a sling to the downed helicopter. Within minutes, everything and everyone were gone. The last time we saw the stranded chopper, it was dangling under the flying crane on its way back to Da Nang.

In the meantime, the war continued. Lima Company was ordered to move west to an area where we could wade across the Than Qiut. We moved back to Route 231 and began heading west. For some reason, there were hundreds of villagers standing along the road watching the progress of Lima Company. Kids were everywhere, begging for food and lining up to have their pictures taken by the marines who had cameras. But for the fact that we were totally exhausted, the mood would have been almost festive. We marched along the road to shouts of "Marines number one, VC number ten!" and "Hey, marine, give me chop-chop!" As we marched west, the skies began to cloud up, and it appeared we were in for another torrential downpour.

We eventually wound up at the river crossing. Second Platoon provided rear security for the column. When we arrived at the riverbank, Rich Muler was huddled with Colonel Turner attempting to come up with a plan of action to cross the river. I took one look at the river and concluded we had our work cut out for us. I don't know why they picked that location to cross the river. The Than Quit looked as deep there as it was where we had set up the blocking position the day before. In addition, the far bank of the river was covered with elephant grass, an ideal location for a VC ambush. Rich had the artillery FO register targets across the river and moved Second Platoon along the riverbank to provide covering fire in case the VC attempted to ambush us as the company waded the river. Despite the precautions, the first elements crossing the river would be dead meat if the VC were waiting on the other side.

When the first group of marines entered the river, I was taken aback by the fact that the river came up to their armpits. They had their rifles and ammunition, along with their packs, held over their heads as they waded the fifty meters across the Than Quat. They were completely helpless in the water, and if they came under attack, their only salvation would be the ability of Second Platoon and the artillery battery to lay down enough firepower to suppress the enemy assault.

The marines reached the far bank without incident and set up a defensive position along the riverbank. After the two platoons from Lima Company along with the battalion headquarters group crossed the river, it was Second Platoon's turn. I was now concerned about us getting ambushed from the rear; if the VC slipped in behind us, we would be sitting ducks out in the river. Luckily, we made it across without incident, and the company started moving north away from the river. The lead element hadn't gone a hundred yards when they started taking heavy rifle fire from several directions. Since Second Platoon was still in the rear, we were in no immediate danger from the attack. We hastily set up a defensive position to cover the company's rear and waited to see what developed. What developed was the sky opened up with a torrential downpour, raining out the firefight between Lima Company and the VC. Word came back that we would be spending the night on the north bank of the Than Quit, and I moved Second Platoon back to the edge of the river to set in for the night.

That was probably the low point of my brief Marine Corps career. We had slept only briefly during the last sixty hours, had only one good night's sleep in the previous five days, were sopping wet from wading the river, and were being soaked by the monsoon rain. The situation was aggravated by the fact that the temperature started to drop. In the past, we got rained on, but the sun always came out shortly after the downpour to bake us dry. That afternoon, the rain did not let up and continued long into the night. The temperature was probably a balmy 60 degrees, but because we were acclimated to the 120-degree temperature of the Vietnam summer, we were chilled to the bone. I was completely exhausted, soaking wet, and freezing to death all at the same time.

A lot has been said and written about the thousand-yard stare on the faces of men engaged in prolonged combat. The men of Second Platoon had developed just such a look. We were both physically and mentally drained. If the VC attacked, I didn't know how much fight we had left in us. We had gone from exhaustion to a state of near collapse, barely able to perform the simplest of tasks. We couldn't go any farther without a night's sleep.

I tried to cook a meal of C rations, but it was raining so hard I couldn't get the heat tab to light, so I wound up eating a can of cold ham and lima beans. After this gourmet treat, I got the bright idea of trying to light a heat tab under my poncho in hopes of trapping enough heat to warm myself. After several attempts, I managed to get the heat tab lit only to be asphyxiated by the fumes from the burning tab.

After several attempts to warm myself, I gave up and rolled into my poncho and tried to get some sleep. I was lying in a depression in the sand and was able to sleep until the rain filled up the hollow, at which time I had to get up and bail out the rainwater. This continued until the rain finally stopped sometime after midnight. When I awoke the next morning, the sky was still overcast, threatening additional rain. Because of the rain and cloud cover, the resupply chopper could not come in.

We had a meeting at the company CP shortly after 0600 hours, and Rich gave us our marching orders. We would initially move northwest to the railroad right-of-way, at which time we would sweep north and then back east to link up with Kilo Company. We started out in a wedge formation with Second Platoon on point. After thirty minutes, we switched to a column formation led by Second Platoon. The undergrowth was just too thick to maintain a tactical formation, and we were reduced to traveling in single file as we hacked our way through the brush.

The lead element radioed they had the elevated railroad bed in sight, and I instructed them to swing north. We were moving slowly, trying to pick our way through the entangled maze of elephant grass, vines, and bamboo thickets. Suddenly, we received a hail of rifle fire from the area of the railroad bed. I immediately hit the ground as the bullets were cracking overhead. I had learned to distinguish between the different sounds of incoming rifle fire. When bullets are coming directly at you, they make a cracking noise, as opposed to a popping sound when they are being fired in your vicinity. The bullets that day were coming right at my position. I could see them striking all around me. If I didn't find better cover, I would soon become a casualty. About ten meters to my right rear was a bomb crater, and I managed to crawl over to it, followed by my radioman. My initial inclination was to crawl to the bottom of the crater and curl up in a fetal position and hope the firing would stop. The fitful night's sleep had little effect, and I was about to reach my limit of endurance. I had lost my will to fight, and my only desire was to survive another day. I forced myself up to the edge of the crater and got on the radio to First Squad to try to find out what was happening.

An explosion erupted on the other side of the bomb crater I was occupying. The crater was less than five meters across, and the noise left my ears ringing. I initially assumed we were being mortared and thought we would be reliving our experience of Operation Swift. Another explosion detonated to my left front, and I realized we were being fired on by an M79 grenade launcher from the area of the railroad tracks. Whoever was firing the blooper had us zeroed in, and I could hear the rounds leaving the launcher, followed by a nearby explosion. The rounds kept hitting the far side of the crater we were occupying, and I was convinced it was only a matter of time before one of his rounds would land directly on top of us.

I called for an M79 man to come to my position, and before long, the grenadier from Third Squad was in the crater with me. We attempted to locate the VC who was firing at us, and shortly, we had a duel going between the two grenade launchers. Someone to my left front started calling for a corpsman, and Doc Blake went running past me in that direction. I now had Lima Six on the radio demanding to know what was going on and a Blackcoat overhead asking for targets. I should have gotten out of the crater and crawled to my lead elements to take charge of the situation, but I just couldn't bring myself to do it. Maybe it was the exhaustion; maybe I just didn't have the courage, but I refused to leave the security of the crater. I again contacted First Squad to find out where the firing was coming from with little results. I noticed Second Platoon wasn't returning a lot of fire, while the enemy rounds continued to crack overhead and hit around the crater.

It was apparent Second Platoon was not responding like they should. They were pinned down and not attempting to suppress the VC fire. It was up to me to get up and rally the troops. Instead, I remained in the security of the crater, trying to direct my troops by making inquiries over the radio. I finally determined most of the firing was coming from the railroad right-of-way, and shortly, the Blackcoat was dropping artillery rounds on that target. This was followed by napalm from a pair of F-4s, which ended the firefight.

After assessing the damage, I discovered we had a marine from Second Squad with a bullet wound in his calf. Other than that, we came through the battle unscathed. Lima Six set up a perimeter, and we had the wounded marine medevaced in short order despite the cloud cover. The wounded marine was another new guy that had joined us during Operation Swift, and once again, I didn't know his name. We now had several new guys in the platoon as a result of the casualties we had taken over the previous weeks.

I was concerned about the performance of Second Platoon, as well as my inability to appropriately react to the situation at hand. We were simply worn out. We needed some time to rest and recuperate from the rigors of the battles we had recently faced.

After the wounded marine was medevaced, we moved to the railroad right-of-way to assess any damage we might have inflicted on the VC. Once again, we could not find any evidence of VC casualties. As we checked the area, the reason became obvious; the enemy had been in fortified positions along the railroad bed. The VC with the M79 had been crouched behind a concrete embankment, and there were two dozen spent cartridges scattered about his position. The only way we could have gotten him was with a direct hit while he was standing to fire his M79. The remainder of the time, he was squatting behind the concrete shelter reloading his weapon. As usual, the enemy was able to choose the terrain and circumstances under which the battle was fought, and on cue, they beat a hasty retreat before we could effectively use our air and artillery support.

As we examined the VC position, Sergeant Presno shouted we had a problem. I went to his location to see what was the matter. He informed me he thought he was standing on a "Bouncing Betty" mine. He had felt the stem from the mine when he stepped on it and heard it click as he put his weight down. The Bouncing Betty was designed to detonate when the pressure from his weight was released, at which time it would bounce in the air and explode, sending shrapnel several feet in all directions. We cleared the area, and Sergeant Presno dove off the mine in an attempt to escape injury. The mine did not explode, and we checked the thing out. Sure enough, three prongs were extending out of the ground, indicating the presence of the mine. Fortunately for Sergeant Presno, the mine was a dud.

After checking out the VC ambush site, word came down to get ready of move out. The clouds continued to build, and it looked like we were in for a repeat of the previous day's weather. We started sweeping north, parallel to the railroad bed, when once again we came under fire. We were less than a hundred meters from our previous battle site when the tree line in front of us erupted with small-arms fire. The VC with the M79 was back, and he once again began to lob rounds in on top of us. The firefight lasted for some thirty minutes. Because of the rain clouds, we didn't have the use of a Blackcoat or other air support. We were finally able to call in an artillery mission, which brought an end to the VC attack. When the firing was over, we discovered Lima Company had two casualties—a marine from First Platoon had been shot in the chest, while a member of the company CP group had taken a piece of shrapnel from an M79 round.

By now, the sky had filled with thunder clouds and was pouring rain. We attempted to get a medevac and were told nothing was flying and wouldn't be until the storm abated. The marine with the shrapnel in his arm was able to walk and could accompany us to link up with Kilo Company. I had my doubts about the casualty from First Platoon.

Two corpsmen were working on the wounded marine, and I was told he had a sucking chest wound. None of his other organs had been hit, and as soon as they patched the hole in his chest, they would decide whether or not he could walk. After several minutes, it was determined the marine was well enough to move out with the rest of the company. We saddled up and started moving east to link up with Kilo Company.

Once again, the terrain dictated the order of march. Instead of being in a tactical wedge, we were strung out in a long, unmanageable column stretching several hundred meters. Ideally, we would have moved in a formation two hundred meters long and two hundred meters wide. Instead, we were one man wide and six hundred meters long. The thick undergrowth simply did not allow us the luxury of spreading out vertically to our line of march, and the best we could do was follow in the footsteps of the man in front of us.

Another problem arose; as a result of the rainfall, all the streams in the area were at flood stage. What should have been a small stream was now several feet deep, and we were forced to find crossing points shallow enough to wade. The rest of the day was spent fighting the rain and wading chest-deep streams. Once again, we were soaked to the bone, but the continued humping kept us warmer than the evening before.

At 1600 hours, we linked up with Kilo Company just as the rain let up. Thankfully, someone had realized the troops needed a rest, and by 1700 hours, we were set in for the night, trying to dry out and get some much-needed sleep. Mother Nature cooperated, and the rain clouds left the area as nightfall set in. The stars came out, and hopefully we would be resupplied the next morning and the wounded would by medevaced.

I joined the company CP for our nightly meeting. The marine with the chest wound was being attended to by the company medic and sounded horrible. He was struggling for every breath, and I was told the lung that the bullet passed through had collapsed. He was operating on one lung, and the hump to link up with Kilo Company had taken its toll. It didn't sound like he would make it through the night, but I was assured he would be all right. Regardless, I was glad to leave the CP and get away from the sound of his labored breathing. By 2000 hours, we had our watches assigned, and everyone not on watch was sound asleep.

The night's sleep worked wonders for Second Platoon. Everyone was able to get at least eight hours of relatively dry sleep, and our spirits were lifted by the dawning of the new day. In addition, the cloud cover was gone, and we were looking at clear skies and sunny weather. In the past, the sun was not an ally, but with two straight days of drenching rain, it was good to feel the warmth of the Vietnamese morning. In addition, the resupply choppers and medevacs were flying, and we had our casualties heading toward Da Nang by sunup. The resupply choppers showed up, but their arrival was a mixed blessing. They brought much-needed C rations and ammo, but somehow the supply requests got mixed up.

Since we had not been resupplied since crossing the Quan That, another resupply request had been sent in the night before. When the supply choppers dropped off their cargo, it was discovered they had filled both requests instead of only one. The daily resupply was designed to keep each marine equipped with the maximum amount of ammo that he could effectively carry. As a result of the additional resupply request, we would be substantially bogged down with twice as much ammo as needed.

We met with Rich at 0600 hours, and he informed us Battalion wanted Kilo and Lima Companies to sweep abreast of each other back west toward the railroad tracks. Kilo would be on the right, and Lima would be on the left. Rich put Lima Company in a wedge formation with Second Platoon on point. We would start our sweep as soon as the artillery prepped the area to our west.

At 0630 hours, the artillery barrage began, and by 0650, we were saddled up and sweeping west. We had traveled a couple of hundred meters when Sergeant Presno came up on the radio, saying, "Lima Two, you need to get up here and take a look at this."

I went forward to the point where I observed what was left of a VC ambush. First Squad had been guiding on a large trail that ran east and west. Several marines were standing in an area where the trail entered a small tree line, examining the ground around the trail. As I entered the tree line, it was apparent artillery rounds had recently landed in the area. I could still smell the cordite, and the debris from the explosion was everywhere. Lying on the ground was the body of a dead VC cradling an M60 machine gun. The body had been decapitated by the exploding artillery round, and the head was nowhere to be found. Sergeant Presno directed my attention to the left of VC's body, where there were two feet cut off at the ankles. I examined the body of the VC, and he had his feet attached, so we had two confirmed kills from the morning's artillery bombardment. A lucky round had landed on top of the VC waiting to ambush us as we walked down the trail. The troops were jubilant. There was nothing like a couple of dead VC to make your morning.

I reported our find to Lima Six and was getting ready to move on when Rich came back on the radio requesting I examine the feet to see if they were a matched pair. If they did not match, we could chalk up another kill. I was not an expert on matching feet, but as I looked at them, they appeared to be the same size, and one was a left and the other a right. I radioed back that as best I could tell they came from the same person and we only had two kills.

The morning artillery barrage made a big difference for Second Platoon. The VC had picked an ideal spot for an ambush and would surely have inflicted casualties on our point squad, who would have walked into the teeth of the machine-gun fire. Instead, we had two confirmed kills, as well as the capture of an M60 machine gun. The sun was shining, and we had just had a good night's sleep. If it wasn't for the extra ammo that we were humping, it would have been the perfect morning.

We continued to move west, adjacent to Kilo Company. The lucky artillery barrage must have taken the fight out of the VC, because we had no contact with them for the rest of the morning. We were making little progress with our company-size sweep due to the terrain. Because of the thick underbrush, we were once again reduced to hacking a route through the tangled vegetation, following each other in single file. When we reached the railroad bed, it was decided we would break up into platoons and saturate the area with patrols to see if we could generate enemy contact. Each platoon was given a patrol route with instructions to rendezvous at a predesignated site at 1500 hours.

Second Platoon was to patrol along a trail leading northeast for several hundred meters and then north through what appeared on the map to be an isolated section of dense jungle. After clearing the jungle, we would move to the east, crossing several streams to link back up with Lima Company. India Company would be doing the same thing, except they would be moving in from the east. Hopefully, one of the platoons would make contact with the VC, and we could converge on the enemy from several directions.

As we moved along our route, we uncovered several pits dug into the trail lined with punji stakes designed to injure anyone unlucky enough to fall on them. They were pretty crude traps but could inflict substantial injuries on their intended victims.

As we proceeded north into the jungle, I was introduced to an entirely new terrain. Before, we had operated on relatively open ground. The patch of jungle was something I had not experienced before, and it caused me some serious navigation problems. There was no outside reference point from which we could determine our location, and I was reduced to relying solely on my compass. I set a course for due north and had to estimate how far we had traveled to have any idea where I was. After traveling three hundred meters, we exited the jungle, and I was surprised to learn we came out pretty close to where I thought we would. Not being used to the jungle, I was uncomfortable with the fact that I couldn't verify my location while passing through the thick foliage.

A Blackcoat, which was assigned to the operation, would periodically fly over our position as we continued our patrolling. I could not raise him on the radio, so I assumed he was on someone else's net. At 1530 hours, he flew over and dropped a red smoke grenade on top of us, which was the universal signal for enemy troops. We immediately went into a panic, frantically calling to Lima Six to find out what radio net the Blackcoat was on. I could envision an artillery barrage being called in on top of us in the next couple of minutes. After firing several green flares to indicate friendly troops, we were contacted by Lima Six and told not to worry. Apparently, the Blackcoat had run out of green smoke and was using the red smoke to mark our position for the battalion headquarters group who was close by. At this point, I became agitated; if battalion wanted to know where we were, all they had to do was ask. I had regularly reported my position to Lima Six, and I didn't want every VC in the vicinity to know where the hell Second Platoon was. Rich laughed at my concerns. He explained the battalion headquarters group was lost and Second Platoon was the closest platoon to them. They used the red smoke to try to reestablish their location. Of course, if Second Platoon had gotten themselves lost, there would be hell to pay, and I was sure Battalion wouldn't allow red smoke to be dropped on their position.

As we approached the rendezvous site, I noticed we had a couple of small streams to cross before getting to our destination. As usual, the streams were swollen by the recent rains, and what should have been a simple crossing became a search for a crossing point that wouldn't drown the entire platoon. At best, we were wading through waist-deep water, and on some occasions, the water came to our armpits. We finally arrived at the rendezvous site soaking wet, but at least the sun was out, and we weren't freezing to death.

I noticed several men from Second Platoon were starting to limp, and I asked Doc Blake to look into the situation. He reported we were going to have problems with immersion foot, which was once called trench foot. The men's feet had been continually wet for the last couple of days as a result of the rain and the wading of the streams. We wore special jungle boots, which were fast drying to help reduce the casualties from immersion foot. Because of the extreme conditions of the last few days, we were faced with a small crisis. I reported the problem to Lima Six, and he informed me we would be setting in for the night, and hopefully, we could get the men some dry socks with the next supply chopper. By 1700 hours, we had set up our perimeter and were anxiously awaiting the resupply chopper.

The chopper showed up, and as promised, we had new socks for everyone in the platoon. Doc Blake had each man take off his shoes and socks, and he inspected their feet before he issued them a new pair of socks. After this process was completed, he informed me we had two men who weren't going to make it much farther if they didn't get their feet taken care of. I passed this information to Rich, who told me our problem may be solved. We were about to wind up the operation, and if the men could make one more short hump, we would have them back at Hill 63 by the following afternoon. I checked with Doc Blake, and he said he thought the men could go one more day.

Because we shut down early, the men had plenty of time to set up their nightly fortifications. As I walked our perimeter, I was almost overcome with emotion as I observed the men going about their nightly task. These men had been operating under the most adverse of conditions for the last month—fighting during the day and humping all night—and yet there they were, digging in for another night without complaint, thankful their country had provided them with a dry pair of socks. The sacrifices these men were making were beyond belief. They risked injury, disease, and death, asking nothing in return—not for a hot meal, not for a day off, not even for a pat on the back. Why did they do it? For God, country, and Mom's apple pie? No. They did it for each other; they did it because of the pride they took in being Marine Corps grunts. Each man knew he would have to carry his share of the load, and his fellow marine would carry his. I had never been prouder to be part of something as I was that evening as I walked the lines, visiting with the men of Second Platoon.

As the sun was going down, the VC began to probe our lines with sporadic rifle fire. This was a golden opportunity for Second Platoon to burn some of the excess ammo they had been humping all day. I passed the word that the next time we received incoming fire, every man should return the maximum amount of fire for as long as he could. Sure enough, we received a couple of rounds of incoming and returned several thousand rounds over a ten-minute period. Battalion was on the phone wanting to know what the hell was going on; it sounded like we were involved in a major battle and about to be overrun. I can only imagine what the poor VC who fired at us must have thought; apparently, he concluded we couldn't take a joke, because we heard no more from him for the rest of the night.

The next morning, it was time to pack it in and head back to Hill 63. Battalion did not want to airlift us out of our present location, so we were required to hump back across the Than Quit to an area known as Liberty Bridge to be picked up by CH-53 helicopters and ferried back to our base camp. Liberty Bridge spanned the Thu Bon River, linking An Hoa with the city of Da Nang and was some eight klicks from our present position. The only real obstacle between us and the bridge was the Than Quat. Since we had previously waded across it to get to our present position, presumably we should have little trouble getting back across. As usual, I was overly optimistic.

We arrived at the north bank of the Than Quat shortly before 1300 hours. For whatever reason, Battalion chose a different crossing point than that which we had used previously. The river must have been swollen from the monsoon rains, because it didn't resemble the river we had crossed three days earlier. The current was substantially stronger, and the river appeared to be deeper. The battalion headquarters group was attempting to find a place where we could cross the river. They would send a marine out into the river, and after several steps, the water would be over his head. The logical thing to do would have been to change our pickup point from the Liberty Bridge to the north bank of the Than Quat. In the Marine Corps, logic doesn't always enter into the equation. We were supposed to be airlifted at the Liberty Bridge, and by God, we would hump to the Liberty Bridge, regardless of how many marines we drowned on the way.

A crossing point that was shallow enough to allow most of the men to wade the river was finally located. The only problem was the river current was stronger in that particular area. To demonstrate their dedication to the cause, several members of the battalion headquarters group, including the battalion commander and the battalion S3, formed a human bridge to assist us in crossing the river. I noticed the water was up to everyone's armpits as the units in front of us waded across the river, I looked at a couple of the shorter marines in Second Platoon and realized we were going to have problems.

I passed the word that whoever was still humping excess ammo should drop it in the river as we were wading across. There were several marines who still had full ammo cans in each hand, despite our attempts to use up the excess in the previous night's "firefight." If I had been caught giving this order, I probably would have been court-martialed, but we had carried that ammo far enough, and it was time to unload it in the bottom of the river. In addition, this would give everyone two free hands to negotiate the river. Second Platoon was the last unit to enter the river, and I positioned myself behind Private First Class Slater, who was barely five feet tall. Halfway across the river, he was bobbing up and down in an attempt to keep his head above water. The current knocked his feet out from under him, and when he surfaced, he no longer had his rifle. He grabbed on to the human bridge and was able to cross the river by dragging himself from one man to another.

When we got across the river, the excess ammo problem was solved. Unfortunately, we had one fewer M16 than when we started. I didn't give this too much thought. Slater had a choice of letting go of the rifle or drowning in the river. Battalion would later take a different view of things, and they attempted to court-martial Slater for losing his rifle. Apparently, Slater should have gone down with the rifle just like a captain with his ship. I was glad Slater let go of the damn rifle and saved himself from drowning.

We continued on with our hump to Liberty Bridge and arrived there shortly after 1400 hours. We were instructed to standby for an airlift back to Hill 63 sometime later that afternoon. Since Liberty Bridge was in a secure area, we did not bother to set up a defensive position and spent the rest of the afternoon lying around on the riverbank. The choppers had us back at Hill 63 by 1700 hours for our first hot meal in well over a week. We were assigned to the troop tents and given a ration of beer.

Wading the River

14

ALL GOOD THINGS HAVE TO COME TO AN END

THE NEXT MORNING, OUR WORLD was turned upside down. After eating breakfast, I was returning to the company area when Lance Corporal Moreno told me there was a meeting at the Lima Company CP. When I arrived at the CP, Rich Muler and Lee Gounds were engaged in an animated conversation. When I approached, Rich turned to me and said, "You won't believe what's happened."

"What's that?"

"We've all been assigned to Battalion."

I didn't get the drift of what Rich had said and asked, "Lima Company's been assigned to Battalion?"

Lee joined in. "No, the three of us have been assigned to Battalion."

I still wasn't clear on what was going on. "The three of us have been assigned to Battalion? Who's going to run Lima Company?"

Rich replied, "Apparently, they have a bunch of new officers coming in, and we're being kicked upstairs to Battalion."

It was finally starting to sink in. I asked, "New officers are being assigned to take our place in Lima Company?"

Lee replied, "Yeah, and you haven't heard the rest of it. We're leaving Hill 63."

"The three of us are leaving Hill 63?" I asked.

"No, Third Battalion is leaving Hill 63," answered Rich.

I was more confused than ever. I sat down and asked them to start over. They explained the Fifth Marines were moving north and Third Battalion would be replacing First Battalion, First Marine Regiment in their firebase twelve miles south of Da Nang. At the same time, new officers had been assigned to Third Battalion, and the three of us would be taken out of the field and replaced by a new contingent of officers.

I was dumbfounded. I couldn't believe they would replace every officer in Lima Company at one time. I asked, "You mean they're going to replace us with a bunch of boot officers?"

Rich replied, "It looks that way. It doesn't sound like a real smart idea, but we will be moving into a pretty secure area—nothing like what we've been dealing with out here. I've heard the entire area was pacified years ago, and the villagers are actually on our side instead of theirs."

All of it was finally starting to sink in, and I felt like I had been kicked in the stomach. I should have been elated that I was finally getting out of the field to a safer job with Battalion, especially in light of the fact we were moving into a secure area. For some reason, I didn't look at it that way. I felt like my family was being taken away from me. Who was going to look after the raggedy-ass bunch of marines in Second Platoon? Surely they couldn't survive without me. Hadn't I gotten them through the last several months? Who was going to take care of them? Certainly not some boot lieutenant who didn't know his ass from third base. I finally said to Rich, "Isn't there something we can do to keep this from happening? I mean, they're going to replace all three of us. They won't have any experienced officers."

"I understand the problem, and I tried to explain that to Colonel Turner. Unfortunately, his mind is made up. He has to put the new officers somewhere, and we've been in the field longer than any of the other officers in the battalion, so it's our turn to move on up the ladder. Captain Burke from India Company is also being replaced by a new company commander, and a couple of other lieutenants are being moved to Battalion to replace the officers rotating back to the States."

I still wasn't satisfied and said, "Well, I still want to talk to Colonel Turner. Maybe I can change his mind."

I returned to Second Platoon in a state of shock. Officers being rotated out of the field was a fact of life in an infantry battalion. Second lieutenants, fresh out of Basic School, were being shipped to Vietnam, and room had to be made for them; at the same time, experienced officers were being rotated back to the States, and someone had to replace them at the battalion level. I had been in the field longer than I could reasonably expect, and it was time for me to be moved on up to Battalion. I could have accepted that but for the fact that all the officers of Lima Company were being replaced. The company was being placed in the hands of inexperienced officers, and the troops were the ones who would have to pay the price.

I ran into Sergeant Green and told him the news, both about me leaving the platoon and the battalion leaving Hill 63. He did not react to the news one way or the other. He had been in Vietnam long enough to know lieutenants came and went, and this would be the fourth or fifth time Battalion had picked up and moved since they landed at Chu Lai. In certain ways, the enlisted men were like cattle. They had little control over their destinies and were subject to the whims of their superior officers. The one thing they could be sure of was they would spend their full thirteen months in the field; the luxury of being moved to Battalion headquarters was not in the cards for them.

Sergeant Green wished me well and asked when I would be leaving the platoon. I told him I didn't know. I had decided to request a hearing with Colonel Turner, asking him to reconsider his decision to transfer me to Battalion. If I had expected Sergeant Green to be overcome with emotion by my loyalty to Second Platoon, I was sadly mistaken. He turned to me and said, "Lieutenant, they won't change their minds. They don't really give a shit about what happens to the men of this platoon." He then laughed and said, "Besides, I can remember when you showed up as a boot lieutenant. Hell, you're the guy that took the mortars on a platoon-size patrol."

We both laughed at his remark, and he ended the conversation by saying, "I'll tell the troops what's happening. I'm sure they'll be glad to get off their damn hill and closer to Da Nang."

I was still having a hard time dealing with the recent turn of events. I knew I wasn't going to be the platoon commander of Second Platoon forever, but I never really gave much thought to the circumstances under which I would leave. We had been through so much together, and I couldn't imagine a life without the platoon. They had become a part of me. They were my platoon, and I couldn't accept the fact they would now belong to someone else. I was now even more determined to talk Colonel Turner out of his decision to transfer me to Battalion.

I marched to the battalion CP, determined to plead my case. Surely Colonel Turner would listen to reason and allow me to stay with the platoon at least through the transition period until the new officers get their feet on the ground. When I arrived at Battalion headquarters, I discovered I had to go through my old nemesis Major Franks, the battalion XO, in order to talk to Colonel Turner. Major Franks immediately asked me what I wanted, and when he learned of my request, a smirk came over his face. He said, "Lieutenant, the decision to transfer you to Battalion has already been made. There is no need to discuss it with Colonel Turner."

It was obvious Major Franks was enjoying the conversation. A lowly second lieutenant had little bargaining power with the battalion brass, especially a smart-ass one like me. I had been led to believe every member of the battalion had a right to demand an audience with the battalion commander, and I pushed my request to see Colonel Turner.

Major Franks's mood went from amused to ominous. He turned to me and said, "Look, Lieutenant, I told you Colonel Turner was busy right now, and he does not want to be bothered about a decision that has already been made. Maybe you didn't understand me. I do not want you to take up the colonel's time with your useless demands. Is that clear?"

So much for being able to demand a hearing before the battalion commander. I acknowledged I understood and returned to Lima Company with my tail between my legs. I found Sergeant Schwartz, the source of all knowledge, and asked him if he knew when we would be replaced by the new officers. He told me the information he had indicated it wouldn't happen until we moved north to take over our new base. This softened the blow a little bit. At least I would have a couple of more days to spend with the platoon. I asked him if he knew when we would be moving north.

He said, "Some of the battalion headquarters group left yesterday to take a look at our new headquarters. I imagine we won't be moving for at least a week. Someone will have to stay here until the army unit arrives to take over the hill."

This brought me to my next question. "Who's going to take our place here on Hill 63?"

"I've been told it will be a brigade from one of the air cavalry divisions. If it is, it won't take them long to move in here with all their helicopters."

I then asked Sergeant Schwartz what he knew about the area where we were moving to. He replied, "From what I hear, it will be a big change from where we're at. The First Marines have been there for a long time, and they have fixed it up pretty nice. They even have a generator, which provides electricity to the compound, which means cold beer and electric lights. This will be a good move for Battalion. The monsoon is about to set in, and at least we will be able to sit out the rain in some semblance of comfort."

"How about the VC?" I asked.

"The area is supposed to be pretty well pacified. We will be patrolling just north of the Go Noi Islands, but from what I've been told, the VC stay out of our new TAOR. The local farmers don't like the VC and won't support them. With the monsoons coming, our biggest problems will be trying to keep dry. Of course, in your new position, you won't have that problem; you'll be spending all your time in a dry hooch."

I knew Sergeant Schwartz was kidding, but I still felt bad about leaving Second Platoon and Lima Company. I then asked, "What the hell are you going to do without Rich, Lee, and me to keep your sorry ass out of trouble?"

He laughed and said, "Lieutenant, I've broken in more officers than you've ever met. Hell, I'll have the new CO squared away in no time. Besides, I'm the one that runs this company, not the officers. I just let them think they run things."

He continued to joke, saying, "The day the officers start running the Marine Corps is the day I hang it up. I'm not going to let these new officers fuck up Lima Company any more than I let you guys screw things up."

Sergeant Schwartz then became serious and said, "Lieutenant, I know how you feel about leaving, but things will be all right. These troops are tough, and they know how to take care of themselves. The new officers will figure things out pretty quickly, and we'll have plenty of time to break them in with the monsoon coming on. Don't worry about Second Platoon. They'll be okay."

I felt a little better about things after talking to Sergeant Schwartz and decided to make the best of the next couple of days until it was time to leave Second Platoon. I went over to the company CP to try to find out what we would be doing to get ready to move north to our new TAOR.

I ran into Rich, and he told me he had a special assignment for me. He explained the tank platoon stationed at Hill 63 would not be accompanying Third Battalion on their move north. They had been transferred to support Third Division up at the DMZ. They would be traveling south to Chui Lai and then boarding a ship to be transported north to join up with Third Division. They needed an infantry platoon to accompany them on their trip to Chu Lai, and Second Platoon had been chosen.

Although in the past I had not had the best of experiences with the tankers, I looked at this as one last opportunity to lead Second Platoon and was grateful for the chance to take them out one more time. Rich told me to check with the battalion S3 for details on the trip to Chu Lai and to let him know when we were taking off. I was tempted to run over to the S3 tent to get briefed on my last mission with the platoon, but I kept myself in check long enough to inform Sergeant Green of the recent development and instructed him to make sure the platoon was ready to go. I then went to find out what lay in store for Second Platoon. I was directed to the assistant S3 officer who had the particulars on our assignment. He told me it should be a no-sweat assignment. We would be traveling with the Tank Platoon down Highway 1 to Chu Lai, which was less than forty miles to our south. Since we were riding on the tanks, we ought to be able to make it to Chu Lai in a day. When we got there, we would spend the night and then return by choppers back to Hill 63. The whole thing shouldn't take more than two days.

It wound up taking us four days, but we arrived safely. I got the men set in for the night, although I knew they would be at the enlisted men's quarters knocking back more than a few beers. Around 1730 hours, I wandered over to the officers' club for the drink I was promised by the captain from the S1 shop. The club was crowded with clean-shaven officers dressed in starched utilities. I stood out like a sore thumb in my filthy clothes and muddy boots. In addition, I was carrying my M16 as I entered the bar; I didn't have anywhere else to leave it. I was immediately spotted by the captain, and he invited me to join his group at a nearby table. I was well treated by the officers sitting at the table, and they insisted on buying me several rounds of drinks. The conversation turned to what was happening in the field, and when they discovered I was in Operation Swift, I was deluged with questions about the fighting in the Que Son Valley. Apparently, they had all heard about the operation and were interested in a firsthand report. The discussion continued for several minutes when the S1 captain said, "It's too bad about the way the operation ended."

I assumed he was referring to the fact we had gotten the shit kicked out of us by the NVA and replied, "Yeah, a lot of good men died for nothing."

He gave me a quizzical look and said, "No, I mean the part about the NVA getting away."

I hadn't the faintest idea what he was talking about and asked, "How did they get away?"

"We heard you had them surrounded and were ready to stick it to them when they broke out through the ARVN's position."

For a moment, I was speechless. That was one of the most preposterous statements I had heard in a long time. I asked, "Where did you hear that?"

"That's the word we got. If it hadn't had been for the ARVNs, we would have annihilated an NVA division."

I felt like telling him what really happened on Operation Swift. How 138 marines died in a meaningless battle over a shithole place like the Que Son Valley. That over 350 marines were wounded in a battle that decided nothing. How the NVA outmaneuvered us at every turn and left the battlefield on their terms and not ours. That we never had anyone surrounded and we were the ones surrounded most of the time. How America's finest young men were killed and wounded fighting for a cause they didn't understand and probably wouldn't have believed in if they had understood it. Instead, I said, "Yeah, if it hadn't have been for the ARVNs, we really would have fucked them up."

The innocent statement of the captain from the S1 section knocked me for a loop. The people back in the rear envisioned a magnificent battle in which the marines chased the NVA through the Que Son Valley, finally surrounding them, only to have them escape through the ARVN lines. Nothing could have been further from the truth. If that was the story they were getting there in the war zone, what was being told to the American people? Did they know their sons and husbands were getting killed and maimed by a well-disciplined and highly motivated force that was trying to reunite their country? Was the sacrifice we were making really worth it? These questions put a damper on the rest of the evening, and after answering several more questions, I excused myself and returned to Second Platoon without stopping at the chow hall. I fixed myself a meal of C rations, lay down on the cot, and went to sleep wondering where the war was really headed.

Around 0200 hours, I was awakened by the noise made by the men of Second Platoon returning from the enlisted men's club. They were all pretty drunk and in a boisterous mood. I found Sergeant Green, who had obviously done his share of celebrating, and requested he make sure all the men hit the sack. I didn't want them wandering around the base in their present condition. He said he would make sure the men didn't get in any trouble. He also related that the men had been treated like royalty at the EM club. They were bought round after round of drinks by the local marines. By the looks of the men, it was apparent the local desk jockeys must have spent a lot of money. It was good to know there was somewhere the grunts were appreciated. I returned to my tent feeling thankful the men had a good time.

I was awake at 0430 hours the next day, rousting the men out of their racks. Since the mess hall wasn't open, we had to eat a breakfast of C rations. Unfortunately, no one had any. We had planned on a one-day trip down to Chu Lai, and all of us had consumed more than our allotted two meals a day, and we were out of rations. There wasn't anything we could do, and at 0500, the trucks showed up. Oh well. We would be back at Hill 63 shortly, and surely we could get something to eat there. We loaded onto the trucks, and by sunup, we were sitting in a staging area next to MAG 13 awaiting our ride back to Hill 63.

I didn't know what time the choppers would arrive. I was told to wait there and, ultimately, we would be picked up. I found a comfortable place on the ground, covered myself with my poncho, and went back to sleep.

Around 0900 hours, things started coming alive in our little area. Most of the men in Second Platoon were still asleep as a result of their late-night partying. I looked around and found a fifty-five-gallon drum that was being used as a garbage container. Upon examining its contents, I discovered it contained discarded cans of C rations.

Apparently, this area had been used in the past by personnel awaiting airlift to some unknown location. They must have been given C rations to eat while they waited. Most of the C rations found their way into the Dumpster. It wasn't like REMFs to stoop to eating these tasteless meals. I, of course, had discovered a bonanza. I turned the drum over and spilled its contents on the ground, and soon, the men of Second Platoon were scrounging through the debris looking for meals to their liking. There wasn't enough to give each man a full meal, but at least everyone got something in their stomachs.

Shortly after 0900 hours, they opened a small portable PX, which was adjacent to our staging area, and the men thought they had died and gone to heaven. The men swarmed the building trying to buy one of everything they had. I didn't give it much thought and assumed the men would behave themselves. Unfortunately, I was wrong. At 1000 hours, a captain pulled up looking for the commander of the motley group of marines. No one said anything, and soon, the captain was going from marine to marine, asking him who was in charge. Finally, I volunteered I was the person he was looking for. He said, "I've received a report that your men are harassing the employees of the PX."

I hadn't paid much attention to what the men were doing in the PX, but I noticed they had two female employees working in the store. I asked the captain, "How's that, sir?"

"They have been making lewd remarks to these ladies working for me in the PX."

"I am sure my men wouldn't do anything like that, but just in case, I will have a talk with them. I certainly wouldn't want to leave a bad impression with the local gooks."

This really set him off. His attitude went from arrogant to nasty. He looked around at the men and demanded, "I assume those weapons are unloaded. This is a secure area, and loaded weapons are not allowed."

"Captain, I would be very surprised if their weapons aren't loaded. We try to keep them that way most of the time."

He said, "I order you to tell your men to unload their weapons immediately. If they don't, I will have the MPs up here to take care of the problem."

By this time, I was getting pissed and answered, "Captain, I will have my men unload their weapons, but if you send the MPs up here, you'd better make sure their weapons are loaded, and you'd better bring a bunch of them. We're not here to be fucked with, and if you attempt to, you'd better stand by for a long afternoon."

The captain was taken aback by my reply and demanded to know my name and what unit I was with. I answered, "My name and unit are none of your fucking business. You're not dealing with some rear-echelon motherfuckers. We'll be out of here pretty soon, and until then, you need to leave us alone. My men will unload their weapons and stay away from your PX. In the meantime, stay the fuck away from us."

By this time, a crowd was gathering, and the captain realized he was being backed into a corner. There really wasn't much he could do, and calling the MPs would be a real mistake. He turned and stormed off to the PX, which he immediately locked up, after which he got in his jeep and left along with the two female employees. I decided I had the problem solved, but I really wanted to get out of there, because there was no telling when the captain might return and who he might return with.

After the captain left, two gunnery sergeants who had been watching the entire incident walked up to me. The laughed at the antics of the captain and commented that the men of Second Platoon looked like a pretty salty bunch. I visually surveyed the platoon and had to agree. They were filthy dirty with their clothes in tatters, but they had that certain look about them. They were a typical grunt outfit, not very pretty to look at but as hard as nails inside, and it's what was inside that counted out in the field. I answered the two sergeants, "Yeah, they're pretty salty."

I told Sergeant Green to make sure the men unloaded their weapons just in case the captain came back. As the men went about clearing their weapons, I was once again amazed by the amount of armaments carried by a marine platoon. Bullets, grenades, and rockets were spread all over the ground as the men removed the ammunition from their weapons.

At 1430 hours, we heard the sounds of approaching helicopters, and pretty soon, we had four of them on the tarmac. I ran out to the choppers and talked to the crew chief, and he informed me they couldn't carry the entire platoon on one trip. I returned to the platoon and divided them into two groups and sent the first group on with Sergeant Green while I remained behind with the second group. The helicopter crew chief told me he would be back in about thirty minutes to pick us up.

As I was sitting there waiting for the choppers to return, who should drive up in a jeep but my old friend the captain from the tank platoon that we escorted down from Hill 63. He approached me and said, "Did you get our pistol back this morning?"

The truth of the matter was that I had completely forgotten about the lost pistol. I explained to the captain I hadn't gotten around to asking the troops about the pistol and apologized for my negligence, but that wasn't good enough for him.

He said, "Goddamn it, Lieutenant, I want that pistol back."

I assured him I would confront the men of Second Platoon just as soon as I got back to Hill 63. This also wasn't good enough.

He said, "Lieutenant, I want you to search every man in your platoon until you find the pistol."

I agreed to make every effort to find the pistol once I got back to Hill 63, and he stormed off to his jeep. It seemed like it was my day to take a ration of shit from my superior officers. As far as I was concerned, they could all fuck themselves. What were they going to do, send me to Vietnam? Pretty soon, the helicopters returned, and I loaded the rest of the platoon on the choppers for our return to Hill 63.

As we landed at Hill 63, I was flabbergasted by the transformation that had occurred in the previous few days. When we left three days prior, Hill 63 was a sleepy little firebase out in the middle of nowhere.

Now it was a beehive of activity. Helicopters were everywhere, and troops were busily coming and going, except they were soldiers and not marines. There were more helicopters there than I had seen anywhere in Vietnam—or in the United States, for that matter. Transport helicopters were ferrying in supplies in what seemed like a never-ending stream. Sitting next to the LZ was a mountain of C rations, enough to feed a battalion of marines for a month. Other gear was stacked around the LZ in mammoth proportions. It was obvious that when the army occupied a firebase, they really occupied a firebase. What took the Marine Corps several months to build and supply, the army fully occupied in a couple of days.

The rest of Second Platoon was waiting for us on the LZ, and they excitedly pointed out the provisions. We took a special interest in the mountain of C rations, and it was decided that this was an opportunity that could not be passed up. I sent several of the men over to the stacked provisions in an effort to steal as many as they could. Just as they were in a position to grab several cases, an army staff sergeant appeared out of nowhere and demanded to know what we were up to. I decided the truth was the best approach, and I explained we hadn't eaten all day and were going to help ourselves to the C rations. I also told him we were only going to take enough for one meal. The sergeant replied, "Hell, who in their right mind would steal C rations? Take all you want. There's plenty more where they came from."

With that, each man in the platoon helped himself to a case. With our newfound booty, we marched back to the LZ, where I had Sergeant Green form up the men in something that resembled a platoon formation. I explained the tank platoon was missing a .45-caliber pistol, and they thought someone from Second Platoon had stolen it. I told them if anyone had it, I wanted it turned into Sergeant Green, and no questions would be asked. Having said that, I marched the platoon over to a corner of the perimeter set aside for the marine personnel who were still at Hill 63. It was a strange sight as each man marched along with a case of C rations slung over his shoulder.

I ran into Lee Gounds, who, along with First Platoon, was still at Hill 63. He brought me up to date on what had been happening since I left for Chu Lai. Most of the battalion was now at our new TAOR south of Da Nang. The army showed up two days prior, and since then, it had been nothing but chaos with choppers coming in and out of the perimeter on a twenty-four-hour basis. The remaining Third Battalion marines would be choppered out the following morning. Since it was approaching 1700 hours, we decided to head for the mess tent to grab a bite to eat. On the way, we passed a helicopter unloading a pony, which we later learned was the battalion mascot. We were befuddled by what they could possibly be doing with a pony in the middle of Vietnam.

Another strange ritual we observed was every time the soldiers passed each other, they muttered something we could not understand. We initially thought they were saying "Carry on," which seemed rather unusual. We finally gathered enough nerve to ask one of the enlisted men what he had just said. He informed us it was customary in the air cavalry to great each other with the term "Gary Owen." I wanted to ask him who in the fuck Gary Owen was, but I didn't want to show my ignorance. After that, every time we heard a soldier say "Gary Owen," we responded with "Chesty Puller"—at least we knew who he was.

The next morning, I had Second Platoon at the LZ at 0600, waiting to be airlifted to our new home. As usual, the helicopters were late, and as I sat there, I looked around at what was now becoming a huge firebase. My thoughts returned to the day I arrived there in early June when the place was nothing but an isolated hill in a forlorn part of Vietnam. I remembered walking off the helicopter to the battalion command post and getting my assignment to Lima Company. I recalled getting lost on my way up the hill to join my new unit and that first night on top of the hill with my trepidation about my future command. Most of all, I remembered the men who had transformed this hill into what it was that day.

It had finally hit me that it was probably my last day as the platoon commander of Second Platoon. I had grown to love the bunch of men who had been mine for what now seemed like a very short time. There had been a Second Platoon of Lima Company for a long time before I took over, and there would be a Second Platoon for a long time after I left. For a brief period in the summer and fall of 1967, they were my marines. I was their father, mother, and confessor all rolled up in one. They depended on me for guidance, and I depended on them for my very life. I would never again be part of something as significant as my stint with Second Platoon. No matter what happens to me in the future, I can look back and say, "At one time, I was the leader of the finest group of men anywhere on earth." No matter how difficult a situation I may face, I can always say, "Hell, I once took a platoon of marines into the Que Son Valley. If you can do that, you can do anything." No matter how bad things get, I can truly say, "I've seen worse."

Pretty soon, the helicopters showed up, and I loaded the platoon on board for our short trip north. When we landed, I marched the men over to our assigned area. There was a day and night's difference between our new quarters and Hill 63. Plywood hooches were everywhere, and the men would have tents to sleep in instead of reinforced bunkers. Although there was a series of bunkers surrounding the perimeter, they were only manned at night and not designed to be lived in. Life there would be a lot easier than what we had experienced back at Hill 63.

I had been told by Lima Six to deliver the platoon to their bivouac area and to report to the battalion S3 for my new assignment. That was it—the last time I would be able to call myself Lima Two Actual. I gathered the men of Second Platoon around me for a few last words. It was very difficult to express my feelings. The last thing I wanted to do was walk away with tears in my eyes. Marines don't cry, especially in front of their troops. I told the men they would be getting a new lieutenant and they needed to help him along as best they could. I explained the new lieutenant would be doing things his way and it was their job to adjust to the way he did things. I assured them things would work out for them and that, in a short time, they would have forgotten I had ever been their platoon commander.

Finally, I told them how proud I was to have had an opportunity to lead them over the last several months. I explained, "Lots of people never made it to Vietnam, and lots of those that did never made it to the bush. You guys have done something you can be proud of. You went toe-to-toe with the best that the enemy could throw at you. You never once backed down. You never ever gave up. You did your job with honor and valor. I'll never forget you guys, and I can't thank you enough for what you've done for me, for the Marine Corps, and for your country."

I really couldn't continue. I turned and walked away toward Battalion headquarters hoping the marines of Second Platoon couldn't see the tears welling up in my eyes.

The End

Rich Mueler on the left, Lee Gounds on the right and a handsome guy in the middle

CPSIA information can be obtained at www.ICGtesting.com
Printed in the USA
BVOW02s2133270815

415482BV00001B/4/P